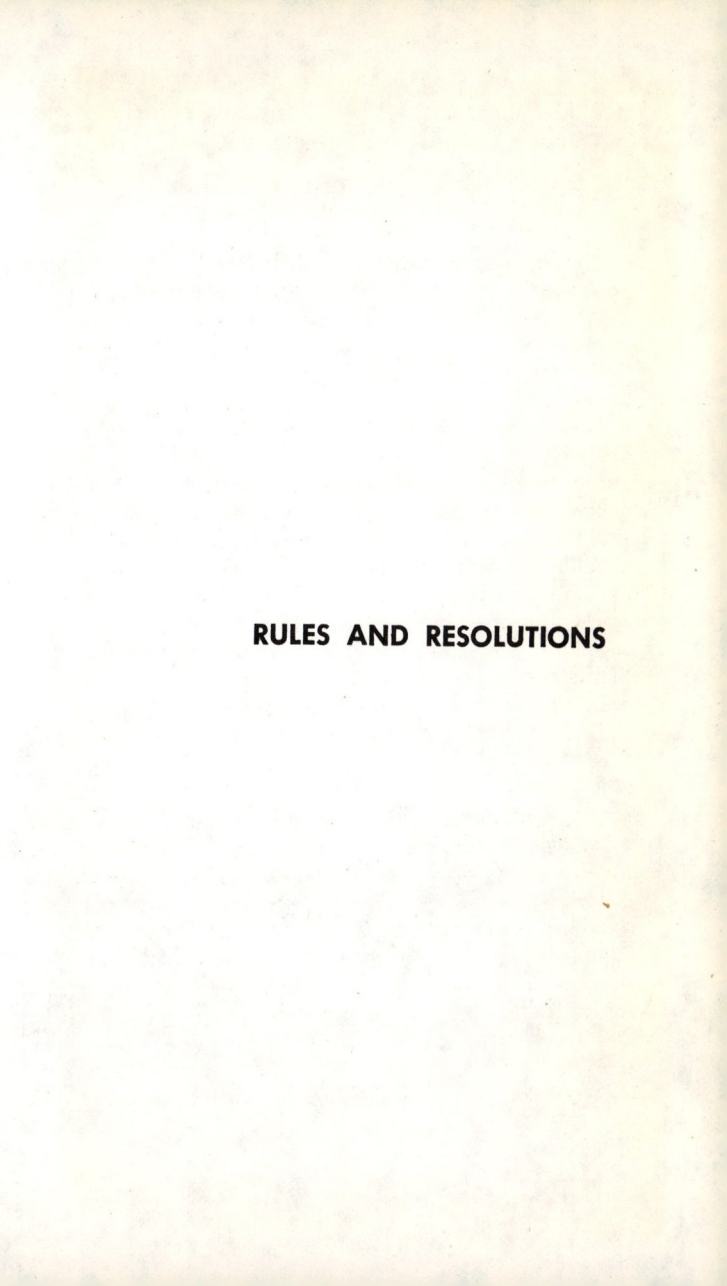

RULES AND RESOLUTIONS

Reorganized
CHURCH OF JESUS CHRIST
of Latter Day Saints

Rules and Resolutions

1980
HERALD HOUSE
Independence, Missouri

Copyright © 1980
HERALD PUBLISHING HOUSE
Independence, Missouri

Revised, 1957, 1964, 1975, 1980

All rights in this book are reserved. No part of the text may be reproduced in any form without written permission of the publishers, except brief quotations used in connection with reviews in magazines or newspapers.

Library of Congress Catalog Card No. 74-84765
ISBN 0-8309-0136-1

Printed in the United States of America

Contents

RULES OF ORDER—SECTION ONE

Foreword to Rules of Order	7
Church Organization, Purpose, and Membership	9
A Theocratic Democracy	11
Conferences and Assemblies	16
Rules of Representation	18
General Church Missions and Regions	21
Stakes	23
Districts	26
Branches	29
Further Instructions Concerning Branches and Districts	32
Amendments	34

GENERAL CONFERENCE RESOLUTIONS—SECTION TWO

Foreword to General Conference Resolutions	35
1862	37
1870	38
1880	44
1890	48
1900	55
1910	60
1920	70
1930	92
1940	110
1950	121
1960	147
1970	182
1980	253

APPENDIXES

Appendix A, Articles of Incorporation of the Reorganized Church of Jesus Christ of Latter Day Saints (1872)	265
Appendix B, Articles of Incorporation of the Reorganized Church of Jesus Christ of Latter Day Saints (A reincorporation)	270
Appendix C, Incorporations: Canada, etc.	273
Appendix D, Australasian Incorporation	276
Appendix E, Articles of Incorporation of Graceland College (A reincorporation)	278
Appendix F, Articles of Incorporation of Independence Sanitarium and Hospital	289
Appendix G, Church Court Procedure	292
Index	320

FOREWORD
To the Rules of Order

The World Conference of 1950 authorized the appointment of a committee to consider previously published statements on church procedure, "making such changes as they shall deem wise, and submitting them to the First Presidency for publication at an early date" (Conference *Daily*, page 109).

The committee thus authorized was constituted by action of the Presidency, the Council of Twelve, and the Presiding Bishopric so as to include Elders F. Henry Edwards, C. George Mesley, Henry L. Livingston, Ward A. Hougas, and E. Yewell Hunker.

A ruling of the Chair at the time the committee was authorized indicated that the function of the committee was "to produce a work that would become final and binding on the body." Nevertheless, the nature of some of the matter covered was such that the committee preferred to bring their "statement of Rules of Order for the approval of the [1952] Conference" (Conference *Daily*, page 70). The recommendations of the committee were therefore discussed, amended, and approved at the World Conference of 1952 (Conference *Daily*, pages 99-100, 103, 109, 110).

Amendments to the Rules of Order have been authorized by numerous World Conferences since 1952 relative to representation at the Conference, the nature of the Conference, and the nature of field jurisdictions.

It should be noted that the final paragraph of the Rules of Order provides that the said "Rules may be amended at any General Conference provided that at least sixty days' notice of the effort to amend" has been given in the *Saints' Herald*.

THE FIRST PRESIDENCY

RULES OF ORDER

Adopted April 5, 1952

I. Church Organization, Purpose, and Membership

1. The Church of Jesus Christ was "regularly organized and established agreeably to the laws of our country, by the will and commandments of God," April 6, 1830. This was in fulfillment of commandments "given to Joseph Smith, Jr., who was called of God and ordained an apostle of Jesus Christ, to be the first elder of this church; and to Oliver Cowdery, who was also called of God an apostle of Jesus Christ, to be the second elder of this church, and ordained under his hand: and this according to the grace of our Lord and Savior Jesus Christ, to whom be all glory both now and for ever."[1]

2. The Restoration of the gospel was heralded in these terms:

A marvelous work is about to come forth among the children of men, therefore, O ye that embark in the service of God, see that ye serve him with all your heart, might, mind, and strength, that ye may stand blameless before God at the last day; therefore, if ye have desires to serve God, ye are called to the work, for, behold, the field is white already to harvest, and lo, he that thrusteth in his sickle with his might the same layeth up in store that he perish not, but bringeth salvation to his soul; and faith, hope, charity, and love, with an eye single to the glory of God, qualifies him for the work.[2]

and

Keep my commandments, and seek to bring forth and establish the cause of Zion: seek not for riches but for wisdom; and, behold, the mysteries of God shall be unfolded unto you, and then shall you be made rich. Behold, he that hath eternal life is rich.[3]

3. The early elders bore testimony to the world:

That the Holy Scriptures are true, and that God does inspire men and call them to his holy work in this age and generation, as well as in generations of old, thereby showing that he is the same God yesterday, today, and for ever. [4]

The testimony continued:

And we know that all men must repent and believe on the name of Jesus Christ and worship the Father in his name, and endure in faith on his name to the end, or they can not be saved in the kingdom of God. [5]

4. Those who received this testimony were received into the church in harmony with the following instructions:

No one can be received into the church of Christ unless he has arrived unto the years of accountability before God, and is capable of repentance. [6]

and

All those who humble themselves before God and desire to be baptized, and come forth with broken hearts and contrite spirits, and witness before the church that they have truly repented of all their sins, and are willing to take upon them the name of Jesus Christ, having a determination to serve him to the end, and truly manifest by their works that they have received of the Spirit of Christ unto the remission of their sins, shall be received by baptism into his church. [7]

5. The church continues to function in harmony with these principles:

All are called according to the gifts of God unto them; and to the intent that all may labor together let, him that laboreth in the ministry and him that toileth in the affairs of the men of business and of work labor together with God for the accomplishment of the work intrusted to all. [8]

---

1. Doctrine and Covenants 17:1
2. Doctrine and Covenants 4:1
3. Doctrine and Covenants 6:3
4. Doctrine and Covenants 17:2
5. Doctrine and Covenants 17:6
6. Doctrine and Covenants 17:20
7. Doctrine and Covenants 17:7
8. Doctrine and Covenants 119:8

II. A Theocratic Democracy

6. **The church**, as defined by the late President Joseph Smith, is a theocratic democracy—not man-made, but of divine appointment and origin.[1] It was brought into being by command of God, is guided and administered by his authority, is sustained by the light of his Spirit, and exists for his purposes; but notwithstanding the primary rights of Divinity in his church, our heavenly Father has committed to the Saints an important share in the responsibility of governing his church.

Neither shall anything be appointed unto any of this church contrary to the church covenants, for all things must be done in order and by common consent in the church, by the prayer of faith. [2]

7. **The government of the church** is by divine authority through priesthood.[3] It should be noted that the government of the church is *through* priesthood, not *by* priesthood. The distinction is important. Ministers must first of all be disciples. They must learn the will of God and make this their own. In no other way can their claim to divine authority become rich and meaningful. This is clearly written into the law of the church. For example, an important revelation concerning the functions of the presiding quorums is followed by this instruction:

The decisions of these quorums, or either of them, are to be made in all righteousness, in holiness and lowliness of heart, meekness and long-suffering, and in faith and virtue and knowledge; temperance, patience, godliness, brotherly kindness, and charity, because the promise is if these things abound in them, they shall not be unfruitful in the knowledge of the Lord. And in case that any decision of these quorums is made in unrighteousness, it may be brought before a general assembly of the several quorums which constitute the spiritual authorities of the church. [4]

8. **The reality and extent** of priesthood authority are indicated in such statements as the following:

Whatsoever ye shall bind on earth shall be bound in heaven: and whatsoever ye shall loose on earth shall be loosed in heaven.[5]

Whatever God commands man to do the command carries with it the authority to do the thing commanded to be done. When the church was instituted . . . the Melchisedec priesthood was conferred for the last time before the second and final coming of Christ. . . . This priesthood so conferred was endowed with all the rights, privileges, and authority to bring forth the church of Christ, conduct its expansion, and watch over its development and welfare until the coming of Christ should bring its work to a triumphant and glorious consummation.[6]

9. **The government of the church** includes administrative, legislative, and judicial functions. There are also other ministerial functions such as those of the evangelist and other members of the standing ministry. For the sake of convenience these may be regarded as contributory ministries within the administrative field.

10. **Administrative Functions**

Administration is through members of the priesthood, acting according to their several callings and with the consent of the church. These may be grouped as follows:

The Presidency, who administer the affairs of the entire church.[7]

The Twelve, who represent the Presidency in organized fields and are assisted in this work by stake presidents, regional administrators, district presidents, and branch presidents in their respective responsibilities. The Twelve also direct the missionary work of the church with the members of the Seventy as their chief assistants.[8, 9]

Bishops, who administer the temporal affairs of the church, consisting of

The Presiding Bishopric, who have administrative and trustee responsibilities covering temporal affairs of the entire church, and

Stake, Regional, District, and Branch Bishops.[10]

11. In church administration the rights of the body are safeguarded under the law as follows:

1. By the guidance of the Holy Spirit in calling members to the priesthood.

> Every elder, priest, teacher, or deacon is to be ordained according to the gifts and callings of God unto him; and he is to be ordained by the power of the Holy Ghost which is in the one who ordains him. [11]

2. By the requirement that "no person is to be ordained to any office in this church, where there is a regularly organized branch of the same, without the vote of that church."[12]

3. By the right of approval and recall which rests with the people who are asked to sustain General Church leaders at General Conference, and local leaders at local conferences and business meetings.[13]

4. By the requirement that all things shall be done with due regard for the duties and privileges of other ministers and members and in harmony with the legislative enactments of the body.[14]

5. By the special provisions of the law. For example, that General Conference approves the budget according to which General Church funds are expended.

6. By the provisions for correcting disorder.[15]

7. By the growing understanding that—for the good of all—properly selected administrative officers must be allowed to do their work without undue interference, subject always to the provisions made to cover special situations.[16]

12. Legislative Functions

Legislation is considered and enacted in General Conference, mission, stake, and district conferences, and branch business meetings. These assemblies meet at the call of the responsible administrative officers, at times and places determined by the bodies concerned, or in emergencies at times and places set by these responsible administrative officers.

Every such assembly has authority to legislate for those it represents as long as it does not usurp rights lawfully centered elsewhere. For example, no branch business meeting can legislate for the district, such as requiring certain acts on the part of district officers; no branch or district can enact binding legislation on matters of General Church importance, such as setting up the conditions of church membership; and no branch business meeting or district, stake, or General Conference can change the basic law of the church, such as the law concerning the mode of baptism.

No legislative body can rightfully take to itself administrative or judicial functions such as initiating calls to the priesthood or trying a church member accused of transgression. These matters are specifically placed elsewhere, as is required by the necessities of good organization.

13. Right to Nominate

It is the right of all members to make nominations in filling elective officers in the branch, district, stake, and general church, but this action in no sense denies the right of presiding officers to present concurrent nominations for the filling of such elective offices.

14. Judicial Procedure

All members of the church have right of access to the courts of the church for protection or redress.

Elders' courts are convened as courts of original jurisdiction where no bishop's courts can be had conveniently.

Bishop's courts are standing courts and have original jurisdiction or hear appeals from elders' courts.

High councils exist in stakes and in the General Church. These have original jurisdiction in some matters and may hear appeals from bishop's courts.[17] However, the First Presidency or stake presidencies "have power to determine whether any such case, as may be appealed is justly entitled to a rehearing, after examining the application for appeal and the evidences and statements accompanying it."[18]

In branches or districts where a branch or district bishop is available, all initial court actions should be referred to the bishop's court. In stakes the high council may take original jurisdiction in some actions.[19]

Where no branch, district, or stake bishop, or competent high priests or elders are available, inquiry should be sent to the First Presidency requesting information concerning competent ministers from elsewhere who may be made available to compose a court. Where charges are such as might involve expulsion from the church, the Presidency will do their utmost to make a bishop available.

---

1. Matthew 16: 19, Inspired Version; Doctrine and Covenants 1: 5; I Nephi 3: 221; III Nephi 10: 1
2. Doctrine and Covenants 27: 4
3. Doctrine and Covenants 104; Acts 20: 28 (See General Conference Action of 1925)
4. Doctrine and Covenants 104: 11
5. Matthew 18: 18 (See also John 20: 23; Doctrine and Covenants 19: 1; 83: 6, etc.)
6. *Saints' Herald*, May 21, 1902, page 497.
7. Doctrine and Covenants 104: 4; 107: 39; 122: 1, 2.
8. Doctrine and Covenants 16; 104: 11, 12, 13, 30; 105: 7, 8; 120: 1, 3; 122: 3, 7, 8, 9; 125: 12; 133: 2; 134: 6, etc.
9. Doctrine and Covenants 107: 42; 120: 2, 4, 7; 125: 10.
10. Doctrine and Covenants 42: 8-11, 19; 48: 2; 58: 4, 7, 11, 12; 72:3, 4; 104: 32, 33, 35, 40; 114: 1; 122: 5, 6; 126: 5, 10; 128: 1, 9; 129: 8; 130: 6, etc.
11. Doctrine and Covenants 17: 12
12. Doctrine and Covenants 17: 16
13. Doctrine and Coevnants 120: 2; 121: 2
14. Doctrine and Covenants 120: 4; 125: 14; 27: 4
15. Doctrine and Covenants 122: 10; 126: 10
16. Doctrine and Covenants 120: 7; 125: 4, 14
17. Doctrine and Covenants 99: 1
18. Doctrine and Covenants 99: 14
19. Doctrine and Covenants 68: 3; 122: 10

III. Conferences and Assemblies

15. Conferences are Legislative Assemblies of the church. They may be regular or special. Regular conferences may be held annually, semiannually, or otherwise, as agreed upon by those who constitute their membership. They may represent the church at large, missions, stakes, or districts, and bear names accordingly, as General Conferences, mission conferences, stake conferences, or district conferences. They are subject to the jurisdiction of the First Presidency, ministers in charge, stake presidents, and district presidents.

16. General Conference is the highest legislative body in the church and should be organized with primary reference to its legislative functions.

The General Conference is constituted according to the provisions of the rules of representation and is empowered to act for the entire church. Delegates may present such questions as they have been especially instructed to offer, or only request them, and ask consideration and decision thereon.

17. The General Assembly is a convocation of the priesthood organized as quorums. This is the highest and only authoritative body known to the church as an assembly.[1]

18. Who presides. In the General Conference and in a general assembly, the First Presidency should preside. In case of the absence or disqualification of the First Presidency, the Council of Twelve should so function.

19. Stake and District Conferences are regular gatherings authorized by the general authorities concerned or by stakes or districts or their presiding officers. They have to do with the common interests of the branches and church members within the specified areas.

20. Special Conferences may be called by the First Presidency for the General Conference; by ministers in charge for missions; by stake or district presidents for stakes or districts, or by the bodies concerned. In emergencies special conferences may also be called by general authorities having jurisdiction. The call for special mission, stake, or district conferences should specify the purpose of the conference.

21. Where no previous organization has been effected, members of the Presidency, Twelve, and Seventy take precedence in that order, or in harmony with their specific assignments.[2]

---
1. Doctrine and Covenants 104: 11
2. Doctrine and Covenants 122: 9

IV. Rules of Representation

22. Ex officio members of the World Conference. All high priests, the seventy, division directors, commissioners, staff executives, national ministers, the church secretary, superannuated ministers, district presidents, branch presidents, congregational presiding elders in stakes, and World Conference appointees not included in the foregoing are ex officio members of the World Conference and are entitled to voice and vote in the World Conference upon registering with the Credentials Committee. (Adopted April 1, 1976)

23. Delegates to General Conference. Stakes and districts are authorized to appoint, at their conference or business meeting next preceding the sitting of General Conference, delegates to General Conference who shall be entitled to represent said stake or district. Delegates are members of the General Conference to which they are appointed and are entitled to voice and vote at its sessions.

Conference and business meetings are also authorized to elect up to one alternate delegate for each elected delegate or at least two alternate delegates, said alternates to have full delegate rights if and when they shall be seated with their delegation on recommendation of the Credentials Committee. (Adopted April 1, 1976, GCR 1138)

24. Basis of representation. Each stake and district shall be entitled to one delegate for every one hundred members of said stake or district, and one vote in Conference for each delegate.

Each mission abroad not organized into a district or districts shall be entitled to one delegate and to one additional delegate for every one hundred (100) members above the first one hundred (100); and to one vote in Conference for each delegate,

Regularly organized branches of the church not included in a district shall be entitled to at least one delegate, who shall have the same privileges as other delegates. When the membership of such a branch exceeds one hundred, that branch shall be entitled to one delegate for each one hundred members. The selection of these branch delegates shall be made in regular branch business meetings or in special business meetings of which due notice shall have been given as to time, place and purpose.

25. **Qualifications for delegates.** The only qualification for eligibility as a delegate to the General Conference shall be membership in good standing in the church.

26. **Certification of delegates.** Delegates shall be entitled to act upon registering with the Credentials Committee. This Committee should be supplied with a certified list of delegates, bearing the signatures of stake or district president and secretary; or bearing the signatures of the branch president and secretary if they represent branches in unorganized territory.

This certified list of delegates shall indicate the delegate receiving the smallest number of votes in the election of delegates. In the event that one more than is allowed has been elected, the one so designated becomes the first alternate.

The alternate delegates certified to the Credentials Committee shall be listed in the order of the votes cast for them at their election, and shall be seated by the Committee in place of regular delegates who cannot attend, in the order of such listing; it being understood that the action of the Credentials Committee in this regard shall be based on a written statement signed by the administrative officer and secretary of the conference or business meeting concerned, indicating which properly selected delegates cannot be present. This statement must be in the hands of the Credentials Committee not less than ten days prior to the opening of General Conference.

If a permanent vacancy occurs due to emergency during the ten days prior to or while Conference is in session, the Credentials Committee may seat the next listed alternate if requested in writing by the administrative officer of the Conference or business meeting concerned or his designate. (Adopted April 1, 1976, GCR 1138)

The Credentials Committee shall certify delegates to the General Conference, up to the number to which the stake, district, mission, or branch is entitled.

27. Rules and restrictions of delegate voting. The delegates present at General Conference shall be entitled to cast the full vote of the areas which they represent.

In case of divergence of views among the members of any delegation, the vote of the area shall be divided in the same proportion as the members of the delegation are divided.

No delegate shall be entitled to cast more than twenty delegate votes in the same Conference.

28. (Rescinded by G.C.R. 1011)

29. Organization and membership of delegate district conference. Districts may organize their conferences in harmony with these rules, by providing for delegate conferences, in which the basis of representation shall be determined by the district.

V. General Church Missions and Regions

30. General Church Missions and Regions are administrative units of the General Church. The First Presidency appoints members of the Council of Twelve, or other members of the Melchisedec priesthood, to preside over these administrative areas. The designation of such presiding officers other than members of the Council of Twelve is subject to the approval of the Joint Council of First Presidency and Twelve.

31. Missions and regions may be organized for legislative and educational functions where it is desirable or necessary to facilitate the work of the church; but no such organization invalidates or supersedes branch, district, or stake organization already existing. The conferences of missions and regions are designed to promote the common interests of the area concerned.

32. The designation of the field jurisdictions comprising missions and regions is a function of the First Presidency (with the counsel of the Joint Council of First Presidency, Council of Twelve, and Presiding Bishopric).

33. The minister administratively in charge of the mission or region should be elected president of the conference unless there are good reasons to the contrary. Organization should be held to a minimum, other officers being appointed or elected only as they are found to be necessary.

34. The legislation of mission and regional conferences is confined to matters of concern to the area as a whole and must be in harmony with and subject to General Conference action. Recommendations may also be adopted for reference to the General Conference. Reports should be made to the mission or regional conference by the officers of the mission or region, by the districts and the branches not in districts, and by the

General Church appointees assigned to the mission or region.

These conferences may be organized as delegate conferences according to the provision of Section IV (Rules of Representation), the basis of representation and designation of ex officio members being determined by the conference. (Adopted April 12, 1972, GCR 1108)

VI. Stakes

35. The Nature of Stake Organization

Stakes are the most highly co-ordinated units of church organization. Ideally, a stake is not an association of branches but a well-integrated organization of related congregations. For this reason it is advisable that all the congregations in the stake shall be under the supervision, direct or indirect, of the stake presidency. The presiding officers of these congregations being assistants to the stake presidency, the selection of these congregational presiding officers should be made at the stake conferences, with the right of nomination resting concurrently with the stake presidency and the people. The value of the high priestly ministry in stake organization cannot be fully enjoyed except when these high priests and their associate ministers operate freely throughout the stake under the direction of the stake presidency.

36. Stakes are formed in major centers of gathering for more complete systematizing and honoring of the law of Christ in both spiritual and temporal affairs than is possible in branches and districts. They are "for the curtains, or the strength of Zion."[1] They are not necessarily contiguous.

37. Stakes are organized on recommendation of the First Presidency approved by the Joint Council of the First Presidency, the Council of Twelve, and the Presiding Bishopric, then by General Conference and by the members of the proposed stakes.

In approaching the organization of stakes the following factors are considered: There should be available a sufficient number of members of mature experience in the church, who live in close proximity to a given center; a sufficient number of ministers of high priestly caliber to provide personnel for the presiding councils.

There should also be a sufficiently stable economy to assure permanence, and the possibility of definitely relating the contribution to be made in the area to the advancement of our Zionic program.

38. **A fully organized stake** includes a stake presidency, a stake high council, and a stake bishopric. The stake presidency consists of a president and two counselors, all of whom are high priests. The stake high council is composed of twelve high priests presided over by the stake presidency. The stake bishopric consists of the stake bishop and his two counselors. The latter may be high priests or elders. All of these are ordained and set apart to their respective ministries by the imposition of hands.[2]

39. **The stake presidency** presides over the stake and has immediate charge and oversight of all spiritual activities within the stake and is responsible for the welfare and spiritual discipline of all church members within the confines of the stake, subject to the advice and direction of the general spiritual authorities of the church.

40. **The stake high council** serves at the call of the stake presidency as an advisory board in both spiritual and temporal matters within the stake. This high council is also the highest judicial body in the stake. It has both original and appellate jurisdiction. Appeals are taken to the stake high council from the stake bishop's court in cases which have not been settled by that court to the satisfaction of the parties. Ordinations to the high priesthood within the stake must receive the prior approval of the stake high council.[3]

41. **The stake bishop** is the chief financial officer within the stake, having immediate charge and oversight of General Church finances and properties, and

is responsible to the Presiding Bishopric as trustees. The stake bishop should also be chosen to have charge of stake finances, and in this relationship he is responsible to the stake presidency and to the stake conference for the administration of such finances as trustee in accordance with budgetary appropriations.

However, regarding those matters in which the bishop has specific trustee responsibility he is directly responsible to the stake conference.

The stake bishop is also a judicial officer, the stake bishop's court having original jurisdiction in cases of a local character within the stake. Appeals from the decision of the stake bishop's court may be made to the high council of the stake.

42. If for any cause a **vacancy occurs** in the office of stake president or stake bishop, the First Presidency present to the Joint Council of the First Presidency, Council of Twelve, and Presiding Bishopric their recommendation concerning the filling of such vacancy and, upon approval by the council, this recommendation is presented to the stake conference for consideration and approval. If such approval is obtained, the necessary ordination or ordinations are authorized.

43. Stake conferences are authorized to transact business relating to the maintenance and spread of the work within the stake boundaries, but subject always to the resolutions of General Conference and to the advice of the general authorities in matters committed to these authorities under the law. They may also consider legislation relating to General Church affairs and recommend its enactment by General Conference. Notices of date of conferences should be sent to general officers having jurisdiction.

---

1. Doctrine and Covenants 98: 4
2. Doctrine and Covenants 125: 10
3. Doctrine and Covenants 17: 17;   104: 14

VII. Districts

44. District organization. Districts are organized by the First Presidency of the member of the Council of Twelve concerned, after approval of the organization by the Joint Council of First Presidency, the Council of Twelve, and the Presiding Bishopric.[1] Reasonable notice of the organization meeting must be made available to all who are concerned, stating purpose, time, and place of meeting.

45. The district president is the co-ordinating administrative officer of the church in the district over which he presides. He is entrusted with the care and direction of the branches and district missions through the properly constituted officers of these branches and district missions, and of the nonresident members of the district directly or through the nonresident pastor. It is his duty to plan the extension and development of the work of the church within the district.

All district officers should report to the district president and hold themselves subject to his general direction and counsel.

District bishops and bishop's agents have specific trustee responsibilities in which they are subject to the direction and counsel of the Presiding Bishopric, but, where either a bishop or a bishop's agent serves as trustee of a district or branch, he is responsible for such trusteeship to the district or branch conference, and to the district or branch president according to the provisions of the district or branch budget.

The district president should be kept fully informed of the condition of all branches of the district and should have frequent consultation with the branch presidents concerning their plans and difficulties. He should be informed of the business meetings of the branches of the district and invited to attend and offer any suggestions or nominations he may desire to present. In emergencies, and especially when the branch president is incapacitated or the branch shall have fallen into decay, he may request or call a branch business meeting; in this or any other necessary situation he may recommend procedure, present nominations for office, or do such other things as will best protect the interests of the church. When these interests shall require, he may take over direction of the branch for a time, administering the work thereafter—either directly or indirectly—until a more permanent arrangement can be made. If the district president is thought to have proceeded unlawfully in any of these matters, appeal is to the next higher administrative officer.

In all his work the district president may be assisted by one or more counselors chosen from among the elders and sustained by the vote of the district, provided always that the responsibility of decision in the district presidency shall rest on the district president and shall not be transferred from him to a majority of the district presidency by any action of that presidency.

The district president should seek the counsel of the General Church officers concerned, and should respect this counsel, subject to the appeal provided in the law.[2]

46. **District conferences** are authorized to transact business relating to the maintenance and spread of the work within the district boundaries, but subject always to the resolutions of General Conference and to the advice of the general authorities in matters committed to these authorities under the law. Notice of such conferences should be sent to the First Presidency, the apostle in the field, and to such other general officers as might be concerned with the business to be transacted.

47. **Who shall preside.** The district president presides over the district conference. At his request, or in

his absence, his counselors may preside. Members of the First Presidency or Council of Twelve, or their authorized representatives, may be asked to preside as a courtesy or in view of special circumstances. [3]

48. Duty of the presiding officers. It is the duty of the presiding officers to bring to the attention of the conference such matters as require the consideration or action of the body; to require observance of the rules of order with decorum and propriety; and to secure, as far as he is able, a due respect and regard for the laws governing the church as contained in the Bible, the Book of Mormon, the Doctrine and Covenants, and General Conference enactments.

49. An appropriate order of proceedings for a district conference is as follows:

Opening worship
Reading and approval of the minutes
Reports, communications, and suggestions from the presiding officer
Communications or reports from the First Presidency, the minister in charge or his assistant, the Presiding Bishopric, or other General Church officers (with precedence in the order named)
Reports of the officers of the district, other than the presiding officer
Reports of standing and special committees
Business made the special order of the meeting
Unfinished and new business
Business deferred subject to call
Election of officers
Action on time and place of the next meeting
Adjournment

---

1. Doctrine and Covenants 120: 1; General Conference Minutes 1930, page 130
2. Doctrine and Conference 120: 4
3. General Conference Resolution 580

VIII. Branches

50. Organization of branches. The branch is the primary field organization of the church. It may be a single congregation or it may consist of two or more closely related congregations under a single presidency. Branches are formed by the authority of the First Presidency or of any member of the Council of Twelve having jurisdiction, or by their direction when circumstances prevent them from being present. Multiple congregation branches shall be organized only after approval of the Joint Council of First Presidency, Council of Twelve, and Presiding Bishopric. (Adopted April 13, 1972, GCR 1111)

51. Branch officers. All persons who are to have official status in organized branches should be chosen by vote at a regular meeting of such branch, or at one specially called for that purpose, of which due notice shall have been given.

52. What may be discussed in branch business meetings. Branches may consider legislation relating to branch affairs. They may also consider legislation relating to district affairs and recommend its enactment by district conference.

53. Who shall preside. The branch president presides over the branch business meeting. At his request, or in his absence, his counselors may preside. Members of the First Presidency, Council of Twelve, ministers in charge, or members of the district presidency may be asked to preside as a courtesy or in view of special circumstances.

54. Duties of the presiding officer. It is the duty of the presiding officer to bring to the attention of the body such matters as may require consideration or action; to enforce observance of the rules of order with decorum and propriety; to secure, as far as he is able, a due respect and regard for the laws governing the church as contained in the Bible, the Book of Mormon, the Doctrine and Covenants, and General Conference enactments.

55. Business meeting—when held. Branch business meetings should be held annually or at such other times as are determined by action of the body. Special business meetings may be called by the branch president.

In a multiple congregation branch the basic legislative authority is vested in the general business meeting attended by members of all the congregations. Congregational business meetings are by nature permissive and are called by the officers concerned and deal with issues related solely to the congregation concerned. (Adopted April 13, 1972, GCR 1111)

Authorization of metropolitan branches requires a vote of the members concerned, and all procedural descriptions having a bearing on this type of organization will be developed accordingly. See World Conference Minutes, April 13, 1972.

All branch business meetings shall be scheduled by the branch president in cooperation with the district president. Notice of branch business meetings should be sent to the district bishop or bishop's agent, and to any other district or general officer concerned.

56. Number constituting a quorum. For the transacting of all branch business, unless otherwise provided, six or more members present at any properly called meeting shall constitute a quorum.

57. Duty of members to attend. It is the duty of

every member of the branch to attend branch business meetings, both regular and special.

58. A suggested order of proceedings for the branch business meeting is as follows:

Opening worship
Reading and approval of the minutes
Reports, communications, and suggestions from the presiding officers
Communications or reports from the First Presidency, the minister in charge or his assistant, the Presiding Bishopric, or other General Church officers, and the president or secretary of the district (with precedence in this order)
Reports of officers of the branch other than the presiding officer
Reports of standing committees
Reports of special committees
Business made the special order of the meetings
Unfinished business
Business deferred subject to call
New business
Election of officers
Adjournment to a given date other than the regular time of meeting
Adjournment

IX. Further Instructions Concerning Branches and Districts

59. **In both branches and districts** the presiding officers should be considered and respected in their offices. Nevertheless, the traveling presiding councils of the church, being made by the law, their calling, and the voice of the church the directing, regulating, and advising authorities of the church, and representing it abroad, should when present in either district or branch be regarded and considered as the leading representative authorities of the church, and be respected as such. Their counsel and advice should be sought and respected when given. In cases of conflict, or extremity, their decision should be listened to and regarded, subject to the appeal and adjudication provided for in the law.

He that heareth him that is sent heareth the Lord who sent him, if he be called of God and be sent by the voice of the church.

In these matters, there is no conflict in the law.

In matters of personal importance and conduct arising in branches or districts, the authorities of those branches and districts should be authorized and permitted to settle them; the traveling councils taking cognizance of those only in which the law and usages of the church are involved, and the general interests of the church are concerned. "Where cases of difficulty are of long standing, the council may require local authorities to adjust them; and in case of failure to do so may regulate them as required by their office and duty; and this that the work and church may not be put to shame and the preaching of the word be hindered."[1]

Branches and districts are to be conducted according to the rules given in the law as directed in a former revelation: "They shall take the things which have been given unto them as my law to the church to be my law to govern my church. And these affairs are not to be conducted by manifestations of the Spirit unless these directions and manifestations come through the regularly authorized officers of branch or district. If my people will respect the officers whom I have called and set in the church, I will respect these officers; and if they do not, they can not expect the riches of gifts and the blessing of direction."[2]

---

1. Doctrine and Covenants 120: 4, 5, 6, 7
2. Doctrine and Covenants 125: 14

X. Amendments

60. **The rules and orders** of the Book of Rules may be amended at any General Conference, provided that at least sixty days' notice of the effort to amend in manner and form be previously given in the *Saints' Herald*, the official organ of the church.

FOREWORD

To the General Conference Resolutions

The First Presidency introduced a communication to the General Conference of 1934 with the following statement:

> The compilation of General Conference Resolutions at present issued by the church contains many actions having relation to local or temporary conditions or which have become obsolete through the passage of time or changed practice or by the enactment of fresh legislation. It also includes a number of resolutions defining mission and district boundary lines which the Conference of 1930 provided shall henceforth be determined by administrative action. The Conference has already instructed that further compilations of Conference Resolutions shall be prepared with the idea of guidance in Conference and branch legislation and administration. The Presidency now therefore gives notice of intention to request the General Conference of 1934 to authorize elimination of resolutions listed in the following groups:
>
> 1. Resolutions covered in subsequent revelation
> 2. Resolutions changed by subsequent enactment
> 3. Resolutions dealing with district and mission boundaries
> 4. Resolutions of a temporary nature or the provisions of which have been fulfilled
> 5. Resolutions having become obsolete with the passage of time or changed practice
> 6. Resolutions of historical interest only
>   —*Daily Herald,* April 6, 1934, p. 19.

This request was granted (April 11, 1934, p. 104). The deletions of additional resolutions were authorized by the World Conferences of 1936 (April 15), 1952 (April 1), 1964 (April 11) and 1970 (April 10).

The present compilation is presented in harmony with these actions, the resolutions being numbered to correspond with the earlier publications.

Conference Resolutions, or portions thereof, referring

to Rules and Representation are now included in the Rules of Order. Those dealing with the corporate structures of the church, Graceland College, and the Independence Sanitarium and Hospital are in the Appendixes.

This edition includes all changes authorized by World Conferences through 1980.

It is intended by the Presidency that after the close of each World Conference a supplement will be published containing the Conference enactments.

THE FIRST PRESIDENCY

RESOLUTIONS

General Conference Resolutions

Ordinance of Baptism
Adopted October 7, 1862

48. That whoever administers the ordinance of baptism should use the precise words given in the law of the Book of Covenants, and not substitute his own words in place of the words of God.

Spiritual Authorities
Adopted April 6, 1866

61. That this body [General Conference], now assembled, is a body of spiritual authorities within the purview of the law found in the fifth paragraph of Section 99 of Book of Covenants. (Now D. and C. 104: 11.)

Elders Legal Acts
Adopted April 8, 1868

90. That the legal official acts of elders, though in transgression, are valid till they are officially silenced by proper authority.

Close Communion
Adopted April 9, 1868

91. That unbaptized persons, whether children or adults, are not entitled to partake of the sacrament of bread and wine.

Intoxicating Drinks and Tobacco
Adopted April 9, 1868

92. That this conference deprecates the use of intoxicating drinks (as beverages), and the use of tobacco, and recommends, to all officers of the church, total abstinence.

Quorum Ordinations
Adopted April 8, 1870

109. That all presidents of quorums, and counselors to presidents of quorums, be set apart to their offices by ordination.

Branch Presidents
Adopted April 9, 1870

111. That the law does not make it necessary for high priests to preside over branches, although they have the right to preside when chosen by the branch.

Church Secretary
Adopted April 12, 1870

115. That there be appointed a Secretary of the Church of Jesus Christ of Latter Day Saints, whose duty it shall be to sign all documents authorized by general provisions of General Conference, to sign licenses and certificates issued by the First Presidency, and to perform any and all other duties coming properly within the province of an organized government.

Members in Debt
Adopted April 8, 1871

120. That the members of the Church of Jesus Christ of Latter Day Saints shall not be counted in good standing who will contract debts without a fair prospect of being able to pay the same.

Laying On of Hands
Adopted September 23, 1871

132. That the law of the Lord does not authorize

the administration of the ordinance for the healing of the sick to be performed by any person in the church, except those holding the Melchisedec priesthood.

133. That when a person already a member of the church is baptized to satisfy the demands of conscience, or because of informality in the first baptism, his membership and his priesthood, if he hold any priesthood, should be again confirmed upon him by the laying on of hands.

President of Church
Adopted April 12, 1873

153. That this conference accept and sustain Elder Joseph Smith as President of the High Priesthood of the Church of Jesus Christ of Latter Day Saints, by virtue of which office he is Prophet, Seer, and Revelator to the church.

Gospel to All Mankind
Adopted April 10, 1875

171. That it is the opinion of this assembly that the gospel is to be offered to all mankind, irrespective of color, nationality, sex, or condition in life; and that elders in Christ are not justified in making, or insisting on being made, any separation in church privileges, worship, or sacrament, other than is made in the church articles and revelations in regard to ministerial ordinations and labor; and that we advise all officers of the church to be governed by the spirit and tenor of this teaching and this resolution.

Bread and Wine Use
Adopted April 10, 1875

172. That the bread and wine used at the sacrament

are simply blessed for the use of those who at the time, and with an understanding of its purpose, partake of it, in no way relating to its subsequent use; therefore it is unnecessary to pass the bread until all be taken.

Secret Society
Adopted April 10, 1875

175. That in the opinion of this body, this church has no right to subvert the liberties of its members by prohibiting their membership with what is known as "a secret society," unless such society shall first be condemned by either a decision of the General Assembly of the church or by the law of the land.

Sealing Up to Eternal Life
Adopted April 12, 1877

202. That we know of no law of the church creating or authorizing "sealing up to eternal life" as an ordinance; other than such sealing as may be found in the "laying on of hands for the gift of the Holy Ghost," in confirming members into the church. We therefore decide that such persons as may have performed a rite supposed to be one of "sealing unto life," as an ordinance of the church, have erred, but such error is not of such a nature as to become a crime against the law governing the church, as the fact of such "sealing up unto eternal life" cannot be determined as to its truth, or falsity, except at the judgment day, when the acts of all are to appear for arbitration and decision; therefore the act of those men referred to in the inquiry submitted to us, and of which complaint is made, is not such an act as demands official inquiry and condemnation.

That while there is no ordinance of the kind referred to known to the law, the written law of the church, it is therefore of the things of the unwritten law, if the right exists at all to seal up unto eternal life, other than in confirmation by the laying on of hands for the gift of the Holy Ghost, the performance of such an ordinance, or other solemnizing of such a rite is of doubtful propriety, and should in no case be done except upon unqualified directions of the Spirit. Further, that elders should not teach nor practice such rites as a rule of the church.

Procedure in Baptism
Adopted September 11, 1878

212. That all baptisms, in order to be legal, must be done by both the administrator and the candidate going down into the water, according to the instructions in the Bible, Book of Mormon, and Doctrine and Covenants; and if there are any now numbered with the church who have received the ordinance with any less than the above requirements, that they are hereby required to receive the administration of the ordinance in the above form.

Inspired Version of Bible
Adopted September 13, 1878

214. That this body, representing the Reorganized Church of Jesus Christ of Latter Day Saints, does hereby authoritatively indorse the Holy Scriptures, as revised, corrected and translated by the Spirit of revelation, by Joseph Smith, Jr., the Seer, and as published by the church we represent.

Standard of Authority
Adopted September 13, 1878

215. That this body, representing the Reorganized Church of Jesus Christ of Latter Day Saints, recognize the Holy Scriptures, the Book of Mormon, the revelations of God contained in the Book of Doctrine and Covenants, and all other revelations which have been

or shall be revealed through God's appointed prophet, which have been or may be hereafter accepted by the church as the standard of authority on all matters of church government and doctrine, and the final standard of reference on appeal in all controversies arising, or which may arise in this Church of Christ (see 222).

Tobacco
Adopted September 13, 1878

217. That this body declares that the use of tobacco is expensive, injurious and filthy, and that it should be discouraged by the ministry.

Standard of Authority
Adopted September 29, 1879

222. That the free rendering and meaning of the resolution passed at the semiannual session of 1878 (215) is that:

Whereas, Certain rumors had obtained currency that the church had not at any time so attested the Book of Doctrine and Covenants, and the later revelations given to the church, by vote and affirmation, that they should form with the Bible and Book of Mormon, a standard of reference in case of controversy and difference of opinion upon questions of doctrine and practice in the church; therefore to remedy this defect, if it existed, the resolution referred to was introduced and passed.

Further, it is not the intent and meaning of the said resolution to make a belief in the revelations in the Book of Covenants, or the abstract doctrines possibly contained in it, a test of reception and fellowship in the church; but that the things therein contained relating to the doctrine, rules of procedure and practice in the church should govern the ministry and elders as representatives of the church.

And further, while it is not intended, or indeed practicable to bind, or proscribe the liberty of conscience, whereby violence is done to the honesty and integrity of the people by prescribing dogmas and tenets other than the plain provisions of the gospel, as affirmed in the New Testament, Book of Mormon, and Doctrine and Covenants, and set forth in the Epitome of Faith and Doctrine; it is clear to us that it is destructive to the faith of the church, and inconsistent with the calling and dignity of the ministry, to decry, disclaim, preach, or teach contrary to the revelations in said Book of Covenants, or to arraign them in such a way that the faith of the people of the church is weakened and they thereby distressed.

The elders should confine their teaching to such doctrines and tenets, church articles and practices, a knowledge of which is necessary to obedience and salvation; and that in all questions upon which there is much controversy, and upon which the church has not clearly declared, and which are not unmistakably essential to salvation, the elders should refrain from teaching; or if called upon, in defense of the church, or when wisdom should dictate, they should so clearly discriminate in their teaching between their own views and opinions, and the affirmations and defined declarations of the church that they shall not be found antagonizing their own and others' views as a conflict in teaching upon the part of the church.

The advancing of speculative theories upon abstruse questions, a belief or disbelief in which cannot affect the salvation of the hearers, is a reprehensible practice and should not be indulged in by the elders; especially should this not be done in those branches where personal antagonisms must inevitably arise, to the hindering of the work of grace; and should be reserved for the schools of inquiry among the elders themselves.

Until such time as vexed questions now pending are definitely settled by the competent quorums of the church, the discussion of them should be avoided in all places where the elders labor, in the world and in the branches, and should only be had in solemn conclave when necessary to examine them for settlement, under proper rules of restraint.

Divorce and Remarriage
Adopted April 9, 1884

272. Whereas, We believe that marriage is ordained of God, and that the law of God provides for but one companion in wedlock, for either man or woman—except in cases where the contract is broken by death or transgression; therefore

Resolved, That it is our understanding that in case of separation of husband and wife, one of which is guilty of the crime of fornication, or adultery, the other becomes released from the marriage bond, and if they so desire may obtain a divorce and marry again.

Quorum of Twelve Decisions
Adopted April 11, 1884

280. That the Quorum of the Twelve, as a judicial body, have the right, collectively or individually, to render decisions involving the law and usages of the church, in their various fields of labor, and when such decisions are made by individual members of the quorum, said decisions are binding on the church, and should be respected until brought before the quorum and its decision had.

Local Commandments
Adopted April 11, 1884

282. That the commandments of a local character, given to the first organization of the church are bind-

ing on the Reorganization, only so far as they are either reiterated, or referred to as binding by commandment to this church.

Drinking Intoxicants
Adopted April 9, 1885

297. Inasmuch as some of the members of this church are in the habit of visiting saloons and drinking intoxicants, which habit seems to hinder the spread of the work, therefore be it

Resolved, That . . . it be made a test of fellowship for any member of this church who will persist in this practice. (Presented by the Third Quorum of Elders.)

"Saints' Herald" Editorial Policy
Adopted April 10, 1885

298. With regard to certain measures proposed concerning the publication of articles in the *Saints' Herald,* it was resolved

(1) That the enforcement of ironclad rules and arbitrary decisions by persons who were not governed in their work by broad and liberal principles of toleration, as is shown by the history of societies in the past, has had such a tendency to subvert the liberties and retard the progress of the race, as to make the enactment of any set of rules to be followed under all circumstances of doubtful propriety and final good.

(2) That in our opinion there is a just and proper line to be drawn between the positions of permitting a fair hearing of the views of any and all through the church paper, and the abuse of the sacred principle of toleration and freedom adhered to by the church by using to excess the columns of the church paper, in making a series of attacks upon the life of the body, or an undue effort to enforce personal views upon the people, when

they are clearly in part antagonistic to the accepted faith of the body; and that the responsibility is upon the editor and Board of Publication to see that this line is truly made in their discrimination, the improper exercise or abuse of such discretion, or agency, to be remedied by the selection of such persons for these positions as will fill them in wisdom and fairness to all.

(3) That where radical differences of opinion occur between leading representatives of the body, the discussion of them should take place in quorum capacity, and not through the columns of the *Herald*.

(4) That in the acceptance of articles for publication through the *Herald,* the parties doing the same should exclude all such as make special attack upon the supposed private views and character of the dead, or that impugn motives and question the integrity of the living; there being neither sound argument nor wisdom attained by such methods.

(6) That any man who accepts appointment and ordination as a representative of the church is under obligations to teach, sustain, and seek to establish the faith of the church; and no one, be he whosoever he may be, has any right to attack the divinity of the faith in part, or as a whole, as said faith is set forth in the Bible, Book of Mormon, and Doctrine and Covenants.

Doctrines, Commandments, and Opinions
Adopted April 9, 1886

308. (1) That the presentation of individual opinions by elders, or others of the body, such opinions not having been affirmed by the body as a rule of faith or practice, does not make them a part of the faith or belief of the body; but relate to us individually upon the issue of toleration, which toleration, we believe as was manifested in the action of Jesus while dealing with men here in his ministry, should be so broad as to make no occasion for persons to wish to withdraw from the body by reason of these individual differences of opinion.

(2) That we know of no temple building, except as edifices wherein to worship God, and no endowment except the endowment of the Holy Spirit of the kind experienced by the early saints on Pentecost Day.

(3) That "baptism for the dead" belongs to those local questions of which the body has said by resolution:

"That the commandments of a local character, given to the first organization of the church, are binding on the Reorganization only so far as they are either reiterated or referred to as binding by commandments to this church." And that principle has neither been reiterated nor referred to as a commandment.

(4) That tithing is a law applicable to the church in the sense set forth by the Savior in the sixteenth chapter of the Gospel recorded by Luke, that we are stewards of our heavenly Father so far as the riches of this world are concerned, and that as such we should render an account of our stewardship here; the rendition is in all cases, however, necessarily voluntary on the part of the member complying with the law.

(5) That we know of no "consecration" by which individuals are made legal heirs to the kingdom of God, or church of Christ, when the rewards are apportioned; except that of a life consecrated to the service of the Master as ordained in his word together with the consecration of properties for the aid of the poor, preaching of the gospel and establishment of the said kingdom, as a member of the same has so to impart.

(6) That the sole mouthpiece of the church is Jesus Christ. We are to receive commandments as a church only as Christ communicates the same; and we are entitled, as a church, to be first satisfied that Christ did

give any commandment purporting to come from him, before accepting, or receiving, the same.

(7) That "plenary inspiration" has never been affirmed by the church; but we believe in the so named "authorized" books of the church as true and proper standards of evidence in the determination of all controverted doctrines in theology.

(8) That the doctrine of "cursing" and "avenging enemies," we accept only as explained in paragraph 3 and 4 of Section 102, Doctrine and Covenants, the section referred to by the brethren, wherein the Lord is made the sole executor in behalf of the children of Zion as follows . . .

(9) That we believe in an "imperial dynasty" only, wherein Christ is to be King, and the reigning of such of his servants who keep the faith here with him when he shall come with his rewards. . . .

Ordinations Void When Rebaptized
Adopted April 11, 1888

329. (Note: Part of this resolution was superseded by action of the 1956 General Conference. See paragraph 69 of the Church Court Procedure.)

That in the event of a necessity for baptism, for a renewal of the gospel covenant, the former ordinations of the individual thus baptized become null and void.

Witnesses of Adultery
Adopted April 9, 1891

343. Whereas, There is a difference of opinion existing in the minds of the Saints regarding the requirements of Doctrine and Covenants 42: 22, relating to the trial of parties charged with adultery, some holding that two or more eyewitnesses to the act charged are necessary before conviction, and others believing differently,

Resolved, That . . . the law referred to does not require eyewitnesses to the act charged, but if there are found members of the church who as witnesses testify concerning facts or circumstances bearing upon the case, whose evidence is of a character to remove all reasonable doubt as to the guilt of the parties charged, from the minds of the elders trying the case, it is sufficient. If one eyewitness be found willing to testify in addition to the above it is better, though not absolutely necessary.

Missionary Moves
Adopted April 15, 1892

367. Whereas, A question has arisen in regard to the right of a missionary in charge to move a missionary placed under him from one subdivision of his field to another, after the General Conference has ratified his appointment to the first subdivision, and,

Whereas, The missionary in charge is expected to direct the labor of all under him for the best good of the cause throughout his mission,

Resolved, That in our opinion the authority is vested in the missionary in charge to make all such changes of the above character as in his judgment are necessary to advance the church work, and in so doing he does not violate the sense of the General Conference action regarding the missionary whose field of operation is thus changed.

Authorized Publications
Adopted April 15, 1892

368. *Resolved*, That we recognize the Bible, Book of Mormon, and Doctrine and Covenants as the only standard works of the church; and it is our opinion that every other book, pamphlet, or other publication should

simply rest upon its own merits, the church being responsible only for that which it authorized to be done, or which it accepts after it is done.

Writers-Editors Conform to Law
Adopted April 14, 1893

379. That general church ministers who labor in the literary concerns of the church should conform to the provisions of the law in the Book of Doctrine and Covenants, as found in Sections 70: 3 and 72: 4.

Further, that the Board of Publication be instructed to carry this resolution into effect in its management of the Herald Publishing House.

Report of Joint Council
Adopted April 12, 1894

386. The Joint Council of the First Presidency, Twelve, and High Priests, which had been holding sessions during this conference, presented the following report, which was thereupon adopted by the Conference:

(1) Office in the church of Christ is not conferred to distinguish, or glorify, or increase the importance of the person on whom it is conferred.

(2) Office in the church is conferred for the purpose of accomplishing certain results designed in the instituting and establishing the church.

(3) All offices in the church come properly under the head of the priesthood. Under this general head all the officers are arranged, there being two orders of priesthood: the Melchisedec and the Aaronic.

(4) The scope of the present council is confined to an inquiry into the calling, duties, and prerogatives of the First Presidency, Twelve, and the Quorum of High Priests.

(5) The President of the church is primarily appointed by revelation.

(6) This appointment is confirmed by the vote of the church properly taken.

(7) The Presidency is the leading quorum in the church. That the duty of presiding over the church devolves on that quorum. That it is the prerogative of the President to preside over the whole church, to bear the responsibility of the care and oversight of the work of the church in all its different departments; and through the constituted officers of the church in their various callings, according to the laws, rules, and regulations in force and recognized by the church.

(8) It is the prerogative of the President to receive revelations from God and give them to the church for the direction and government of the affairs of the church.

(9) The members of the Presidency are leading interpreters and teachers of the laws and revelations of God, and are of right presidents of the General Assemblies of the church.

(10) The members of the Presidency are to preside over the High Council, and in the exercise of this duty to render decisions on important causes submitted to that council.

(11) It is the prerogative of the Presidency to receive revelations from God through the President and present them to the church.

(12) The Presidency are the counselors of the Twelve and exercise the right of presidency by direction and council to that quorum.

(13) The calling and duties of the high priests are those of standing or local presidency of branches, dis-

tricts, conferences, or stakes, to the presidency of which they may be called, or appointed by the constituted authorities of the church, in accordance to the law.

(14) "The Twelve" is the second quorum in authority and importance in the general work of the church; and is the leading missionary body of laborers, under the direction and counsel of the Presidency, whose duty it is to preach the gospel, win souls to Christ, administer in the rights of the gospel, carry the gospel to this and every other nation, take charge of and direct other missionaries; and to do any work within their calling, which the necessities of the work and general welfare of the church may demand.

Ministry to Preach Gospel
Adopted April 14, 1894

387. That it is the sense of this Conference that our ministry should confine themselves to the preaching of the gospel, and that they desist from preaching that which cannot be fully sustained by the standard works of the church.

Doctrine of Resurrection
Adopted April 19, 1894

391. The Presidency to whom the resolution on the subject of the resurrection was referred, report:

That, while we are of the opinion that the standard books of the church clearly teach the unconditional resurrection of man, we believe it to be of doubtful propriety for the church to put unnecessary restrictions upon the ministry as to the manner of their teaching those doctrines and matters of faith which are of secondary importance; for, while possible injury may accrue to individuals, here and there, who may be inquiring for the word, from the advocacy of individual views held by some of the laborers in the field; we think such injury less hurtful to the general work than that which would result from the creation of a creed, or the putting restrictions upon the ministry in the form of resolutions restraining the liberty of inquiry and investigation and censuring those who may venture into such investigation, upon what seems to them to be fair grounds.

We therefore recommend that the Conference go no further than to say that it is the belief of the church that the doctrine of the resurrection provides for the rising from the dead, of all men, each in his own order, through the atonement wrought by Jesus Christ.

We cite from the Scriptures such passages as may be aids to understanding upon the subject: Doctrine and Covenants 28: 7, 8; 43: 5; 45: 10; 63: 13; 76: 3, 4, 7; 85: 6, 29. Book of Mormon: II Nephi 6: 24-40; Mos. 8: 80-91; 11: 133-142; Alma 8: 89-107; Alma 19: 21-36; III Nephi 11: 28-33; Mormon 4: 66-74. Bible: John 5: 28; Acts 24: 15; I Corinthians 15: 21-26; Revelation 20: 5, 12, 13; 21: 8; 22: 15.

Emblems of Sacrament
Adopted April 12, 1895

401. That the act of conveying the emblems to those partaking forms a part of the work of "administering the sacrament," and, under the law, neither teachers, deacons, nor laity have right to serve in that capacity.

Church Secretary
Adopted April 12, 1895

411. The office of the Church Secretary was designated as "Secretary of the Reorganized Church of Jesus Christ of Latter Day Saints."

Preaching by Teachers and Deacons
Adopted April 9, 1898

449. Whereas, The law contained in Section 17, paragraph 11, Doctrine and Covenants, clearly authorizes teachers and deacons to "take the lead of meetings, . . . to warn, expound, exhort, and teach, and invite all to come unto Christ"; and

Whereas, In Section 42, paragraph 5, teachers are required, together with elders and priests, to teach the principles of the gospel; and in Section 120, paragraph 2, either of said officers is permitted to preside; and

Whereas, In our judgment said duties include in their performance what is commonly understood to be preaching; and

Whereas, In Section 83, paragraph 22, teachers and deacons are limited in their duties to local service,

Resolved, That in our judgment teachers and deacons are authorized by the law to labor as preachers within branches to which they belong, when they are presidents thereof, or with the advice and consent of the chief presiding officer.

Appointee Standards
Adopted April 16, 1898

463. Whereas, The Lord has spoken against the use of tobacco and strong drink on different occasions; and

Whereas, In all our appointments we ought to show respect unto said counsel. Therefore

Resolved, That henceforth we recommend no man for General Conference appointment whom we know to be addicted to either of the above evils.

Quorums and Departments History
Adopted April 11, 1900

470. *Resolved,* That this Conference request each of the several quorums and all other departments to prepare a record of their work for the Church Historian for each year's report.

Duties of Deacons
Adopted April 12, 1900

471. The following was adopted by a committee of the Conference and later by the Conference as a statement of the Duties of Deacons.

"Every branch must have a place of meeting. This place of meeting, if a public building, hall, or meeting house, or church, must be in the actual possession of the association of church members worshiping there, at least during its occupancy while worship; and if the property is owned by the church, someone must have constructive possession at all times.

"What particular officer of the church has precedence of right in this constructive possession? The right to carry the keys; open the doors; conduct visitors, either those belonging or not belonging to the church; to see that the floors, doors, windows, pulpit or stand, seats, table or stand, lamps and other fixtures are clean and in good order; to open the doors at the hour of gathering for preaching, fellowship, prayer, or business meetings; to see that the lamps or candles are trimmed, lighted, and burning in time for evening meetings; to see that the members coming in find seats; to keep watch over the Saints during meetings, repressing loud talking, whispering and laughing, reproving the thoughtless, and rebuking the giddy; putting a prompt stop to rude, indecent, and boisterous acts by which the propriety, solemnity, and peace of the meetings may be disturbed; to exercise kind and diligent supervision over the health and comfort of the Saints while in meeting by securing a proper ventilation of the room; to light and keep burning the fires by which the room is kept warm; to have charge of the treasury; to receive, disburse, and account for the contributions of the Saints intended for necessary and incidental expenses of the association of members; to keep, preserve from damage, and account for all personal effects of the association; to visit the poor, ascertain their needs and report the same to the church; and in fact, to perform any and all of those necessary duties by which the welfare of the Saints is secured through a careful administration of the outward ordinances, a faithful employment of the talents entrusted to that man. It follows then of a necessity that the right, the duty of the performing these acts, these unwritten but essential things of the law, devolve upon the office of deacon."

District Historians
Adopted April 21, 1900

498. Whereas, The Church Historian recommended the appointment of district historians in districts, to assist him; therefore be it

Resolved, That he be empowered to appoint such persons and in such places as he may deem proper, according to his discretion.

Private Publication of Literature
Adopted April 14, 1904

550. *Resolved,* That the writing and publishing of literature as private enterprises by parties whose time belongs to the church by virtue of ordination or appointment, where the profits of said publication are appropriated to their private ends, is unwise and should be discouraged. (Reaffirmed April 15, 1912).

Stake Officers
Adopted April 14, 1904

551. That stake officers when presenting themselves to the appointing powers for appointment may be appointed as missionaries, but to appoint the stake presidency or bishopric outside the limits of the stake, thus interfering with the operation of local organizations, would be unwise.

That for stake organizations to choose General Church officers or men under General Conference appointment and ordain them stake officers without consent of the general body is improper.

All missionaries under General Conference appointment, whether in stakes or out, are under the general direction of the minister in charge, but the stake presidency has the right to direct local laborers within the stake not under General Conference appointment.

Age for Baptism
Adopted April 15, 1904

552. That children under eight years of age are not eligible for baptism in the church.

College Day
Adopted April 8, 1905

558. That one day in each year be set apart, to be known as College Day, upon which offerings, in the manner of collections, shall be taken up in all districts and branches of the church, to aid the college work, the same to be forwarded to the Bishop of the church to be devoted to such purposes.

Superannuated Ministers
Adopted April 15, 1905

560. Whereas, The general missionary list has those on it who by reason of age and other disabilities are unable to travel and perform satisfactory missionary labor in the active field; and

Whereas, It is our conviction that the list should be kept up to the best working condition possible, and the Presidency having advised removing from the list those who are not effective missionaries, the Bishop also requesting us to release those who by reason of lack of ability, infirmities of old age, physical condition, or family surroundings, that make it impracticable for them to do the work of an active missionary in the field; therefore be it

Resolved, That we revise our list, retiring those who are incapacitated for active missionary work, from the general missionary list. Those aged ones, who by long and faithful services are entitled to our special consideration, should be placed on the retired list, known as "superannuated ministers," they to do such labor as their strength and circumstances will permit, in harmony with local authorities under the direction of the missionary in charge; and they should receive the same consideration as the general appointees in the field, if their circumstances require it, they to report their labors and financial condition to the minister in charge annually.

Appointments to this list should be made by the Presidency, Twelve, and Bishopric, in joint session, and published with the balance of the appointments.

Secret Society
Adopted April 16, 1907

593. That we discourage members of the Reorganized Church of Jesus Christ of Latter Day Saints from holding membership in any society or order which requires the taking of oaths or the entering into covenant or obligation to guard the secrets, purposes, or doings of its organization.

Member-Branch Responsibility
Adopted April 16, 1907

594. That members of the church are under the jurisdiction of, and amenable for their conduct to, the branch and district where they are residents, temporarily or permanently, and must answer to complaints duly filed with the officers of the branch or district where they are residing at the time when the acts complained of are performed though their homes and branch membership may be in some other branch.

And further, that all church members are amenable to the branch most convenient to the place where they may be residing or sojourning, and if there is no organized branch, then to the district, or General Church authorities, and should answer to such local authority for their conduct.

Speculative Enterprises
Adopted April 17, 1907

595. That we disapprove of our ministry giving their attention to speculative mining or other ventures or their promotion; and that we advise all persons who may decide to invest in any enterprises of this kind to do so only after such investigation as shall be fully satisfactory to themselves as to the safety of their venture, the same as in other business enterprises, and not upon their confidence in the ministerial position of those who seek to interest them therein.

Financing Ministers
Adopted April 15, 1908

606. Whereas, The law of God specifically predicates ministerial support upon the law of necessity (see Doctrine and Covenants 81: 4; 77: 1; 70: 3; 51: 1); and

Whereas, There is no provision in the law for any minister receiving financial aid from the church not based upon his actual needs; therefore be it

Resolved, That hereafter all those engaged in General Church or ministerial work be supported in harmony with the aforementioned provisions of the law.

Credentials Committee
Adopted April 9, 1909

617. That the First Presidency be authorized to appoint a committee on credentials prior to the convening of General Conference.

High Priests, Calling and Ordination
Adopted April 8, 1910

638. (Submitted by the First Presidency on request)

The ordination of high priests is to be by direction of a high council (either a stake high council or the Standing High Council) or the General Conference (see Section 17, paragraph 17, Book of Covenants; also Section 120, paragraph 2). The call of high priests is the same as provided for others that is, by revelation, as see Hebrews 5: 4. But we find no direction in the revelations and rules of the church determining the manner in which the call and recommendation for ordination are to be made. (See GCR 1051 for paragraphs 2, 3, and 4.)

Referring of Petitions
Adopted April 11, 1910

640. Whereas, Courtesy and justice, as well as the rules of the church, require that petitions, addressed to the body receive recognition from the body; and

Whereas, The reading of them often consumes time without profit;

Resolved, That the president of the Conference be authorized to announce to the body the nature of such petitions and if no objection is urged refer them to committees or quorums having jurisdiction without reading.

Conference Reports
Adopted April 12, 1911

666. Only quorums which are general in organization need report directly to General Conference. Others should report to the conference of immediate jurisdiction, whether stake or district.

Each quorum should file regular reports with the First Presidency and such matters concerning the quorums as are necessary to reach the General Conference can do so through the Presidency or the local conferences.

Ordinance of Blessing
Adopted April 9, 1913

701. That the ordinance of blessing should not be administered to children who are old enough to be baptized.

Sacrament Wine
Adopted April 9, 1913

702. That fermented wine should not be used in the Sacrament services of the church, but that either unfermented wine or water should be used, and so be in harmony with the spirit of the revelations. (See Doctrine and Covenants 26: 1; 86: 1; 119: 5.)

Requirement for Baptism
Adopted April 15, 1913

705. That all that is required of a candidate requesting baptism is for the candidate to satisfy the church authorities that he is worthy, and that it is not necessary to make a public request.

Publication of Prophecies
Adopted April 18, 1913

709. Whereas, the collection of prophecies and statements other than those which are accepted and approved by the General Church, claiming to be of spiritual origin, some of which may be of doubtful character, and the records of what may be regarded as miracles, and the publishing of such in books or pamphlets and so parading them before the public partakes of the nature of boasting, which is contrary to the instructions of the Master: "But a commandment I give unto them, that they shall not boast themselves of these things, neither speak them before the world; for these things are given unto you for your profit and for salvation" (Doctrine and Covenants 83: 11); and

Whereas, We believe that such publications are detrimental to the best interests of the church and encourage an undue desire for such experiences; therefore be it

Resolved, That we look with disfavor upon such publications and recommend that the resolutions which are already on record have the respectful consideration and observance of the brethren who are affected thereby. (See General Conference Resolutions 368, 550.)

Bishopric Terminology
Adopted April 18, 1913

710. The term "The Bishopric," as used in the revelations to the church, refers to the Presiding Bishopric, and also to the association of men holding the office of bishop under a presiding head; therefore, be it

(1) *Resolved,* That when reference is made to the Presiding Bishop and his counselors, the term "The Presiding Bishopric" be employed. Be it further

(2) *Resolved,* That when reference is made to the bishop of a stake and his counselors, the title "Stake Bishopric" should be used. Be it further

(3) *Resolved,* That when the association of all the bishops and their council is referred to, the term "The Bishopric," or "Order of Bishops" be applied. (See 788.)

Filing Adultery Confessions
Adopted April 19, 1913

713. That in cases of adultery where the guilty member has repented, and the matter is not publicly known, a written confession duly signed and witnessed by one or two officers of the church shall be sufficient to establish the fact of the first offense; said confession, and associated statements by the officer or officers, to be forwarded to the First Presidency's office to be filed in the archives, which are not open to any other officers than the Presidency. The offense should not be made a matter of record in the home branch or district and should not be published by these officers receiving the confession.

If, however, the person should later fall into delinquency, then there should be some way to protect the interest of the church in the operation of the law which requires that the second offense of adultery shall not be forgiven, but there would be no way for the first offense to be known unless there was provision made whereby the officers could be acquainted with the first offense. This can be reached in the instance above cited if the request recently made by the First Presidency will be complied with by local officers; namely, that whenever charges of a serious character are preferred against a member, the Presidency shall be immediately notified of the charges. This would enable the Presidency to notify the officers in the case that they had record of a previous offense unknown to the officers who had formulated the later charges. We think the filing of the confessions with the Presidency would be safer than having them filed with either branch or district presidents, as there is less likelihood of their becoming public property if lodged there than if lodged with a local authority.

Church Is True Exponent of Christ
Adopted April 21, 1913

718. That this representative body—the Reorganized Church of Jesus Christ of Latter Day Saints—is the true exponent of the faith and doctrine of the New Testament Scriptures, as left by Jesus Christ, as corroborated by the blessings of direct revelation in all its forms to us and our immediate predecessors in these latter days.

Certificates of Stewardship
Adopted April 8, 1914

722. That the Presiding Bishop be authorized to issue certificates of stewardship.

Printing Advertisements
Adopted April 11, 1914

725. That we instruct the Board of Publication not to accept for printing in the church papers any advertisements of real estate dealers or banking institutions, mining stock, and other projects of a speculative character.

Validity of Charges Filed
Adopted April 8, 1915

743. That when charges are filed against any [member], with any responsible officer of the church, it should be left to the discretion of such officer to decide as to the validity of the charges and the advisability of empaneling a court of investigation, subject to appeal as provided for in the law.

Individual Sacrament Service
Adopted April 8, 1915

747. That the individual Sacrament service be used throughout the church, as the authorized form of service, in conformity with the laws of health as prescribed by the health officials of the United States.

Labor of Superannuated Ministers
Adopted April 7, 1916

755. That the labor of superannuated ministers should be in the vicinity of their residence, under the local authorities, and of the missionary in charge where such labor is missionary in character; and that where any superannuated minister desires to labor in fields other than his residence, he should secure the consent of the First Presidency and the missionaries in charge of the fields concerned.

Oblation
Adopted April 10, 1917

773. That every branch should comply with the law by receiving oblations at Sacrament services, as found in Doctrine and Covenants 59: 2, and that the amount so received should be placed with the Bishopric in harmony with Doctrine and Covenants 42: 8.

Appointment of Department Heads
Adopted April 6, 1918

782. That the directing heads of the several departments of church work be hereafter appointed by nomination from the Presidency of the church, approved by the General Conference, in so far as their appointment may not already be provided for in articles of incorporation under which they may be working.

Agreements of Working Harmony

[With Church of Christ]

Adopted April 8, 1918

783. (Included for historical value. See GCR 858)

1. Agreed, that we believe in the restoration of the gospel, and the angel's message through Joseph the Seer.

2. Agreed, that so far as the fundamental principles of the gospel of Christ are concerned, both organizations believe the same, as per copies of the epitome.

3. Agreed, that the Book of Mormon is a divine record, and the redemption of Zion must be by purchase.

4. Agreed, that we indorse the revelations contained in the 1835 edition of Doctrine and Covenants.

5. Agreed, that we indorse the revelation found in the letter from Joseph Smith, the Seer, to W. W. Phelps

concerning the "one mighty and strong," dated November 27, 1832.

6. Agreed, that we indorse the articles on Marriage and of Governments and Laws in General, in the 1835 edition of the Doctrine and Covenants.

7. Agreed, that we believe that there are individuals in the different factions who hold the priesthood.

8. Agreed, that where there are six or more regularly baptized members, any one of which is an elder, there the church exists.

9. Agreed, that an organization is necessary and such an organization as the number of members, and the will of God enables them to attain to.

10. Agreed, that wherever a branch exists the power of church extension exists also to its fullest extent, when acting in harmony with the law.

11. Agreed, that any man holding the priesthood, and possessing the proper qualifications, may be chosen by the church, by acting in accordance with the law to act in any specific position.

12. Agreed, that faith and righteousness and the call of God are the chief essentials for the possession of the Melchisedec priesthood.

13. Agreed, that in the opinion of this council, in order to accomplish the work of the Lord committed to his people, it is necessary for them to unite in one organization, in harmony with the law of God.

14. Agreed, that the city of Zion will be built at Independence, Missouri, and that the Saints of God will gather there.

15. Agreed, that the principle of consecration is necessary to the establishment of Zion.

16. Agreed, that the law of Christ requires that every

man be made a steward, and that none are exempt from this law who belong to the church of the living God, whether officer or member, and that all shall be equal in temporal things, and that not grudgingly, in order to be united according to the law of the celestial kingdom; and that the time has fully come to apply this law in Zion; and that we will labor together to see that it is enforced as soon as possible.

17. Agreed, that we believe in the literal gathering of Israel, and the restoration of the "Ten Lost Tribes."

18. Agreed, that Christ will reign personally upon the earth, and the earth will be restored to its paradisaical glory.

19. Agreed, that the question of who the one "mighty and strong" is, whether Christ or man, be left an open question until further revelation from God shall definitely determine who it is.

20. Agreed, that the doctrine of baptism for the dead (by proxy) be not taught as a part of the faith and doctrine of the church unless commanded by a revelation accepted by the church.

21. Agreed, that what is known as the "King Follet sermon" and the book of Abraham be not accepted as the basis for doctrine.

22. Agreed, that the branch of the Church of Christ on the Temple Lot, which was presided over by Elder Granville Hedrick and his successors, shall be continued, and that no change be made in the custody of the Temple Lot.

23. Agreed, that all other minor points of difference in belief and practice, that may exist between the officers and members of the two organizations, be left to the

elders for settlement as they assemble in council from time to time.

24. Agreed, that whereas the Church of Christ and the Reorganized Church of Jesus Christ of Latter Day Saints consist of members who have been baptized by men holding authority, conferred by ordination under the hands of the servants of God, called during the ministry of Joseph Smith, who have remained true to the original faith of the church, organized April 6, 1830, and, whereas, both organizations stand for and maintain the same fundamental doctrine and practice, and have the same purpose and ideal in their church government and work; therefore, be it mutually agreed, that each recognize the standing of the other as representing Christ, the Master, and the priesthood of each as legally constituted, and the administration of each as equally binding before God, when done in accordance with the law.

Church Architect
Adopted April 9, 1918

784. That the Presidency be authorized to appoint a Church Architect.

Order of Bishops
Adopted April 12, 1918

788. Whereas, Some misunderstanding and confusion have arisen over the statement in Doctrine and Covenants 129: 8, and the Conference Resolution 710, concerning the personnel of the Bishopric, therefore be it

Resolved, That the term "Bishopric," as used in Doctrine and Covenants 129: 8, has reference to the men holding the office of bishop under a presiding head and that these should constitute the Order of Bishops.

Church Insurance
Adopted April 17, 1919

800. That we look with favor upon the church carrying its own insurance on church properties, the details of which are to be worked out by the Presiding Bishopric.

Presidents of Seventy
Adopted April 18, 1919

802. Whereas, The method of selecting Presidents of Seventy is provided for by the Lord in the Doctrine and Covenants, Section 124, paragraphs 5, therefore be it

Resolved, That the Presidents of Seventy shall not be restricted or prevented from making such selections in harmony with the said provisions, subject to the approval of the church.

Elders Expense Reports
Adopted April 18, 1919

804. That each general officer and Conference appointee shall keep an itemized account of all receipts and expenditures for personal and traveling expenses and make report thereof monthly to the Presiding Bishop, upon blanks to be furnished for that purpose, to be prepared by the Presiding Bishopric.

Conference Time and Place
Adopted April 9, 1920

808. That the recommendation of the President of the Church relating to time and place of holding of General Conference be adopted. (The place, Independence, Missouri; the time to be named on consideration.)

Common Consent
Adopted October 9, 1923

834. Inasmuch as question has arisen in the church over the meaning and application of the law of common consent; and

Inasmuch as the church of Christ is a theocratic democracy, in which the will of God is executed by divinely appointed ministers, with the consent of the members; therefore be it

Resolved, That we, the officers and delegates of the Reorganized Church of Jesus Christ of Latter Day Saints in General Conference assembled, reaffirm our belief in and our adherence to the principle of common consent as set forth in the Doctrine and Covenants, the Book of Mormon, and the Holy Scriptures; and be it further

Resolved, That this Conference affirm the right of the membership to nominate in filling all elective offices in church, stake, district, and branch organizations in the various conferences and business meetings, general and local; and be it further

Resolved, That this action shall in no way be interpreted as denying the right of presiding officers to present to the appropriate conferences or business meetings concurrent nominations for the filling of such elective offices.

Appointments
Adopted October 11, 1923

839. *Resolved,* That all general representatives of the church receiving appointments shall have such appointments submitted to General Conference for ratification.

That nothing in this action shall be so construed as

to prohibit the appointing powers from making changes or other appointments between Conferences.

Stewardship Responsibilities
Adopted October 13, 1923

847. Whereas, The law of God teaches that the earth is the Lord's and the fullness thereof; therefore:

(1) All men are of necessity stewards.

(2) The law of stewardships applies individually to each and every member of the church (D. and C. 42: 9; 70: 3; 101: 2; 118: 4). Therefore be it

Resolved, That the Order of Bishops believe it to be the duty of every member of the church to acknowledge his stewardship by complying with the law as given in the Scriptures:

(1) Filing his inventory
(2) Paying his tithe
(3) Paying his surplus
(4) Making his offerings
(5) And thereafter giving an account of his stewardship annually as required by the law of God.

In accordance with the foregoing, the members of the church, "who are willing and desirous" (D. and C. 128: 1), under the general supervision of the officers ordained of God for this purpose, may establish such organizations as are contemplated in the law whenever and wherever circumstances warrant this procedure.

In order to accomplish these purposes, we deem it the duty of each individual to endeavor as far as is consistent with wholesome standards of living to establish a plane of living that will make possible an annual increase.

Church Government
Adopted April 11, 1925

849. This church, as defined by the late Joseph Smith, is a theocratic democracy—not man-made, but of divine appointment and origin (Matt. 16: 19; D. and C. 1: 5; I Nephi 3: 221; III Nephi 10: 1).

The government of the church is by divine authority through priesthood (D. and C. 83: 3; 104; Acts 20: 28). The government in its objective is beneficent, and its purpose is betterment of human conditions. The divine authority becomes operative through the consent of the governed—the common consent indicated in the law (D. and C. 25: 1; 27: 4). It is divine government among the people, for the people, and for the glory of God and the achievement of his purposes toward ideal conditions.

God directs the church through clearly indicated channels (D. and C. 43: 1, 2; 27: 2); and his voice is the directing power of the church; but to this the assent of the people must be secured.

In organic expression and functioning there must be recognized grades of official prerogative and responsibility (D. and C. 104; 122: 9), with supreme directional control resting in the Presidency as the chief and first quorum of the church (D. and C. 122: 2, 9; 104: 42). This control it is presumed is beneficent. Protection against prostitution of this power is amply provided in the law.

To carry into effect the purposes of the church, effective administration is imperative, and organic solidarity is maintained only by effective discipline, which is in consonance with the beneficent purposes of the church, but yet strongly enough administered to prevent the purposes of the organization being frustrated by individual caprice and rebellion. Authority to be effective must be respected.

This view of the organization of the church affirms

the interdependence of departments and co-ordination of action and holds General Conference as the instrument of the expression of the will of the people. (See G. C. R. 861, April 10, 1926.)

Zionic Program
Adopted April 13, 1925

851. *Resolved,*

1. That we favor the immediate initiation of a program looking toward the establishment of Zion and the application of the law of stewardships, which program is as follows:

2. That the Bishopric secure completed financial statements by the selection of a corps of men qualified by special training (if possible) who shall be assigned territory with a view to securing these financial statements by personal contact.

3. That financial statements be provided which are especially designed to serve these purposes.

4. That the members of the church be requested to file their financial statements annually.

5. That arrangement for the payment of tithes due the church should be made at the time of filing of the inventory.

6. That all who are willing and desirous should be placed upon the stewardship basis, either individual or group, as they shall manifest the essential qualifications.

7. That books, tracts, etc., expressing the social ideals of the church should be published without delay.

8. That ministerial propaganda of the church include the presentation of the social ideals of the church with

specific reference to the law of tithing and consecration, that they may co-operate in the education of the Saints, particularly young people and inquirers.

9. That the people of the church should be urged to gauge their expenditures in accordance with definite budgets to be formulated with the idea of maintaining an equitable standard of living consistent with the attainment and perpetuation of their maximum efficiency and the needs of the group.

10. That in looking to the completion of the surveys of man power, capital, markets, territories, etc., a bureau of research and service should be established.

11. That the determination of the order of economic development should be given immediate consideration.

12. That the surplus consecrated from stewardships in operation should be set aside for, or at once used in, the establishment of other stewardships.

13. That in view of the extension of our social organization, there will be necessity for providing vocational guidance and training.

Presidency as Editors
Adopted April 13, 1925

852. *Resolved,* That the Board of Publication should recognize the First Presidency as being in general editorial charge of the various periodicals of the church. (Earlier part of a larger resolution adopted this date, the remainder being rescinded by G. C. R. 911, April 9, 1932, and this part retained.)

Standing High Council Members
Adopted April 14, 1925

853. *Resolved,* That in the selection of members of

the Standing High Council, Section 99 of the Doctrine and Covenants be reaffirmed as the constitutional law of the church, and that the Presidency be authorized to fill vacancies in the Council, to act temporarily (subject to ratification by the body) that cases before the Council may be heard. (Restated from G. C. R. 341, 565, 566, 656 and 853; this latter resolution reinstating parts of earlier resolutions which had previously been rescinded.)

Appointees to Be Affirmative
Adopted April 14, 1925

854. Whereas, The law of God has warned the church that no person is to be permitted "to frustrate the commands of the body in Conference assembly," and has directed that those who oppose what may be presented to the Conference should voice their objections in the conferences and not in the fields of labor (Doctrine and Covenants 125: 16); therefore be it

Resolved, That the Conference appointees and ministry be requested to go forward from the Conference with an affirmative message in consonance with the voice of the church as set forth in the constitutional laws and legislative enactments.

Agreements with Church of Christ Rescinded
Adopted April 7, 1926

858. Whereas, The Reorganized Church of Jesus Christ of Latter Day Saints and the "Church of Christ" people at their respective General Conferences in 1918 adopted what were termed "Articles of Working Harmony" (see G. C. R. 783), these articles having previously been adopted by committees representing the two organizations, and being the outgrowth of committee meetings extending over a number of years and of a mutual spirit of fraternity that seemed to be developing and increasing at that time; and

Whereas, Unfortunately, more recent events have greatly disturbed that spirit of "working harmony" to the point where the question of rescinding the "Articles of Working Harmony" is thrust upon our attention; and

Whereas, At a meeting of a committee representing the "Church of Christ" and a committee representing the Joint Council of Presidency, Twelve, and Presiding Bishopric of the Reorganized Church of Jesus Christ of Latter Day Saints, held October 4, 1925 (Clarence Wheaton, A. O. Frisbey, A. E. Himes, and T. J. Sheldon composing the committee first named and Elbert A. Smith, J. A. Gillen, J. F. Curtis, Israel A. Smith, and Mark H. Siegfried constituting the committee lastly named), we are informed for the first time by Clarence Wheaton, as spokesman for the "Church of Christ" Committee, and joint chairman of the meeting, and by other members of the committee, that the "Church of Christ" had by conference action, taken about 1921, greatly modified if not abrogated article four of the "Articles of Working Harmony," and

Whereas, Article four bound both organizations to accept the revelations contained in the 1835 edition of the Book of Doctrine and Covenants, and from our standpoint was and is vital to the agreement, and its modification or repudiation without our concurrence or knowledge would tend to vitiate the entire articles of agreement; and

Whereas, Constructions have been put upon the articles of agreement by the "Church of Christ" people which evidently were never by the Reorganized Church intended to obtain, under which we are represented as having made concessions which we do not believe were intended to be made by the Conference which adopted the articles of agreement, which Conference evidently did not intend to concede the "Church of Christ" people on the Temple Lot to be the church in succession or that it had power of expansion to become the church in succession or that its priesthood had authority to include any power of expansion into organized quorums, as the organic church in succession; and

Whereas, We hold and verily believe the Reorganized Church of Jesus Christ of Latter Day Saints to be the church of Jesus Christ in direct succession to the church organized by commandment from heaven on April 6, 1830, so recognized by the courts of the land and so recognized by our heavenly Father whose Spirit is still the guiding force in the work of the great Restoration, its priesthood in organized quorums having been organized, built up, and recruited by divine call and legal ordination until the present day, which fact herein set forth seems not to be consistent with the present claims and policies of the "Church of Christ" people; therefore, be it

Resolved, That the "Articles of Working Harmony" adopted by the Conference of 1918 be and are hereby rescinded and declared null and void and no longer binding upon or representative of the church.

Presidents of Seventy Reorganized
Adopted April 10, 1926

860. (Although the action contemplated in the following resolution was completed, the resolution is included for its significance in any similar situation.)

A joint council of the Presidency, Quorum of Twelve, and the Seventy reported action, as follows:

Under the date of April 9, the President and Twelve by unanimous vote adopted the following recommendations to the Joint Council of Seventy:

"The Joint Council of First Presidency and Quorum

of Twelve have had in mind the matter of reorganization of the Seventy as per resolution of last General Conference, and take the liberty to observe and suggest:

"1. The action of the Conference as we understand refers to the Presidency, Twelve, and Seventy as a council this entire matter of reorganization.

"2. While the Presidency and Twelve under this commitment bear equally with the Seventy this responsibility, it is not the wish of these quorums first named to function further than is necessary in any reorganization thought to be desirable.

"3. It is therefore in our opinion fitting that the Seventy be left free to act largely on their own responsibility, particularly touching the Council of the Seven Presidents, if any change is to be effected in the personnel of this council.

"4. We therefore recommend that the several members of the Council of Seven Presidents be voted upon by the Seventy with a view to sustaining such as they may desire to continue, or all if they so desire.

"5. And that we may proceed in a manner of dignity and fairness to all, and with a view to the least possible friction, we recommend further that when and if a vote is taken, it be by ballot, on each of the names separately, the meeting to be presided over by the president of the Quorum of Twelve.

"This Council has in mind further suggestions for your later consideration, if you so desire."

These recommendations were submitted to the Seventy on April 9 at their meeting at the Liberty Street Church, and were by them approved by unanimous vote. Apostle J. A. Gillen, president of the Quorum of Twelve, thereafter immediately presided over a session of the Joint Council of Seventy, at which time they proceeded to ballot upon each of the members of the Presidents of Seventy, resulting in the sustaining of James W. Davis, E. A. Curtis, and R. L. Fulk.

At a meeting of the Presidency and Twelve, the following recommendation was adopted, as set out in the copy of letter to the Joint Council of Seventy which follows:

"The Council of the Seven Presidents of Seventy one year ago filed with the Presidency and Twelve recommendation looking to the setting apart of Eli Bronson as a member of that council. The nomination is transmitted to you with the approval of the Joint Council of Presidency and Twelve."

This, upon being submitted to the Joint Council of Seventy, was supported by unanimous vote.

The selection of Elder Eli Bronson as a member of the Council of Presidents of Seventy is submitted to the Conference for approval.

Basic Doctrines Affirmed
Adopted April 10, 1926

861. Whereas, Distress and sorrow have troubled some minds and hearts, due to a misunderstanding and misinterpretations of the Document on Church Government adopted by the General Conference of 1925, and

Whereas, Particularly that portion of the document referring to "supreme directional control" as resting with the First Presidency has by some been represented as implying autocracy, papacy, infallibility, monarchy, an invasion of the legislative rights of the people, etc., and

Whereas, Such implications have been foreign to our understanding and in no way representative of the intentions of those who framed and supported the document and in no way representative of the intentions of those who administer it, and

Whereas, We desire as far as possible to promote a clearer and more unified understanding, that wounds may be healed, and all be assisted to find true fellowship and final salvation in the church, therefore be it

Resolved, That we approve the interpretation set forth by President Frederick M. Smith and his associates, which interpretation recognizes:

First, the supremacy of God, who so loved the world that he gave his only begotten Son, and the divine right of that Son as builder of the church militant and the church triumphant to overrule and guide all the affairs of his church through the ministration of his Holy Spirit in testimony to all faithful Saints and through revelation to the one called and ordained to receive revelation for the church;

And which recognizes, second, the undisputed right of General Conference as the chief legislative body of the church in the legislative arm of the church through which the people may speak and either approve or disapprove or initiate legislation;

And which, third, sets forth, in the administrative work of the church only, the right of the Presidency as the chief or first executive body of the church to administer the laws and policies of the church as approved by General Conference;

And which, fourth, disclaims any and all offensive application of the words "supreme directional control" as hereinbefore mentioned, and claims for the Presidency only the authority and the rights set forth under the law of the church as contained in the Three Standard Books of the church, the Bible, Book of Mormon, and Doctrine and Covenants; and be it further

Resolved, That we reaffirm our unshaken belief in the doctrines, the organization, the authority, and the divine mission of the Reorganized Church of Jesus Christ of Latter Day Saints as the church in succession to that body organized by divine commandment April 6, 1830; and be it further

Resolved, That we invite all the honest in heart who before time have made covenant with us in the waters of baptism to cherish the ardor of their first love, to remain true and loyal to the church and her Lord, to have their part in her devotional services in the congregations of the Saints, and to gladly continue or renew their portion of service whether spiritual or temporal, under the admonition that all are called according to the gifts and callings of God unto them, and that minister and laborer and man of business shall all work together for the accomplishment of the work intrusted to all; and be it further

Resolved, That we reaffirm our belief in the gathering of God's people to Zion and the second personal coming of our Lord and Master, and hold ourselves ready with all diligence to build up his kingdom and establish his righteousness, that Zion may be redeemed and a pure people be made ready for his coming.

Administration of Appointees
Adopted April 12, 1926

862. (On April 9, 1926, the Order of Bishops passed the following resolution and submitted it to the Conference:

"*Resolved*, That we the Order of Bishops recommend to the General Conference that in the making of appointments only those be appointed who are in active sympathy and harmony with the General Church program;

"And we further recommend that any appointee who may be found to be using his influence, publicly or privately, against the church be recalled;

"And we further recommend that allowances from the treasury be withheld from those who are actively engaged, publicly or privately, in opposing the work of the church."

This resolution was referred to the Presidency, Twelve, and Presiding Bishopric by the General Conference for consideration and report. The following recommendation of that Council was unanimously approved by the Order of Bishops and was later adopted by the Conference.)

This council is in sympathy with the principle couched in the document from the Order of Bishops and seeks to apply it as considered consistent with the interests of the cause, endeavoring also at all times in the interest of individuals to maintain a proper balance of justice and mercy; for the council is unreservedly committed to the direction of the Lord defining the rights of individuals as follows:

"Their right to free speech, their right to liberty of conscience, does not permit them as individuals to frustrate the commands of the body in conference assembly. They are sent out as ministers to preach the gospel, and their voices if opposed to what may be presented to the conference should be heard in the conferences, and not in the mission fields, to prevent the accomplishment of the object with which the officers of the church have been intrusted."—D. and C. 125: 16.

"Those who go out from the assemblies and solemn conclaves of the church should exercise great care in their ministration abroad both to the branches where they may officiate and in their preaching the gospel to those outside, to avoid sowing seeds of distrust and suspicion either in public ministration or in private conversation."—D. and C. 131: 4.

While the council is in sympathy with the principle above cited, it believes the interests of the cause would be best conserved by leaving its administration to the Joint Council of the First Presidency, Quorum of Twelve, and Presiding Bishopric, with power to act, and we so recommend.

Church Building Fund
Adopted April 12, 1926

863. Whereas, Under Section 42:10 it is provided, "And again, if there shall be properties in the hands of the church, or any individuals of it, more than is necessary for their support, after this first consecration, which is a residue, to be consecrated unto the bishop, . . . Therefore, the residue shall be kept in my storehouse, to administer to the poor and the needy, . . . and for the purpose of purchasing lands . . . and building houses of worship," and

Whereas, In Doctrine and Covenants 122:6 it is provided, "the matter of purchasing lands, building houses of worship, . . . being within the province of the presidency, the Twelve as a quorum, the councils or other officers of the branches or stakes where houses of worship are to be built, the Conferences and general assembly of the church and the direction of the Lord by revelation," and

Whereas, In Doctrine and Covenants 106:1, the tithe, or "one tenth of all their interest annually" is for "my holy priesthood," and therefore should not be used for the building of houses of worship; therefore, be it

Resolved, That a church building fund should be established from the surplus, in the hands of members or of the church, for the purpose of assisting local congregations in the acquiring of suitable church buildings, subject to the approval of the councils and authorities before named.

Expulsion and Readmittance
Adopted April 12, 1926

864. The following statement of Preamble, Ruling, and Decision was adopted by the Standing High Council, February 8, 1926. It was presented to the General Conference by President Frederick M. Smith, and when President Smith was asked if the decision of the Council settled the question without action of the Conference he stated "that the decision of the Council decided the question at issue, but that he had no objection to the Conference registering its approval." The Conference then voted approval.

Whereas, There has long existed in the church an open question as to the interpretation of the law dealing with the so-called "second offense" of adultery stated in Doctrine and Covenants as follows:

"Thou shalt not commit adultery; and he that committeth adultery and repenteth not, shall be cast out; but he that hath committed adultery and repents with all his heart, and forsaketh it, and doeth it no more, thou shalt forgive; but if he doeth it again, he shall not be forgiven, but shall be cast out."—D. and C. 42: 7; and

Whereas, From time to time appeals come up to the High Council from persons who were at one time excommunicated from the church for this "second offense," who have since, in some instances over a long period of years, atoned for the offense with tears and suffering and through true repentance and right living have won back the confidence of the church, and who because of more mature years and experience have passed beyond the zone of greatest danger from temptation, and who wish to re-enter the church by baptism, thus raising in every such instance question as to the propriety and legality of such rebaptism; and

Whereas, This question involves not so much a matter of new legislation, but rather the interpretation of already existing constitutional law, and

Whereas, It is clearly the right and function and within the authority of the Standing High Council of the church to interpret the law governing the church, and

Whereas, This question has to do directly with the interpretation of law in the very realm (the judicial realm) in which the High Council functions as the highest tribunal in the church and with cases constantly to be adjudged by the council,

Therefore, the High Council, after careful study and prayer, at this time and for the reasons previously herein set forth does render the following ruling and decision:

Where the fact of "first offense" of adultery has been established either by court findings or confession to officials, forgiveness may be extended and the offender be permitted to retain membership and standing (D. and C. 42: 7 and General Conference Resolution 713). When the fact of the "second offense" has been established by confession or official procedure, there is no alternative to excommunication: "He shall not be forgiven, but shall be cast out" (D. and C. 42: 7). A person standing excommunicado [expelled] is in the status of a nonmember; and nonmembers requesting admittance to membership are examined as to fitness for such—repentance, faith, intentions are factors to be considered. Where persons excommunicado [expelled] ask for admittance, the determination of qualification for membership must necessarily take into consideration the question of repentance in the light of past record while formerly a member, together with the question of restitution as a factor in repentance. But it does not appear from a critical examination of the law that such persons are forever barred from entrance into the church. The offense was not forgiven; they were cast out. They have suffered the penalty and paid a price for their sin.

Presiding Bishopric as Trustees
Adopted April 14, 1926

866. Whereas, By action of General Conference, the church was incorporated in 1872 in the state of Illinois and in 1891 in the state of Iowa; and

Whereas, On account of such incorporation of the church in these states some confusion has resulted in the matter of titles to real estate in various jurisdictions on account of the wrongful belief that the church was and has been functioning in said other jurisdictions as a corporation; and

Whereas, On account of state constitutions, statutory enactments, and court decisions in some of the states and other jurisdictions, the church as a foreign corporation cannot legally exercise corporate rights and powers therein; and

Whereas, The church can operate legally in all states and foreign jurisdictions as an unincorporated association through the intervention of trustees; now, therefore be it

Resolved, By the Reorganized Church of Jesus Christ of Latter Day Saints in General Conference assembled this 14th day of April, 1926, that this church organization is and of necessity must be an unincorporated association generally throughout the world; and that where the church has been or is incorporated under local laws, such corporations have been and are maintained for the purpose of exercising corporate rights and functions within such jurisdiction, and only such powers as may be exercised under the comity of states in other jurisdictions, and that they do not and cannot have extraterritorial powers in the matter of taking title to real estate or other property by conveyance or otherwise except so far as such powers may be lawfully and regularly exercised by such corporations under the comity of the states. Be it also

Resolved, That the general practice and procedure of the church is found in its organic law, and the corporation of the church in the states of Illinois and Iowa is patterned and copied after such church law, and that the rights, duties, and prerogatives of the various church officers, quorums, and trustees are identical in both forms of organization. Be it also further

Resolved, That the Presiding Bishop and/or his counselors, or either of them, as trustee or trustees, shall have the authority and right to accept, take, hold, mortgage, and convey title to property, either real or personal or mixed, and wheresoever situated, which the church as an unincorporated association may lawfully take and hold, and to which it may assert title and ownership, and from any source whatsoever, either by deed of conveyance or by last will and testament. Be it also

Resolved, That where property is conveyed to the Presiding Bishop or his counselors as trustees for the Reorganized Church of Jesus Christ of Latter Day Saints, it shall be presumed that they take title as trustees of the unincorporated association, the general church, and not a corporation; and even in those jurisdictions where the church has been and is now incorporated, any transfer by deed or will of any real estate or other property to the church shall be presumed to inure to any such corporation only when it is specifically set forth to "The Reorganized Church of Jesus Christ of Latter Day Saints, a corporation." Be it also further

Resolved, That in mortgaging and conveying church property the signature of the Presiding Bishop or his counselors will pass the entire title and interest of the church therein. Any purchaser of property from the Presiding Bishop and has counselors as trustees shall never have any liability to see to the application of the proceeds of the sale.

Stewardship Compliance
Adopted April 7, 1927

871. That the effort started to make the church membership 100 per cent stewards continue to be stressed.

That the membership may have that confidence in their leaders, the priesthood, and as a result comply with the law governing stewards, the priesthood should be urgently solicited to comply with the law. Especially is this true with all General Conference appointees and all presiding officers in Zion, in stakes, in districts, and in branches.

That great care be taken in the selection of church representatives. The financial department of the church is the first to suffer from those who fail to uphold our Zionic program.

Branch Program in Religious Education
Adopted April 7, 1927

872. *Resolved*, That:

1. Inasmuch as the need of the day is the establishment of Zionic homes, and as this task concerns both men and women, the departments co-operate in the formation of parent classes for the study of parent problems.

Further, that these classes be conducted at an hour when it is possible for the babies to be in the care of a trained nursery mother, preferably at the church school hour; that whenever available trained teachers conduct these classes, and that institute work be provided for the training of other parent-teachers.

2. Believing it advisable to enlarge the scope of the Cradle Roll to insure the entrance of children into the public schools with healthy bodies and normal mental development through the use of baby clinics and nurseries and by means of parent instruction, the name "Cradle Roll" be changed to "Pre-School Age."

3. As the program of religious education adopted by the church includes not only pulpit instruction but also classwork and expressional activity for all ages, new church buildings provide such facilities as parlors, kitchens, reading rooms, and nurseries.

4. Since each leader of the departments of religious education, pastor, missionary, church school superintendent, recreation and expression leader, and superintendent of the Department of Women, working alone, to a degree defeats the purpose of the church, these forces work as a council in each branch, analyze the needs of its membership, and supply those needs in which every department or combination of departments can best meet such needs. Thus classwork, expressional activity, and sermon may all combine to inculcate definite Zionic principles, such as the gospel of good health, stewardship, economic soundness in family life, wholesome recreation, the Sunday program, etc.

Planning Field Activities
Adopted April 8, 1927

873. Whereas, There is entailed in the present

method of determination of dates and locations of district conferences, conventions, reunions, etc., considerable waste of time and money and also of opportunity for members of the presiding quorums to be present in the larger gatherings of the Saints; and

Whereas, Much of the present overlapping and duplication can be eliminated by the conjoint arrangement of the dates and locations of such gatherings by the presiding officers of the district concerned and the presiding officers of the church; therefore be it

Resolved, That stake and district executives be requested to consult the First Presidency and the members of the Quorum of Twelve concerned before the dates and locations of district conferences, conventions, reunions, etc., are finally determined; and that district conferences be requested to provide for such consultation when these matters come before them for action.

Annual Financial Statements
Adopted April 13, 1927

878. That the printing of the itemized lists of tithing be discontinued, and that instead the Presiding Bishopric and general church auditor be directed to send an annual statement to each contributor showing his payments on tithing, offering, and special funds for each fiscal year.

Provided always that the foregoing shall not in any way affect the present policy of publishing the annual statements of income and expenditures and assets and liabilities of the church.

Release of Evangelists and Bishops
Adopted October 3, 1928

884. That members of the Order of Evangelists

or the Order of Bishops who resign from these orders or who are released shall no longer function as members of these orders but continue to labor as high priests and members of such quorum in accordance with the provisions of Doctrine and Covenants 129: 7 (as revised April 12, 1932; G. C. R. 921).

Official Church Flag
Adopted October 8, 1928

887. That this Conference indorse the color and design of the official church flag.

Dignity of Sacrament
Adopted October 11, 1928

894. That in the administration of the Sacrament and ordinances of the church every effort should be made to provide both atmosphere and surroundings of fitting dignity and beauty. (The remainder of the resolution was of temporary nature.)

Members Locate Near Branches
Adopted April 8, 1930

895. That wherever possible members of the church should locate in the vicinity of regularly organized branches and should avoid making their residence where it will be almost impossible for them to attend services regularly. When persons are moving from one town to another, or seeking a new location for their family in which to find better opportunities for employment, we suggest that they keep in mind the desirability of moving into the vicinity of a branch of the church where they may have the benefit of association with the Saints and may also make their contributions to the onward progress of the church. We strongly urge that no such moves be made without consultation with properly constituted stake, district, and branch authorities.

Commitment to Missionary Work
Adopted April 11, 1930

897. That it is the sense of this body that every member of the church commit himself by the fact of his baptism and confirmation to the responsibility of spreading the gospel among his friends and neighbors in all the world by his personal life and testimony and by the payment of tithing; and that every member of the church should therefore be encouraged to share in the total missionary task of the church to the full extent of his opportunity and ability.

That it is the sense of this body that missionary work should be regarded not as a separate department of church enterprise, but as one of the essential functions of every department; and that every officer and member of the church in both local and general organizations should therefore seek to impregnate his work with proper missionary significance.

That while the conditions under which the Saints are grouped together make it both necessary and desirable that the emphasis in the work of some General Conference appointees shall be pastoral while that of others shall be evangelistic, it is nevertheless expected that all appointees shall endeavor to create and take advantage of opportunities for direct missionary service as one of the fundamental requirements of their appointment. (Remainder of Resolution rendered obsolete by subsequent action.)

Financial Reports
Adopted April 11, 1930

901. That hereafter all departments and church

associations making business or financial statements to the church shall file their annual reports with the Presiding Bishopric at such times as may be designated by that quorum, in order that all the business of the church may be co-ordinated and embodied in the annual report of the Presiding Bishopric.

Houses of Worship Investments
Adopted April 16, 1930

903. Whereas, The "Gathering" and the establishment of Zion are fundamental teachings of the church, and

Whereas, The building of houses of worship, purchasing of reunion grounds, etc., have a distinct bearing upon such work, therefore be it

Resolved, That the building of houses of worship, purchasing of lands, and all investments made in the interests of the church shall be considered a part of the work of the General Church and under the supervision of the General Church officers provided for in the law having jurisdiction in such matters.

Creating Business Associations
Adopted April 19, 1930

907. Whereas, The Presiding Bishopric, acting in harmony with the General Conference and the leading and directing councils of the church, has endowed certain associations, such as the Holden Development Association, Lamoni Development Association, Central Development Association, and Independence Development Trust, all of said associations being business associations or business estates wherein the trustees hold the legal title to all properties belonging thereunto, and

Whereas, The question has been raised at times with

respect to the authority of the Presiding Bishop Albert Carmichael and his counselors, Bishop M. H. Siegfried and Bishop J. A. Becker, as trustees for the church, in endowing the aforesaid business estates with the legal title to the lands and real estate and other properties involved, and in thus divesting themselves as trustees for the church of the legal title thereto, now therefore be it

Resolved, That the Reorganized Church of Jesus Christ of Latter Day Saints in General Conference assembled does hereby sanction and approve all acts and proceedings of the said Presiding Bishop Albert Carmichael and of his associates and counselors in office, Bishop M. H. Siegfried and Bishop J. A. Becker, who with him comprise the Presiding Bishopric of this church, in the creation of the aforesaid business associations and in vesting in the respective trustees thereof the legal title to the real and other property comprising the corpus or body of said business estates, hereby expressly recognizing the full right and authority of the Presiding Bishop and his counselors to create associations in aid of the work of the temporal department of the church and to endow the same with legal title to church property, retaining the beneficial interests thereto and therein for the use and benefit of the General Church. Be it also further

Resolved, That any purchaser of property from the trustees in whom the legal title is now or may hereafter be vested shall be fully protected therein without inquiring into the authority of such trustees to sell.

Unknown Membership
Adopted April 7, 1932

910. *Resolved*, That when persons have been reported unknown, and after a diligent effort to locate them has been made by the branch, district, and stake officers, and by the General Church office through publication in the *Herald* or other means, without success, the Church Statistician shall be authorized to subtract the total of such unknown names from the total reported membership of the church. Upon any such persons being subsequently located they shall be enrolled with the appropriate branch, district, or stake and added to the total reported church enrollment.

Herald House Trustees
Adopted April 9, 1932

911. That the Articles of Trust Agreement of the Herald Publishing House be modified to provide that the Presiding Bishopric, in their selection of trustees from time to time, elect those only who are sustained by the General Conference; but in event of vacancies in the Board of Trustees by death or resignation between General Conferences, such vacancies be filled by the remaining trustees by and with the consent of the Presiding Bishopric.

Right Use of Finances
Adopted April 12, 1932

915. 1. Whereas, The financial procedure and methods pursued under administrative activities of the past have resulted in great and perilous loss to the church, and

2. Whereas, The disregard or violation of laws, or enactments of the church are subversive of its unity and demoralizing to the confidence and support of its members, and

3. Whereas, The revelations in Doctrine and Covenants 126: 10; 129: 8; and 128: 1, 2, together with other revelations and enactments of the church, make provision

concerning the application of the temporal law as stated by the Bishopric and for the lawful custody and care of the properties of the church, therefore be it hereby

4. *Resolved,* That the Presiding Bishopric shall assume and are hereby directed to assume full responsibility to see that the finances of the church are used strictly in accordance with the laws and enactments of the church, and for the faithful performance of such responsibility they shall be held answerable to the church in General Conference assembled.

Procedure and Objectives in Zion in Her Stakes
Adopted April 12, 1932

917. The law governing the Gathering and the organization of Zion has two aspects, first, the inflexible provisions which are fixed, and second, the flexible provisions, interpretation and administration of which are in the hands of those designated by the revelations.

A. The inflexible provisions cover the following:

1. The commandment to gather
   The Lord has stipulated this as an essential phase of the Restoration movement, and has repeatedly emphasized the need thereof.
2. The place of gathering in its general aspects
   This has been designated as Independence and the regions round about. This contemplates a Center Place and "curtains" or supports in those territories adjoining, such as our stakes.
3. The law pertaining to temporalities, including the principles of tithing and stewardship
   Herein is covered the holding and administration of temporal and spiritual concerns as stewards, and the accounting for and distribution of the proceeds of temporalities.

4. Governing spiritual laws
   Although this document has been written with the idea of the temporal aspects in mind, there should be included here the statement that the principles of the law governing our spiritual concerns and relationships under which temporal concerns are interpreted and administered are also an integral part of the provisions here set forth.

B. The flexible provisions of the law include

1. The choice of agricultural, industrial, or home sites within the regions designated as the place of gathering
2. The methods by which the Gathering will be accomplished
   "All things are to be done in order," and repeated stress has been placed upon the direction to "have all things prepared" before entering Zion. Hereunder, the certification of spiritual standing an attainment of those desiring to enter Zion has already been arranged for. There is now greater need than ever before to consult the Presiding Bishopric before attempting to move Zionward, and every effort should be exerted by the officials of the General Church and local branches to see that this is done.
3. The designation of who should be gathered
   It can be very definitely said at this time that there is no place for the unemployed elsewhere, inasmuch as unemployment is already widespread and economic conditions critical in the gathering place and surrounding territory. Furthermore, there is no place in Zion or her "curtains" for the dependent or semi-dependent of other localities, since the financial condition of the church makes impossible the assump-

tion of additional burdens of moment of this character.

Those who are willing and able to provide the finances and materials necessary for the type of stewardship they contemplate undertaking are eligible for consideration. In this connection it is obvious that the economic necessity for the undertaking and the costs of establishment and continuance are vital factors in determination of acceptance of the candidate.

Those with special training, fitting them for some service urgently required in Zionic development, are also possibilities for consideration. Due to the limited personnel of the Order of Bishops, that personnel is not in a position to assume the active oversight of stewards. It is inexpedient to encourage the filing of stewardship applications from other than selected persons, until this handicap of organization is overcome.

Objectives

The ultimate and immediate objectives may be briefly outlined as follows:

A. Ultimate objectives

1. The building of a society of people inspired with a like faith, hope, and spiritual type of life, having the materials for the daily needs of a people, from the physical and temporal aspects is the ultimate objective placed before the church by the law. The physical and temporal aspects are but the supports for and background of a Christian life of the highest order possible.

2. This society must be provided with means of daily existence, and all steps taken must be for the pur-

pose of providing these fundamentals in the form of food, clothing, shelter, as well as the tools and equipment of work and production, transportation, and communication. Hereunder will be included the continuance of agricultural stewardships, establishment of canneries, creameries, cheese factories, service institutions of various kinds, textile and clothing factories, among others.

B. Immediate objectives

1. The strengthening and broadening out of the Atherton project

   This requires additional stewards, steps to secure which should be pressed forward. It is desirable to have as close a co-operation as possible existing between the representatives of the Presiding Bishopric and the members of the project, as well as between both the Presiding Bishopric and First Presidency. It is recognized that all concerned have a heavy responsibility upon them to move so that the continued success of this venture will be assured, because of its important bearing upon the cause of stewardship before the whole church. This project should have its plans of development finally ratified and every step in connection therewith should be taken as needed with the ultimate development in view, but as cash requirements are provided.

2. The study and possibilities for the development of Lamoni and Lamoni Stake

   The co-operative creamery there is an example of one type of development to which we should give our approval and assistance in so far as is practicable. Related and stewardship projects should be worked out as required and possible.

3. The project in the Ozarks should be carried on for a five years' experimental period, with those who are able and willing to finance themselves under a lease agreement. The church has no funds at this time to support any stewards there, and any undertaking operations at that point should clearly understand this. Serious consideration should be given to disposing of certain acreages which seem unrelated to the general area in which present development seems most feasible.

It should be borne in mind that the foregoing is a quickly prepared statement of matters long under consideration. Revision and more complete and studied statement of this subject is needed.

Teaching Objectives
Adopted April 12, 1932

918. That we reaffirm our belief in the following as the major teaching objectives of the church and request that all church representatives give special emphasis thereto:

1. The message of the Restoration with its distinctive features including such principles of belief as outlined in the "Official Statement of Belief and Epitome of Faith and Doctrines" and "Belief and Practice" with especial emphasis upon such features as continued revelation, divinely authorized priesthood, the Book of Mormon, and the divine mission of the church.

   a. In the teaching of this distinctive message not only the application of, but the authority for, the same should be sought in "life." The message of the restored gospel must not only be expressed in individual and social living but find its essential truth in the nature of life itself. The gospel way is the way of life.

b. This distinctive message should be recognized as a direct challenge to the paganism in the present social order. We should therefore fearlessly proclaim the ethics of Christ, set up his standards of value and conduct—the sinfulness of sin and the godlessness of many institutions and practices.

2. In our teaching, the major objectives of the church should always be brought into clear perspective: the evangelizing of the world and the establishment of Zion.

3. The heart of this gospel message is in true human and divine relationships, and is found in the doctrine of stewardships.

4. The "law of temporalities" should be stressed, kindly and firmly, without equivocation or apology and as impartial in application.

5. We suggest an affirmative spiritual ministry to the Saints, including the urging of
   a. Individual and family devotion
   b. The study of the word of God, especially as found in the Bible, Book of Mormon, and Doctrine and Covenants
   c. Intelligent and regular reading of the church periodicals
   d. Regular attendance at church services
   e. Intelligent, alert, and efficient participation in the work of the church
   f. Financial support of the church through wholehearted compliance with the financial law
   g. Godly walk and conversation

6. The distinctive message of the church is for all. Wisdom should be exercised in the presentation of these principles so that such will be adapted to the age, capacity, and needs of the particular group to which the

"teacher" is endeavoring to minister, the varying needs and capacities of such groups as nonmembers, adults, parents, young people, children, to be clearly recognized in our teaching procedure.

7. This distinctive message should be made to saturate the literature of the church as well as being the keynote of our preaching. The various church periodicals, including the quarterlies, should present the same message, varied only as editors and writers seek to adapt their material to the conditions mentioned in number six.

The Next Steps in Religious Education
Adopted April 12, 1932

919. Definition and Purpose

The Department of Religious Education finds its expression (in the local branch) in the "church school." The purpose of the church school is to assist in accomplishing the educational task of the church within a local branch or congregation. This task we conceive as the building of men and women for the kingdom of God, and equipping them in an organized way to carry on the work of that kingdom among men.

The specific work of the church school consists in providing occasions under guidance for study, instruction, worship, work, and play through which may come the growth and service contemplated in the gospel of Jesus Christ.

In its essential spirit we believe this work to be consistent with the word of God and with the teaching and practices of the church from its very beginning. In harmony with the Conference enactment of 1930 the carrying out of this work becomes and is an integral part of the total work of the church.

Objectives

In carrying out its major objectives, the church school formulates its objectives in terms of certain progressive changes to be brought about in the lives of growing persons in harmony with the gospel of Christ and the objectives of the church.

In other words, it seeks to guide growing persons:

a. In securing a true and adequate concept of God and responsive relationship with him

b. Through developing an appreciative knowledge of Christ and loyalty and devotion to him and his cause

c. In the formulation of and commitment to a Christian philosophy of life as contained in the Restoration message, and the attainment of a Christlike character

d. In the development of the disposition and ability to participate intelligently, actively, and efficiently in attaining the objectives of the church, which includes making a contribution to the Christian citizenship and social order of the community, state, nation, and the world

e. In acquiring a knowledge of the will of God and the development of an appreciation of the best religious experiences of the race, especially as revealed in the Three Standard Books of the church, the Bible, Book of Mormon, and Doctrine and Covenants

Major Emphases

To serve best the interests of the church it is proposed that the following emphases govern the working program of its schools:

a. The unification of all church school endeavor with the major objectives of the church. This shall recognize, both in theory and practice, that the church school program is a definite part of the total program of the church. It is a means set up by the church to carry out specific aspects of its work.

b. The encouragement of a training program which shall make possible the discovery, enlistment, and training of teachers and leaders, including men of the priesthood, that the teaching work of our branches shall be done with increasing efficiency

The training program may well include correspondence courses, supervised reading, local classes and institutes, and regional or church-wide institutes and conventions.

The purposes of such training must be

(1) To furnish the teacher and leader with a clear and ready knowledge of the teachings of the church and of its program

(2) To encourage a personal, spiritual experience and development in a quality of life that will embody the gospel message

(3) To give a mastery of the technique of Christian teaching and leadership

  (a.) A careful consideration should be given to the nature, interests, needs, and capacities of the different age groups of the church school if we are to provide each with the materials, methods, and opportunities for participation best calculated for their nurture and development in the gospel life. Especially in maturing adolescents is it imperative that increasing opportunity be given for participation in the work of the church through actually sharing in its activities and in helping to carry its responsibilities

  (b.) The diffusion of the missionary spirit throughout the church schools, the discovery of prospective members, the establishment of classes for preparing these for full church membership, and other practical missionary endeavors

(c.) The preparation, publication, and distribution of the materials necessary for the carrying on of this endeavor is one of the most difficult and important tasks of the church. The content of such material, the personality of the teacher and the methods employed all have a vital bearing upon the work of the church in the future.

It is essential that the policy of securing the best qualified persons available for the selection and preparation of educational materials should be continued.

The major teachings of the church, as elsewhere set out and approved by this council, should be given the major emphasis in as effective a measure as possible in all outlines, quarterlies, worship materials, etc., prepared for the church school. Other things being equal, members of the priesthood should be given first consideration when selections are made of those who are to prepare these materials.

Expulsion and Excommunication
Adopted April 13, 1932

922. The penalty of expulsion from the church, which is the most severe that can be applied by the church, should only be inflicted in cases of most flagrant violation of church law and standards.

The penalty for lesser offenses should be excommunication, by which we do not mean expulsion but suspension from the rights of fellowship.

Members and Ministers Expelled

Whenever the law of the church permits and a court so recommends, persons expelled from the church and desiring to return should be permitted to apply to the proper church officers for readmission to the church, and should be permitted to re-enter the church without rebaptism.

Ministers expelled from the church should only be reordained after again being called to the priesthood.

Members and Ministers Excommunicated or Withdrawing

Courts which recommend excommunication should state the conditions upon fulfillment of which the person excommunicated can resume the privilege of fellowship.

Ministers excommunicated or withdrawing from the church should not be permitted to resume their ministry upon being restored to fellowship unless and until they are reinstated by proper administrative action. The status of such persons until reinstatement should be that of ministers under silence.

(Portion of resolution concerning withdrawal was deleted by 1952 Conference.)

Financial Policy
Adopted April 14, 1932

925. *Resolved,* That the financial policy adopted by the Board of Appropriations during its sessions of February, 1931, found on page 169 of the *Saints' Herald* (issue February 25, 1931), be ratified and that the policy as summarized in the report of the Presiding Bishopric on page 37, *Conference Daily,* be adopted.

The major points set forth in the policy adopted in February, 1931, and made a part of this resolution are as follows:

1. Enter upon a concerted and concentrated program of debt reduction, with the object of eliminating all interest-bearing credits, especially those held by persons or institutions other than our own members or concerns.

2. Placing, as soon as possible, all notes, bills, accounts payable upon the basis of definite maturity, with suitable plan of amortization.

3. With the reduction of the interest-bearing debt well under way, create definite reserves or surplus funds, and increase these reserves until the appropriations can be had on the basis of money or funds in hand rather than anticipated or probable income.

4. To accomplish the foregoing it will be necessary to agree upon a nonexpansion program until a large enough reserve has been created to justify resumption of expansion program.

5. Limit all building structures whose need is beyond question, and then build only as the money is in hand.

6. Go upon a budget basis which will keep the appropriations within the limits which will make the foregoing possible.

7. Reduce the overhead expenses of both field and local work.

8. Reduce salaries and allowances of stipendiaries, always, of course, with specific factors in view and consideration.

9. Convert into cash, holdings and properties now owned by the church, but which are not needed or used for local or General Church activities, as soon as is practicable without undue loss, and apply the proceeds to reducing the interest-bearing debt, especially where held by nonmembers.

10. Reduce overhead at the general offices.

11. Find work, church or otherwise, for many who are now drawing allowances for which little or no return is made.

12. Increase the efficiency of all workers, departments, and offices, where necessary or possible.

13. To reduce the appropriations to a point where there will be a margin to apply on debt retirement, basing the appropriations on the lowest probable income, will under present conditions be necessarily extended over a long period, and a span of a decade may be required to eliminate the debt and create the desired reserves.

The summary of this policy as set forth in the Report of the Presiding Bishopric to General Conference, dated April 1, 1932, is as follows:

Present and Future Policy

During the Joint Council and Board of Appropriations sessions of February, 1931, a financial policy was adopted which included the following points:

1. Arrest Expansion: Build only when our present obligations have been met and necessary means are in hand to cover cost and maintenance of further work.

2. Liquidate Assets: Turn into cash as rapidly as possible all assets not needed for the major work of the church, and apply the proceeds against our debts.

3. A Balanced Budget: Expenditures must be less than income, permitting a margin of safety in our regular operations.

4. Operate Economically: By stopping leaks arising from expensive operations, or from activities having a cumulatively increasing cost, our major work may more certainly be done.

5. Pay Indebtedness: By adhering to the above it is possible to pay our obligations. A substantial amount should be set aside each year for this purpose, until the entire debt is paid.

6. Create Reserves: That we may assure ourselves of economic security in the future.

Word of Wisdom
Adopted April 10, 1936

933. Whereas, The church has not put its seal of approval on any system of medication, either drugless or otherwise, therefore be it

Resolved, That we reaffirm our belief in the Word of Wisdom as basic in the health program of the church.

Voting on Delegates
Adopted April 13, 1936

936. That the principle of having all delegates selected by vote of the members in the several stakes and district conferences should be maintained against any action which violates this principle by providing that district officers be empowered to appoint part of the delegates.

Financial Policy
Adopted April 11, 1942

940. (Recommendations contained in the report of the Presiding Bishopric were adopted. Some of these were of a temporary nature. The others were as follows.)
Provide for a program for agricultural colonization:
  a. By setting up an agency for the mobilization of capital for land purchase
  b. Through creating an organization for giving supervision and direction to those gathering, this subject to the provisions in Doctrine and Covenants 128: 9, and other revelations and enactments which are a matter of record.

Provide plans for further segregation of funds when the present debt is eliminated.
- a. To assure use of tithes and offerings received for the evangelical, educational, and administrative work of the church.
- b. To segregate oblation funds, that they may be used for the purpose of giving temporary aid and benevolences, and at the same time to make possible their use for the permanent rehabilitation of those who have become physically incapacitated or disabled, and who are worthy of the assistance and help of the church.

Continue emphasis upon the financial law and the need for compliance by an ever-increasing number of church members.

Continue operation of the church upon the basis of the financial policy adopted by the General Conference of 1932, which policy applies both to times of adversity and to times of prosperity.

Special Funds
Adopted April 6, 1944

948. (The Presiding Bishopric presented the following recommendations to the First Presidency and Board of Appropriations and after the approval of this Board was received the recommendations were approved by the General Conference. They are important as indicating the purpose of the funds named, although the amounts involved have been changed by subsequent action.)

2. **Ministerial Reserve Fund** $228,787.13

(Appropriation for age group 60-74—total number of men covered, 24)

For many years the church has operated on a policy of meeting the cost of retirement, death benefit, and premature disability of appointees. Previously such costs have been met out of current income, which did not make provision for accrual of this liability.

The recommendation we are making for this appropriation is to make allocation out of funds now on hand to increase the reserve by the amount figured to meet the costs of the age group from 60 to 74 years, inclusive. This would leave an approximate amount of $146,000.00 to be appropriated from future income to bring our reserves up to an amount sufficient to meet our accrued liability for all ministers under appointment.

3. Operating Fund Reserve $250,000.00

This reserve and the Ministerial Reserve Fund were referred to in the "Epistle from the Joint Council" (see *Saints' Herald* of May 15, 1943). The Operating Fund Reserve goal was set at $500,000.00. Out of funds now on hand, either in the form of cash or Government Bonds, we are recommending the allocation of the above amount, $250,000.00, to be set up as an Operating Fund Reserve, the ultimate purpose of this goal being that of making appropriations for a current year out of cash on hand, rather than on the basis of anticipated income. This would provide for adjustments in operating costs on an annual basis, rather than on an emergency basis.

4. Auditorium Construction $25,000.00

This recommendation is based on the need for finishing three additional office floors—the floors below the First Presidency, one of which is now used by the local offices in Zion, and the floor below that to provide facilities for a research library and the proper cataloguing and filing of the valuable historical documents and books owned by the church; the floor below the general office of the Presiding Bishopric to be finished for additional office space for this department. Some additional improvements should be made on the foyer and/or the radio room.

5. Independence Sanitarium and Hospital $50,000.00

Application has been made for a grant from the United States Government for additional construction work on the old and new buildings. It is necessary for us to participate in the cost; the $50,000.00 would provide for our share of such cost on the basis of our present application. This appropriation, however, we recommend as being made outright so that provision may be made for classroom facilities and laboratory space in the event that our application is not granted.

6. Graceland College $100,000.00

Recommendation is made for the appropriation of this amount of money to be set up as a reserve with which to meet the costs of dormitory facilities that will be needed for this institution. The funds will not be turned over to the College until circumstances and conditions make such construction necessary. From information available at present, this need is pressing, and provision for the cost should, in our opinion, be made with funds that are now available.

7. Lamoni Church Building $30,000.00

The Lamoni Branch for years has provided church home facilities for Graceland College students. Since the loss of the Brick Church by fire in 1931, the branch has used the "Coliseum" building and other classroom space above the Supply Store Building, looking forward to the time when it will be possible to construct a new church building. The branch has now raised the sum of approximately $50,000.00; the estimated cost of the project will be approximately $90,000.00.

The recommendation for the appropriation of $30,000.00 is based upon the fact that the General Church has some responsibility to furnish church facilities to Graceland College; furthermore, it is contemplated that the church building will provide office space for the stake headquarters.

Total..$783,787.13

Church Appointee Program
Adopted April 8, 1944

949. The word of God depicts the church as a militant people on the march toward world evangelism for the kingdom's sake. Always the promise and prophecy of miraculous achievement is wedded to the requirements of great devotion, great sacrifice, and great endeavor. The task of the church is to use her total and growing resources to the best possible advantage, and to this end wisdom and experience must open the way for enlightenment, and careful conservation of our forces must go hand in hand with complete abandon to the demands of our calling. We must conserve in order that we might serve more effectively. It is with these facts in mind that we make the following comments and recommendations:

The guidance and development of the Saints throughout the world require the full-time ministry of general officers and also of appointee high priests, bishops, evangelists, and elders. These should be appointed to their several tasks, but the number of such appointees should be kept to a minimum so that these brethren may lead the local priesthood and not displace them, and so that the remaining resources of the church may be devoted to planned missionary endeavor.

In order that this minimum number of appointees might serve effectively, and for other good reasons, it is of major importance that the Saints shall be grouped in compact organizations in and around Independence and other key centers of church activity. The economy of operation which is thus envisaged is not now fully possible, but it can be approximated; and the major missionary activities of the appointees for the present should be directed toward improving the stability and compactness of the local organizations already established.

Such a policy of appointments as the foregoing will enable us to maintain the established work of the church and thereafter to assign to the field a growing number of missionaries: as many as can be sustained by the contributions of the Saints on the basis of our average income.

In order to free as many appointees as possible for this work, both the ministry and the membership need to be reminded that "in private and in public expenditures" we should "carry into active exercise the principle of sacrifice and repression of unnecessary wants" (D. and C. 130: 7) and that we should do our utmost "to remove the principle of selfishness from the hearts of the Saints and especially from those upon whom rests the burden of the church and its ministrations abroad" (D. and C. 127: 7).

The policy of directing our efforts toward stabilizing our work in centers already opened should be applied in foreign fields as well as in the United States and Canada. Both at home and abroad this will require the provision of reasonable equipment as well as of increased man power.

The presiding authorities have carefully surveyed the domestic and foreign fields with due regard to the factors already mentioned in this report, and it appears that to meet the needs of the church in the fields now open, and to take advantage of the pressing missionary work now possible, will require the appointment of approximately twenty-nine general and departmental officers, 137 high priests (including bishops and evangelists), seventy-six seventies, and forty elders.

The average income of the church such as can be maintained even under adverse conditions, will not yet warrant as many appointments as are here contemplated. And brethren of the high caliber desired are not readily available for appointment, many of our prospective appointees being in service with the armed forces. But additional appointments should be made as soon as conditions warrant, and looking toward this we recommend that:

We continue our program of setting aside reserves to relieve the operating budget of nonproductive costs.

We make further efforts to increase the number of continuous contributors among our present members.

We decrease the costs of appointee ministry in relation to return by more efficient placement and administration.

We increase our membership and contributions by more aggressive and well-placed missionary endeavor, in which every appointee shall be joined by as many of the Saints as will, each in his own place.

The efficiency of the appointees can be greatly augmented through careful selection, training, assignment, and supervision. With these things in mind we recommend in regard to the selection of appointees:

That a definite sense of divine direction precede every ministerial appointment.

That the brethren appointed show reasonable acquaintance with the fundamental beliefs, structure, and procedure of the church.

That two years of college or its equivalent be required of any minister before he is appointed.

In regard to training we recommend:

That as a general rule all new appointees shall first be assigned to a training area where they will work and study under the supervision of experienced ministers.

That in addition to this general preparation, each appointee be required to develop special knowledge and skill in some phase of church endeavor within a specified time, and that these special studies be broadened down the years so as to particularly fit him both for the distinctive work of his calling and for properly co-ordinating his work with that of his fellow ministers.

In regard to assignments we recommend:

That as soon as possible, but with due regard to special circumstances, the various districts, branches, and missionary fields to which ministers may be assigned shall be classified as to their fundamental needs and opportunities, and that appointees shall be assigned to these fields with careful regard to their growing powers.

That with confidence in God, reinforced by the lessons of our history, we shall eagerly expect men of devotion and intelligence to fill positions of major responsibility with distinction while yet in their twenties and thirties, and that appointees be made and supported in this confident expectation.

In regard to supervision we recommend:

That it shall be our general policy to leave all appointees to their own initiative as fully as their abilities, experience, and calling, and the general needs of the church shall warrant; but that during the early years of an appointee's ministry he shall be given specially careful guidance in order to determine whether he is justifying his call to permanent appointment, and that where he fails to do so he shall be released from the field while yet young enough to make his adjustments in the industrial world.

The supply of potential appointees is at present strictly limited because of the war. It is also seriously affected by such matters as:

1. Faulty understanding of the fundamental teachings of the church.

2. Unworthy concepts of the ministerial task, which tend to make the ministry appear unimportant and unrewarding when compared with other life vocations.

3. Lack of incentive for participation and growth in our smaller branches.

4. Inadequate home financing, which frequently leads to the early deflection of young people away from the educational preparation which might otherwise lead to ministerial work.

In view of these facts we call the attention of the church, and particularly of local pastors, to the following recommendations:

1. That we continue to emphasize the faithful performance of religious duties in the homes of the Saints as a necessary means of creating right religious attitudes in our young people.

2. That the local branch in action be the focal point for developing priesthood for General Church appointment.

3. That devoted and experienced ministers who have themselves served under appointment share their experiences with the young people of the church. This process can be given dignity as these brethren seek divine guidance, so that those participating shall have an unmistakable sense of divinity in work.

We believe that we owe it to God and to the church to appoint those who shall be indicated by the spirit of wisdom and revelation, as quickly as these brethren can be made available and as finances will permit. To the task of preparing and assigning and supporting these brethren the church should address itself with unreserved devotion. It is a task which lays obligations on all. As it is fulfilled, the stable Zionic growth of our people should be steadily advanced, and the gospel of the kingdom should be spread abroad to the full measure of our abilities.

Property Purchase and Improvements
Adopted April 9, 1947

954. *Resolved,* That no church site, reunion grounds,

or other church properties be purchased, or church edifices or other buildings, or major improvements erected by any [stake] district, or branch, unless approval is first had of the First Presidency, the Presiding Bishopric, the Apostles directly concerned, and the General Church Architect or other approved architect. (See GCR 1083 removing stakes from this resolution.)

Lamanite Ministries
Adopted April 12, 1947

955. Whereas, Jehovah saw fit to bring forth the record of the Nephites and the Lamanites in the beginning of this Restoration movement and have it translated into our language through the labors of his servant, Joseph Smith and others, and

Whereas, The same unchangeable Creator commanded the church to send Oliver Cowdery to the Lamanites in the year 1830 to carry the message of the "Holy One of Israel" to them (D. and C. 27: 3), and

Whereas, The Reorganization has in the past fifty years baptized several hundreds of these Lamanite brethren, and

Whereas, They are today without shepherds and are fast falling a prey to many evils and other religious movements, therefore be it

Resolved: That the Joint Council of First Presidency, Quorum of Twelve, and Presiding Bishopric be requested to give earnest consideration to the needs of the Indian members of the church, and to the conservation, consolidation, and expansion of the work among the Indians as may be practicable in connection with other interests of the church.

Radio Fund
Adopted April 11, 1947

957. Whereas, Consideration has been given by the Joint Council of the First Presidency, Quorum of Twelve, and Presiding Bishopric, and the Board of Appropriations, to the future needs of the church in the field of radio broadcasting and they feel that further investigation and research are necessary, and have already recommended an appropriation of $7,500.00 to provide for competent engineering and legal services in this connection, and this appropriation has been authorized by the Conference: It is therefore

Resolved, That if, after making such study, it is deemed advisable to make application for FM and/or AM licenses the First Presidency and Presiding Bishopric be authorized to do so, and

In the event the Joint Council of the First Presidency, Quorum of Twelve, and Presiding Bishopric find it advisable to proceed with the building of a station, the Presiding Bishopric be authorized to draw upon the Radio Fund of $110,000.00 for such capital and initial expense as may be needed.

Broadcasting Services
Adopted October 7, 1948

960. *Resolved:*

1. That we continue the development of recorded radio service for places distant from the Center Place

2. That we continue our present schedule of broadcasting with the improvements made possible by the appropriations to be recommended to this Conference

3. That we continue our application for a daytime broadcasting license, subject to the approval of the appropriations recommended in the report of the Appropriations Committee.

Racial Equality
Adopted October 8, 1948

963. All men are God's creatures. He created of one blood all nations and races, and in the presence of God divisions of race are transcended; "There is neither Greek nor Jew, . . . Barbarian, Scythian, bond nor free; but Christ is all, and in all."

Lamanite Ministries
Adopted October 9, 1948

965. *Resolved,* That this Conference go on record as expressing a desire to see the work of ministering to the Indians prosecuted as fast as men can be developed to carry on this work.

Ordination of Seventies
Adopted April 5, 1950

966. Whereas, Under procedure followed in the past, all selections by the Presidents of Seventy for ordination to the office of Seventy, after concurrence of the First Presidency and Council of Twelve, have been submitted for approval to the General Conference, and

Whereas, There is no specific law requiring action by the General Conference in such matters, and such reference often precludes or postpones the ordination of acceptable candidates or nominees for the office of Seventy between Conferences, now, therefore, be it and it is hereby

Resolved, That the ordination of Seventies may be authorized on selection by the Council of Presidents of Seventy and approval by the First Presidency and Council of Twelve.

Lamanite Ministries
Adopted April 8, 1950

970. For many years the leading councils of the church have had under consideration the advancement of work among the Lamanites. It is encouraging that the enthusiasm of the church is mounting toward this historic mission of the Restoration movement. There have been some insurmountable obstacles heretofore which have delayed prosecution of the work among the Book of Mormon peoples. Now, with the church out of debt, growing strength of personnel, and an increasing sense of evangelistic urgency in the church, the Council of Twelve feel the time is ripe to propose the following program, which has the approval of the Joint Council:

1. Let every effort be made to strengthen the church in the domestic field. Only by such a program can those with Indian ancestry, now part of the normal pattern of American life, be ministered to effectively.
2. Let the Saints be encouraged to augment the funds now available for missionary extension by increased support of the financial law.
3. We encourage the expansion of the church into the countries south of the border by the following means:
   a. By the efforts of our people in and adjacent to the universities and colleges to proselytize nationals from these countries and enlist them in the work of the church so that they may be a normal means of extending the gospel in their native countries on their return
   b. By strengthening the church along the Mexican border in such places as seem to be fruitful of contacts in Latin America
   c. By looking toward the purchase of church headquarters in Mexico City or elsewhere as circumstances and wisdom may direct
   d. With a view to opening up the work in a larger sphere among the Book of Mormon peoples, we are recommending that an appointee be authorized as soon as practicable to work among Mexican and other Spanish-speaking nationals now enrolled as students in United States centers of learning or who may be

living in other concentrations of nationals such as Guadalupe Center in Kansas City, Missouri. These, converted and returned to their own countries, could be nuclei of extension, thus making it possible to transfer this appointee and others to Mexico City or such other place as may be advisable.

e. To implement the above policy, we recommend that the translation of the Book of Mormon and selected tracts into the Spanish language be accelerated, and that the Presiding Bishopric be authorized to pay the necessary expenses, not to exceed $25,000.00 from the Missionary Reserve Fund, reporting regularly to the Joint Council on these expenditures. We further recommend that we provide at the earliest opportunity two hundred copies of the Book of Mormon (missionary edition) and other materials to be designated for free distribution, sufficient funds to be drawn from the Missionary Reserve Fund.

4. We look favorably toward the strengthening of the work of the church in branches and missions close to Indian centers in Oklahoma, Nebraska, and such other areas as may be deemed advisable.

5. Let some of our young people possessing an outstanding and intelligent spiritual drive toward work among the Indians, and under the impulsion of the Spirit of God in them, be encouraged to qualify for work in Indian schools and other government agencies, thereby creating places of contact on a high level. Others may well be encouraged to enter into governmental, industrial, or vocational activities on their own in Latin America in order that they may make contacts out of which missionary activities may emerge.

6. We shall see our work among the Lamanites as an inclusive program with the following objectives:

a. To promote the knowledge of Jesus Christ and his gospel and to win mankind to his church
b. To raise the spiritual outlook and moral standards
c. To improve educational and cultural standards
d. To foster and raise social and economic standards
e. To raise health standards
f. To develop members who can contribute toward establishing the total Zionic ideal
g. To enrich the whole church by the sharing of these added peoples in this missionary venture

Radio Station
Adopted April 9, 1950

971. *Resolved*, That in the event the Joint Council of the First Presidency, the Presiding Bishopric, and the Quorum of Twelve find it advisable to establish a subsidiary nonprofit corporation of said church for the purpose of constructing and operating a radio broadcasting station that the First Presidency and the Presiding Bishopric be authorized to create said corporation and proceed to prosecute an application for radio broadcasting facilities; be it further

Resolved, That the Presiding Bishopric in the event a subsidiary corporation is established to construct and operate said radio broadcasting station be authorized to draw upon the radio fund of $100,000.00 for such capital and initial expense as may be needed and transfer said funds to the corporation established in order to carry out the functions prescribed; be it further

Resolved, That in the event the radio broadcasting station is granted and licensed to said subsidiary corporation that the Presiding Bishopric be authorized to draw upon such additional annual radio funds as determined by the General Conference and to transfer the same to the said corporation for operation of the radio broadcasting station.

Home and Family Life
Adopted April 8, 1950

972. (The following excerpt from the report of the First Presidency was approved.)

One of the most important contributions we can make to the establishment of the kingdom is in the refinement of our home and family life. True marriage is a sacrament, and should not be entered into lightly, hastily, or unworthily. In particular, members of the church should not enter into this covenant relationship with persons who do not realize its sacramental nature, or who do not feel deeply their spiritual obligation to abide by its sacrificial demands, as well as to enjoy its happy rewards. Pastors and other ministers of mature judgment will do well to teach these things to our young people before they are called on to choose their life partners. And an ever greater responsibility is carried by Latter Day Saint parents, whose example will go so far to determine the quality and durability of the homes of tomorrow. Let the church be admonished that the kingdom is now seeking expression in the homes of the faithful, and that far more significant for the kingdom, than any material resources we may bring, are such spiritual qualities as industry, forethought, thrift, co-operation, kindness, temperance, patience, and compassion which are best matured in saintly homes.

When divisive forces are already found at work in church families, we suggest most soberly that the Saints who are involved seek out their pastors or other ministers of mature judgment and secure their help in effecting reconciliation before these differences become unsupportable. And ministers who are asked to advise in such delicate situations should take particular care to prove themselves both compassionate and trustworthy. Failure to seek and to give such ministry as is here suggested means that in far too many cases the first official contact of the church with divided homes and with children threatened by the worst kind of insecurity is when someone suggests that punitive measures should be applied.

Church Building Specifications
Adopted April 8, 1950

974. *Resolved*, That

1. We favor church buildings to accommodate a congregation of such size as to be adequately presided over by local leadership, a congregation of about 200 to 350, with the buildings providing for the seating of 100 to 200 members. The seating needs of a junior church are part of the total seating needs of a congregation.

2. We favor churches being built within the visible capacity of the people to pay for them, and use them economically in the period immediately following the construction. Where in the judgment of General Church officers responsible larger buildings seem warranted, consideration should be given to the planning of units as a whole with the building of sections to meet the growing needs.

3. We favor consultation with recognized local architects, and feel that money carefully spent for adequate plans and specifications is money well spent.

4. We feel that every consideration needs to be given to the multiple use of all possible facilities.

5. We do not favor confining our church buildings to one particular style of architecture, but feel that locality, lay of the grounds, available local materials and building skills, zoning laws, and the taste of the particular congregation are all factors to consider in the selection of an architectural style for each congregation.

Racial Equality
Adopted April 8, 1950

976. The resolution before the body (on racial relations) has been studied carefully and prayerfully by the Quorum of High Priests which by unanimous vote has approved the following as a substitute motion:

1. Whereas, The document under consideration has merit as a reminder of the scriptural instruction on racial equality in the eyes of God, nevertheless, we believe it is inadequate as a comprehensive statement of our church belief; and

2. Whereas, In any case of un-Christian conduct on the part of officers or members of the church in mistreatment of others, those offended have recourse through channels of administrative appeal (pastors, district or stake presidents, apostle in charge, First Presidency) and the judicial bodies of the church, regardless of race, color, or nationality; and

3. Whereas, The question of racial equality has legal and international implications and is only one phase in the field of human rights, therefore, be it

Resolved, That we reaffirm the statement adopted by the Conference of 1948 as it appears in the official minutes of Friday, October 8, on page 105 of the *Daily Herald,* which reads in part:

"There is nothing in the law of the church which creates or tends to create racial inequality or racial discrimination.

"To legislate with respect to a specific race raises by implication the presumption that that race has heretofore been unjustly dealt with in our church law and discipline, which we cannot and do not admit.

"All men are God's creatures. He created of one blood all nations and races, and in the presence of God divisions of race are transcended; "There is neither Greek nor Jew, . . . Barbarian, Scythian, bond nor free; but Christ is all, and in all.'" (See G. C. R. 963.) Be it further

Resolved, That: It is the opinion of this Conference that an official expansion of the statement concerning human rights and racial relationships that was adopted by General Conference action in 1948 would be desirable in light of our long-time world-wide program of evangelism and the manifold laws and traditions of the many nations of the earth to whom the gospel is to go. Be it further

Resolved, That: The Joint Council of First Presidency and the Council of Twelve take such action as deemed necessary to implement education in the field of racial relations.

Consecration of Surplus
Adopted April 9, 1950

977. (At the April Conference of 1947 considerable discussion was had at the Order of Bishops meetings regarding surplus. As a result of that discussion Elder G. L. DeLapp, as Presiding Bishop, was asked to make a brief statement which would set forth his opinion relative to surplus and its consecration. The statement of Bishop DeLapp was approved by the Order of Bishops on April 6, 1950, and ordered transmitted to the First Presidency and General Conference. Prior to its presentation to the Conference it was discussed by the First Presidency, Council of Twelve, and Presiding Bishopric in Joint Council and then referred to the General Conference with the recommendation that it be adopted. A complete statement may be found in the *Daily Herald* for 1950, pages 109-110, 113.)

Resolved:

1. That the Presiding Bishopric set up a separate treasury to be designated as the Storehouse Treasury.

2. That surplus be accepted as an outright conveyance to the church without legal obligation by the church to the contributor other than that implied in carrying out the purposes for which consecrated. It is essential that

there be clear understanding between the bishop and the contributor concerned, as to the purpose of the consecration.

3. That the membership of the church be invited to comply with the law of consecration of surplus for specific purposes, and that these purposes be designated as follows:
   a. For the purpose of purchasing lands for the public benefit of the church, such lands to be in addition to those already designated on the books of the church as stewardship lands.
   b. For the completion of the Auditorium.
   c. Either in part or in full for the building of houses of worship which may be considered peculiarly the responsibility of the General Church, such as those presently considered in the capital cities of the United States and Canada, and such further public buildings as may be approved by the First Presidency and the Joint Council consisting of the First Presidency, the Council of Twelve, and the Presiding Bishopric; but that final approval of the use of surplus for such buildings is subject to the approval of the Presiding Bishopric, with the advice of the Standing High Council of the church.
   d. To provide for the costs for economic and community planning; this not to be limited to new communities, but also for studies of existing communities where we have well-established congregations in stakes.
   e. For the development of business, industrial, and agricultural stewardships.
   f. For funds for care of the poor and needy which may provide specific facilities for their rehabilitation or to supplement the Oblation Fund already segregated.

4. That business, industrial, and agricultural stewardship

projects be for the present confined to the Center Place (Independence Stake) and the supporting stakes designated as the Central Missouri, Far West, Lamoni, and Kansas City Stakes.

5. That in all instances the use of surplus be restricted to the purpose for which it was designated at the time consecrated.

6. That the method of determination involving the acceptance and designation of surplus as such be as follows:
   a. That the individual shall have made accounting to the bishop in harmony with the law:
      (1) Filing his financial statement
      (2) Paying of tithing in full and that the determination of the amount which shall be consecrated for surplus, as well as its designation, shall be mutually agreed upon with the bishop concerned and the contributor consecrating it, and understanding arrived at in writing, either in the form of a receipt or by written agreement, to establish the purpose of the consecration. Unless there is such mutual consideration by the bishop and the contributor, contributions other than tithing should be receipted for as offerings —not surplus.
   b. That a common method of procedure be developed relative to the stakes and to the General Church, which shall be commonly understood and complied with
      (1) Respecting stewardship or other projects involving the use of surplus
      (2) Respecting the administration and use of surplus funds

It is understood that all of the foregoing is and must be in harmony with the principle of voluntary, freewill contribution on the part of the individual; and that it is presented for the purpose of interpreting the law of consecration of the surplus to the specific situation which prevails at present.

Graceland College Dormitories
Adopted April 5, 1952

979. Whereas, Previous General Conferences have made special appropriations for constructing a Men's Dormitory at Graceland College, and

Whereas, The General Conference of 1952 has made an additional appropriation for the completion of the Men's Dormitory, and for the construction of a Women's Dormitory and,

Whereas, It is intended that these special appropriations shall be a part of the Endowment Fund of Graceland College, now, therefore, be it

Resolved, That the said appropriations made by this and prior Conferences for dormitory constructions at Graceland College shall be a part of the Endowment Fund of Graceland College.

Graceland College Properties
Adopted April 5, 1952

980. Whereas, The property in Lamoni, Iowa, known as the "Herald Hall," in which the Herald Publishing House was formerly located, has for a great many years been used by Graceland College as a dormitory and will continue to be needed by Graceland College in carrying out the education work of the college; and, whereas there is little likelihood of need for the use of this property by the General Church, and

Whereas, There are a number of vacant lots on the Graceland College Campus to which the General Church has title, and for which the General Church has no need, but the said lots are a part of the Graceland

College Campus and are being used by the College in connection with its educational program, and

Whereas, It is desirable to consolidate all of these properties in the name of Graceland College; now, therefore, be it

Resolved, That the Presiding Bishop be authorized to transfer title from the General Church to Graceland College covering miscellaneous lots upon the Graceland College Campus, together with such other lots on the Campus as may be acquired subsequently, and title to the property above referred to as "Herald Hall," with the understanding that said property is to be a part of the Endowment Fund of Graceland College.

Withdrawal and Reinstatement
Adopted April 5, 1952

981. That in the event any person desires to withdraw from membership in the church, the First Presidency be authorized to make such investigation as may be necessary or desirable through the proper officers of the church, and, if no sound reasons against such action are found, may authorize the Church Statistician to remove the names of these persons from the records of the church, provided that in the event persons whose names have been thus removed from the records of the church shall desire to resume their membership in the church, and no sound reason for denying this request shall be found, the First Presidency may authorize the reinstatement of the names of such persons on the church records.

Local Bishops
Adopted April 5, 1954

982. (In connection with their recommendation for the ordination of three non-appointee bishops, the First Presidency presented the following, which was approved.)

The basic law of the church calls for the ordination of

bishops in districts and large branches (D. and C. 117: 10 b). From time to time a few non-appointee bishops have been called and have served in their home districts. But the number of these local bishops has been comparatively small. In part, this has been due to our concern lest men who are properly ordained to the bishopric might be retained in that office beyond the point where they could serve more effectively in some other high priestly functions.

We have now felt directed to move forward in the ordination of local bishops. It is not our thought that many such bishops shall be called, but only that we shall move forward when we have full assurance of divine direction.

Our thinking in this connection has been brought into focus in the following statement of principles:

Bishops should be selected from among the high priests on the initiative of the Presidency. Only in emergencies should elders be ordained to the bishopric without prior high priestly experience.

Ordination to the high priesthood followed by ordination to the bishopric might well be followed by a lifetime of ministry in the bishopric. But this is not necessarily so. There appears to be no reason in the law why a bishop should not thereafter serve as a high priest without specific bishopric responsibility.

The ministry of non-appointee bishops should not be casual and temporary, but such as is rightly dignified by ordination. Transfers from the work of the bishopric to work in other high priestly positions should be made only when concurred in by the Presidency, Presiding Bishopric, and minister in charge.

We present this statement of principles for the information of the Conference.

Church Court Procedure
Adopted April 7, 1954

983. Printed as Appendix G at the end of this book.

Church Activities Report
Adopted April 9, 1954

985. *Resolved,* That a committee consisting of one member of the First Presidency, one member of the Council of Twelve, and one member of the Presiding Bishopric, together with such others as they may call to their aid, be set up to study methods of informing the members and departments of the church concerning the activities and objectives of all General Church quorums and departments; this committee to report to the First Presidency with a view to the improvement of both general and regional reporting procedure, suggest the form of reporting, and the frequency of such reports.

Use of Local Architects
Adopted April 9, 1954

986. (Following the release of Church Architect Henry C. Smith, the First Presidency recommended) it was

Resolved, That the First Presidency be free, in consultation with the Presiding Bishopric, to solicit the advice of members of the church who are competent architects in the study of architectural questions, and to employ competent local architects whenever specific local building needs so require.

Calls to Priesthood
Adopted April 11, 1954

988. *Resolved,* That the General Conference rescind

the action on procedure in ordination which was adopted April 12, 1932 (G. C. R. 916, page 105), and substitute the following therefor:

Men are called to the priesthood by God through his Son Jesus Christ by the power of his Spirit (Matt. 9: 38, A.V.; Heb. 3: 1; Rom. 10: 15; I Cor. 7: 17; Heb. 5: 4; Alma 19: 115; Moroni 8: 1, 2; D. and C. 17: 12; 102: 10; 124: 7).

Calls to the priesthood must come through those holding priesthood and in administrative authority (D. and C. 43: 1, 2; 99: 5; 125: 14; Mosiah 11: 17, 18).

Calls in unorganized territory must be endorsed by the minister in charge.

Calls to the Aaronic priesthood in branches and districts should be approved by branch presidents, district presidents, ministers in charge, branch and district business meetings. Calls to the Melchisedec priesthood in branches and districts should be approved by branch presidents, district presidents, ministers in charge, First Presidency, branch and district business meetings. In cases of emergency in branches and districts, ordinations may be provided by the minister in charge.

All calls to the priesthood in stakes must be approved by the stake presidencies, the stake high councils, and the stake conferences, and calls to the Melchisedec priesthood must also be approved by the First Presidency.

In cases of emergency within stakes, ordinations may be provided by the stake presidency in consultation with the stake high council and the First Presidency.

Second Quorum of Seventy
Adopted April 9, 1956

990. The Council of Presidents of Seventy is happy to note that for the first time in many years there will be enough Seventies available to necessitate the organization of a Second Quorum of Seventy.

We therefore recommend to this Conference that action be taken providing for the organization of the Second Quorum of Seventy.

Church Court Procedure
Adopted April 10, 1956

991. Printed as Appendix G at the end of this book.

Book of Mormon Language
Adopted April 13, 1956

993. Whereas, Many persons conversant with and friendly to the Book of Mormon believe the language of the same could be improved, made more understandable and effective, now, therefore, be it and it is hereby

Resolved, That the First Presidency be asked to appoint a special committee of three or more persons to consider wherein and if its language and wording may be improved, and make report of their findings and recommendations to the General Conference of 1958. Be it further

Resolved, That if in their judgment the language of the book should be changed in the interest of clarity or for other good reason, the Committee make report of their suggested changes to the same General Conference, or if more time should be required, to the General Conference of 1960.

(Following the introduction of the above resolution, the First Presidency submitted the following)

We wish to recommend that if the motion having to do with editorial changes in the Book of Mormon is approved, it be understood that we will continue to publish the Authorized Version of the Book of Mormon and that any additional version will stand on its merits in relation thereto.

Racial Integration
Adopted April 13, 1956

995. The gospel is for all mankind. It knows no distinction of race or color.

The possibility of sharing the gospel has always been influenced by racial, social, economic, educational, and political factors. This is still true.

The social patterns are changing in the direction of closer integration by the various groups comprising the total population. It is difficult to imagine segregated churches in a society which teaches the gospel of Jesus Christ.

Wherever groups, missions, branches, and congregations are organized they should be formed as a matter of administration and not as a matter of racial discrimination.

There are areas where the church must first build up the will to welcome all races. In such situations discretion is important, but only as an essential factor in breaking down barriers.

The church welcomes all who respond to the call of the Lord from among all races.

Persons of any race who are ordained to the priesthood should function freely according to their gifts and callings. Some may well receive church appointment. Such appointees should be assigned with reasonable consideration for the opportunities for ministry to their own race, but such assignments should not be to that race only.

The appointing authorities should carry the needs of all men in their hearts with ministry being directed according to the spirit of wisdom and revelation in the general, local, and missionary presiding officers concerned.

It should be shared in by the Saints in the spirit of fraternity, which is the spirit of Zion.

Zionic Research and Service
Adopted April 14, 1956

997. Whereas:

A. Part of the twelve-point "Program for the Establishment of Zion" adopted by the General Conference of 1925 and adopted by the Joint Council of April, 1924, included the following,

   9. That in looking to the completion of the surveys of man power, capital, markets, territories, etc., a bureau of research and service be established.

   10. That the determination of the order of economic development should be given immediate consideration. And,

   Whereas:

B. For various reasons the above steps have not been implemented, therefore be it

Resolved, That this General Conference reaffirm its interest and intent that the above points be implemented as soon as practicable.

Memorial to the Prophets
Adopted April 14, 1956

999. Whereas, After the death of President Frederick Madison Smith the General Conference appointed a committee "to draft suggestions for a memorial for the late President Frederick Madison Smith," and

Whereas, The committee has given this matter consideration from time to time, and

Whereas, The matter has been discussed in General Conferences subsequent to the death of the late President Frederick Madison Smith, and

Whereas, Suggestions have been made, for example

that (1) a library be built, to be known as the "Frederick Madison Smith Memorial Library," to be located on the Campus at Graceland College; (2) that the Auditorium be completed and dedicated as a memorial to the late President Frederick Madison Smith; and (3) that the new Science Building at Graceland College be designated as a memorial; and

Whereas, In the opinion of the committee, none of these seem to be appropriate as true memorials to our late President and Prophet, Frederick Madison Smith, although in each there is evidence of his leadership and of his contribution in their final development, and

Whereas, It would seem that a memorial could more satisfactorily be designated which would be in memory of Joseph Smith, Jr., the Prophet of the Church, and Joseph Smith III, the President and Prophet of the Reorganization, as well as the late President and Prophet, Frederick Madison Smith; therefore,

The committee recommends as a Memorial for the Prophets, a campanile located on an appropriate site near the Auditorium, and of sufficient size to include historical data and valuable relics having special significance in the lives of our presidents and prophets;

And the committee further recommends that the plan for the financing of the memorial be kept within the other budgetary and fund-raising needs of the church. A goal of $25,000 per year for a period of ten years, to be received from contributors in small sums, would enable a large number of people to participate in the achievement of such a goal.

Inheritances for Appointees
Adopted April 14, 1956

1001. Whereas, The General Conference of 1928 adopted a resolution (892) setting up rules governing allowances and inheritances for Conference appointees, which in principles established an equitable basis for providing such inheritances; and

Whereas, The intent of this resolution pertaining to inheritances was not carried out except in a minor degree due to the subsequent change in economic conditions and the inability of the church to specifically meet inheritance needs; and

Whereas, There was included in this resolution provision for life insurance and housing; and

Whereas, Provision for life insurance and housing has become commonly accepted, and in many instances our incoming appointees have already assumed obligations for both housing and insurance; and

Whereas, The cost of such housing and insurance is included as necessary items in each current year's budget of our families; and

Whereas, The establishment of the Ministerial Reserve Fund has now made feasible the financing of some of the provisions for inheritances, and

Whereas, There is need for clarification of policy to enable the Presiding Bishopric to administer family budgets equitably and according to the needs of individuals; therefore be it hereby

Resolved, That provision for inheritances may be included in the family budget on the current basis for housing and insurance, and that this policy be considered as in harmony with the intent and purpose of General Conference Resolution 892;

The further intent and purpose of this resolution being that of recognition of a situation which already exists in that a substantial portion of appointees now have both housing and insurance programs which are included in family budgets; and, further, that present longtime purchase programs for housing are now a part of our total economy; the further implementation of this program to be subject to review of the Presiding Bishopric, the Joint Council of the First Presidency, the Council of Twelve, and the Presiding Bishopric, thus harmonizing with the provisions of Resolution 892, which resolution also provided for and set up the methods for consideration of both inheritances and family allowances; and

Further, that Resolution 953, adopted by the General Conference of 1946, regarding the setting of family allowances, be considered as one of the factors included in the 1928 resolution:

Allowance to be made on the basis of needs and just wants, church, government, and other statistics, also the financial condition of the family and the budget request being determining factors.

Book of Mormon Readers' Version
Adopted October 9 and 10, 1958

1002. *Resolved,* That the Conference authorize the appointment of a committee to prepare manuscript for a Readers' Version of the Book of Mormon. Be it further

Resolved, 1. That the Committee should be composed of persons having a deep spiritual appreciation for the Book of Mormon and for its doctrinal and historical message, a reverent and prayerful approach to the problems involved, an aptitude for painstaking research, a willingness to seek out the best scholarship available in semantics, philology, literary criticism, English, Hebrew, and Egyptian to assist them in deciding on the meaning of the original language, and selecting the modern language and sentence structure which best convey that meaning.

2. That any such attempt should be unhurried and thorough; and that it should be the work of people who can devote a goodly portion of their time to the task until it is completed.

3. That the Readers' Version of the Book of Mormon be paragraphed and versified in such a manner as not to break the textual continuity, and that the present system of versification be noted either in the margin or in small superior figures for reference when citing quotations or using concordances and other reference works.

4. That the Readers' Version should have as few changes as possible, compatible with its purpose of offering a more readable and understandable text.

5. That this Committee also compile a system of marginal cross-reference to suggest parallel or related passages in all Three Standard Books—Bible, Book of Mormon, and Doctrine and Covenants, and that these marginal references include notation to all changes or corrections of meaning from the manuscript having any material consequence.

6. That diacritical markings should be placed over proper names and place names for ease and uniformity in pronunciation.

7. That the work of revision should follow the general style as shown on pages 79 and 80 of the General Conference Bulletin, which is a revision of the first chapter of III Nephi.

8. That the First Presidency and Presiding Bishopric be authorized to draw on the Missionary Reserve Fund for such financing as may be needed to implement this project.

Funds for Graceland College
Adopted October 10, 1958

1003. *Resolved,* That the Presiding Bishopric be authorized to sell such lands as may be necessary in addition to funds available in the Stewardship Funds to meet the General Church obligation to Graceland College in the amount of $233,300.00.

Graceland College Bonds
Adopted October 10, 1958

1004. Whereas, The Board of Trustees of Graceland College in a letter to the Presiding Bishopric, dated September 29, 1958, called attention to the needs of Graceland for two buildings, viz:

Food Service Building at an estimated cost of	$400,000.00
Women's Dormitory Building at an estimated cost of	225,000.00
or a total of estimated cost of	$625,000.00

and

Whereas, A suggested source of finances to meet these needs is as follows:

Use of Endowment Funds	$233,300.00
1956 General Conference appropriations	100,000.00
1958 General Conference appropriation	100,000.00
Use of 1958-1959 College Day Offerings, estimated	42,000.00
Issuance of debenture bonds for sale to church members	150,000.00
	$625,300.00

and

Whereas, There is obvious need for these buildings, and

Whereas, The Board of Appropriations has recommended to the General Conference that the Presiding Bishopric be authorized to dispose of such lands as may be considered not vitally essential to the program of the Gathering to provide funds needed in addition to those now available in the Stewardship Endowment

Fund, it being estimated that approximately $100,000.00 could be available from this fund, thus paying off the Endowment Fund Bonds, and

Whereas, The Board of Appropriations has recommended to the 1958 General Conference the appropriation of $100,000.00 as requested by Graceland College, and

Whereas, It is the consensus of this Order (of Bishops) that $150,000.00 of debenture bonds could be sold to members of our church without adversely affecting our financial program, therefore be it

Resolved, That we approve the issuance by Graceland Foundation of $150,000.00 of such bonds to be amortized over a period of $12\frac{1}{2}$ years, with interest at $3\frac{1}{2}$ per cent, guaranteed as to principal and interest by the college, and with funds provided by Graceland College in the amount of $15,000.00 per annum to meet principal and interest payments. Further

That we concur in the use of the 1958-1959 College Day Offerings in the approximate sum of $42,000.00.

Family Allowance and Elders Expense
Adopted October 11, 1958

1006. *Resolved,* That the Presiding Bishopric be authorized to omit from its printed reports to General Conference in years subsequent to 1958 the schedule of Family Allowances and Elders' Expenses, and that instead of such publication this schedule be submitted to the Standing High Council of the church for such advice and counsel as this body may wish to give the Presiding Bishopric (Doctrine and Covenants 122: 6; 104: 35); and further

That such a schedule also be given to the Joint Council of the First Presidency, Council of Twelve, and Presiding Bishopric, which schedule would include the specific information called for in General Conference Resolution 953; it being understood that

Adoption of this resolution would not relieve the Presiding Bishopric or other General Church administrative officers concerned of their responsibility in regard to Family Allowances and Elders' Expenses, nor will such action invalidate or rescind General Conference to Resolution 953.

Local Church Finance Procedures
Adopted October 11, 1958

(This resolution rescinds GCR 905)

1008. *Resolved,* That we request stakes, districts, branches, missions, reunion associations and other church subdivisions to follow the policy of operating on an approved financial budget submitting an audited financial report to the business meeting concerned for approval, and be it further

Resolved, That in the interest of maintaining a more accurate record of individual offerings, local treasurers be requested to issue official local church receipts for all offerings made in the interest and support of local church work, and be it yet further

Resolved, That we recommend the adoption of the duplex envelope system, or a similar system, for the collection and recording of both general and local contributions in the congregations, branches, and missions of the church.

Handling General Church Funds
Adopted October 11, 1958

1009. *Resolved,* That costs arising directly from gathering, processing, and accounting for General Church funds and tithing statements should be borne by General Church funds. Local offerings should provide for all normal administrative expenses of branches, districts, and stakes.

Resolved, That a sufficient amount be set in the budget for gathering and handling of General Church funds and tithing statements. This budget will then include and replace the present "Bishops and Agents Field Expense Account" and will provide funds for direct costs incurred by solicitors, agents, and bishops, and also reimburse stake treasuries for costs incurred in soliciting and handling General Church funds and processing tithing statements. The Presiding Bishop's office will be responsible for recommending this budgetary item to the Board of Appropriations for final recommendation to the Conference.

Resolved, That General Church administrative officers may at any time exercise their rightful prerogatives to define and develop projects in branches, stakes, or districts. General funds for these projects should be made available as project appropriations, and such projects should include by definition some statement of purpose, scope, and termination so that these appropriations will not be regarded as a part of branch, stake, or district budgets.

Resolved, That this policy be put into effect as of January 1, 1960.

Gospel to All World
Adopted October 11, 1958

1014. Whereas, The Conference recognizes the urgency of spreading the gospel as broadly and as quickly as possible into all the world—both domestic and overseas,

Whereas, The Conference further expressed its confidence in the ability and efforts of the General Church officers to properly evaluate the many complex factors involved in choosing between the different areas; and, to wisely determine the time and extent of our commitment in the various areas of need—whether domestic, overseas, missionary, or pastoral, therefore be it

Resolved, That the officers normally making these decisions be free to discharge their responsibility under God without specific requests from the Conference.

Church Court Procedure
Adopted April 7, 1960

1018. Printed as Appendix G at the end of this book.

Worldwide Worthy Assistance
Adopted April 7, 1960

1019. The report of the Committee on World-wide Worthy Assistance was approved with the following recommendations:

That members individually continue their support of reputable local and world-wide charitable organizations;

That they urge their respective governments to continue the support of the United Nations service organizations;

And that most of all they pay their tithing according to the law of the church, and increase their contributions to the offerings (including oblation), whereby church officials may more fully carry on their divinely appointed work.

"World" in Place of "General"
Adopted April 8, 1960

1021. Whereas, (1) The term "World" is more meaningful and descriptive in our world-wide evangel than the term "General" in reference to World Conference, World Church Headquarters, etc., and

(2) There are no legal problems or implications involved in making such a change; therefore be it

Resolved, That we encourage the use of the term "World" instead of "General" in reference to World Conference, World Church Headquarters, etc.

Interest to Operating Reserve Fund
Adopted April 8, 1960

1023. Whereas, Many pressing church needs for special appropriations have resulted in a cessation of appropriations to the Operating Reserve Fund in recent years, and

Whereas, At the same time increasing costs of General Church operations have resulted in greatly reducing the ratio of operating reserves to the annual budget, now therefore be it

Resolved, That all interest earned by the Operating Reserve Fund beginning with the year 1960 shall be retained in that fund, such interest as earned to become a part of the capital of the Operating Reserve Fund.

Higher Education Program
Adopted April 9, 1960

1024. *Resolved* that,
1. As far as possible the total work of the church in the field of higher education be considered as a unit, General Church appropriations and the assignment of

General Church personnel in any area of this field being made with proper regard to our obligations elsewhere in the field, and to the total church program.

2. In addition to the specific appropriations recommended for the church-sponsored institutions of higher education, the Board of Appropriations be asked to recommend to General Conference such allocations of further funds to the Higher Education Reserve as the circumstances indicate to be wise, it being understood that withdrawals from this fund can be authorized by the First Presidency, Council of Twelve, and Presiding Bishopric, in Joint Council, in order to meet such inter-Conference needs as may arise and, particularly, to arrange for ministry in nonchurch-supported institutions which are attended by large numbers of members of the church.

3. This General Conference assure the Board of Trustees of Graceland College of its affirmative interest in
   a. continued emphasis on its two-year programs (pre-professional, terminal, and transfer)
   b. controlled expansion in the upper division in areas of religion and education; i.e., in those areas related very closely to the purposes and program of the church
   c. the extension of the Graceland Campus to the Independence area if further consultation between the Board of Trustees and the First Presidency and Presiding Bishopric shows this to be wise
   d. the provision at Independence of courses leading to a Bachelor's degree in Nursing

4. The Trustees and administrative officers and staff of Graceland College and of the School of the Restoration be requested to plan together concerning the extension to Independence of church-supported work in higher

education, it being understood that the major concern of Graceland College is in Liberal Arts and that the School of the Restoration is in ministerial and leadership education.

5. The church express appreciation of the work which has been done under the direction of the Committee on Ministry to College People, and the church commit itself to give such support to this endeavor as the needs of the students permit.

Conference Organization Committee
Adopted April 9, 1960

1025. (See Rules of Order, Par. 16 a.)

That a committee constituted along the lines of the committee now reporting shall be authorized by each General Conference and shall be instructed to report to the succeeding General Conference on the matter of Conference membership and the effective organization of Conferences, such committee working in close co-operation with the First Presidency and such other quorums and councils as may be involved, and publishing its recommendations in ample time for consideration by the church prior to any Conference at which action is proposed to be taken.

Church Literature in Libraries
Adopted April 9, 1960

1026. Officers of all groups, missions, branches, districts, and stakes, as well as individuals, should promote the placement in all libraries available to them of literature on the recommended lists as may be published from time to time. Where action is initiated by individuals, consultation should be had with the administrative officers concerned so as to avoid duplication of effort.

The placement of church books in libraries shall be financed as follows:

(a) The Herald House provides a 20 per cent discount on all literature ordered for placement in public and institutional libraries.

(b) For placement in public libraries, such as city or county libraries, the discounted price should be paid by the branches, districts, or stakes where such libraries are located.

(c) For placement in the libraries of colleges, universities, seminaries, and other special institutional libraries, 40 per cent of the list price will be paid from the General Church budget, providing that the remaining 40 per cent is paid by individuals, branches, districts, or stakes where such libraries are located.

(d) In unorganized territory and in areas where there is a demonstrated need and church membership is relatively very small, recommendations should be made to the First Presidency through the responsible field administrator for consideration of General Church assistance. When the cost is met in whole or part from the General Church budget, the list of books concerned must be approved by the First Presidency.

General Church Building Commission
Adopted April 9, 1960

1027. Whereas, There is an increasing number of

church buildings being planned and built throughout the church; and

Whereas, Members of the Quorum of High Priests as administrative officers feel the need for more guidance in the design, planning, and construction phases of church building as well as in the education and orientation of the church membership to understand the nature of worship, education, fellowship, and service as related to the church plant; therefore, be it

Resolved, That a General Church Building Commission be appointed by the First Presidency in consultation with the Presiding Bishopric to collaborate with general officers concerned to study the main phases of church design and building process, and to advise concerning all phases of church design and building.

Student Emergency Loan Fund
Adopted April 9, 1960

1028. Whereas, A "Committee on Ministry to College People" has been appointed by the First Presidency of the Reorganized Church of Jesus Christ of Latter Day Saints for the purpose of bringing special ministry to the church students who are attending college and university, and

Whereas, In the furtherance of said ministry the committee has organized students who are members of the church into groups known as Liahona Fellowships on campuses throughout the world, and has assisted in the purchase and establishment of student center buildings to provide student residences and centers of ministry on several major college campuses, and

Whereas, There is a need for the church to provide, where possible, financial assistance as well as spiritual ministry to its students, now therefore be it

Resolved, That the General Conference of the Reorganized Church of Jesus Christ of Latter Day Saints authorize the establishment of a "Liahona Fellowship Student Emergency Loan Fund" to be administered by the committee on "Ministry to College People," subject to general supervision of the Presiding Bishopric. And be it further

Resolved, That said fund be and the same is hereby designated an official fund of said church, the proceeds of which shall be used exclusively for charitable and educational purposes.

Central Stakes Reorganization
Adopted April 2, 1962

1030. Whereas, Stake organization is designed to facilitate the effective ministry of the priesthood, both non-appointee and appointee ministers, within the stake area; to permit free participation of all the Saints in legislative assemblies in the exercise of common consent; and to strengthen the ministries of worship, evangelism, teaching, and financial administration; and,

Whereas, The inclusion of too great a number of members in a single stake leads to awkwardness in administration and the growing difficulty of participation in overlarge legislative assemblies; and,

Whereas, The Jackson County area of Central Missouri Stake is rapidly becoming urbanized in relationship to the Kansas City Metropolitan area; and,

Whereas, The remainder of Central Missouri Stake is not now so fully urbanized, but is characterized by a high degree of homogeneity; and,

Whereas, The Stakes which are adjacent to each other are mutually involved in factors which significantly affect any one of them so that none is free to act independently on matters of joint concern; and

Whereas, The organization of stakes is the primary concern of the presidency and other general officers of the church; therefore be it

Resolved, That the World Conference of 1962 looks with favor upon the reorganization of the Center Stake of Zion and the Central Missouri Stake so as to form three or more stakes, and to make adjustments to boundary lines of contiguous stakes which may be affected; and be it further

Resolved, That the First Presidency, with the consent and approval of the Joint Council of the First Presidency, the Council of Twelve, and the Presiding Bishopric, and of the members of the proposed stakes, be authorized to proceed with such reorganization at such time as they deem wise with "a sufficient number of members of mature experience in the church, who live in close proximity to a given center; a sufficient number of ministers of high priestly caliber to provide personnel for the presiding councils ... a sufficiently stable economy to assure permanence, and the possibility of definitely relating the contribution to be made in the area to the advancement of our Zionic program" (Rules of Order, VI 37).

Insurance Program Study
Adopted April 3, 1962

1031: Whereas, For a number of years the General Church has been implementing in its financial structure protection which is normally carried by insurance companies so that under this self-insurance program fundings have been arranged which provide for appointee disabilty, pensions, and death benefits; appointee life insurance; employee pensions; employee life insurance; and partial automobile collision and comprehensive insurance; and

Whereas, A committee of the Order of Bishops is investigating a program for implementing fire and extended coverage insurance on the houses of worship; and

Whereas, We feel there is need for a continuing study of the whole field of insurance; and

Whereas, The Presiding Bishopric advise that they would welcome the appointment of a committee to work with them in these areas of mutual concern with a view to creative suggestions which can be used in our insurance program;

Therefore the Presiding Bishopric be hereby advised to ask for recommendations from the Professional Insurance Association for members of an advisory committee of three to work with the Presiding Bishopric in further study along the lines hereinbefore outlined.

Committee on Equality
Adopted April 3, 1962

1032. Whereas, The concept of equality is a vital aspect of the gathering and Zionic philosophy of the church; and

Whereas, We believe that the achievement of equality depends on the free cooperation of godly men motivated by an informed awareness of the demands of justice in the social, political, economic, and other fields; and

Whereas, This involves the background, vocation, social situation of each individual and the operation of such principles as the moral obligation to be brotherly and to cultivate one's special gifts and talents, the right of free agency, the responsibility of each individual to function as a steward, to render an accounting of his stewardship, to share in the results of that stewardship through the paying of tithing, the giving of offerings, and the consecration of surplus, this latter being the focal point of beginning of a condition of equality among members of diverse groups; and

Whereas, equality also involves sound understanding in many areas of human relationship and willingness to take the initiative that justice may be gradually extended; and

Whereas, good could be accomplished in the appointment of an advisory committee; therefore be it

Resolved, That the First Presidency in consultation with the Presiding Bishopric be authorized to appoint a committee to consider means of promoting equality along the lines indicated in the resolution, such committee to work with existing committees of the Order of Bishops in conjunction with the Presidency and the Bishopric.

Marriage, Divorce, and Remarriage
Adopted April 6, 1962

1034. 1. Marriage is ordained of God: "Marriage is ordained of God unto man" (Doctrine and Covenants 49:3 a).

2. Divinely approved purposes of marriage are mutual companionship, procreation within families, and mutual fulfillment: "It is lawful that he should have one wife, and they twain shall be one flesh, and all this that the earth might answer the end of its creation; and that it might be filled with the measure of man, according to his creation before the world was made" (Doctrine and Covenants 49:3; see also Genesis 2:27-30; Ephesians 5:31; Doctrine and Covenants 111:2 b).

3. Marriage is intended to be a life-long covenant between one man and one woman. In the event of the death of either spouse, the other is at liberty to marry again: "One man should have one wife; and one woman but one husband, except in case of death, when either is at liberty

to marry again" (Doctrine and Covenants 111:4 b; see also Matthew 19:5-8).

4. Marriage should be entered into soberly, worthily, and after mature consideration. Members of the church should marry only such persons as realize the sacramental nature of the marriage covenant and are willing to abide by its necessary conditions as well as to enjoy its rewards (see G.C.R. 972).

5. God is concerned in every marriage. Marriages should therefore be solemnized with dignity in a setting conducive to worship. To this end, simplicity, propriety, and frugality in the service and its appointments are advised. Civil marriages, though legally acceptable, recognize only the civil significance of the compact and so tend to minimize the spiritual values involved. In order to preserve the sacramental nature of marriage in countries where civil marriages are required by law, a second ceremony is encouraged. This ceremony is to be conducted by authorized priesthood in the recommended worshipful setting.

6. Members of the Melchisedec priesthood or priests of the Aaronic order may solemnize marriages when so permitted civil law (Doctrine and Covenants 111:1 b, c). Officiating ministers should require that they be given sufficient time by the parties seeking their services to enable them to make such investigation and to give such instruction and counsel as they deem helpful in maintaining the sacramental nature of the marriage covenant and of the marriage itself.

7. The church recognizes that the remarriage of an innocent party in a divorce action is permissible when a divorce has been secured for any of the following reasons: adultery, repeated sexual perversion, desertion, such aggravated conditions within the home as render married life

unbearable for the party petitioning or for the children of the marriage.*

8. Though the civil court may have accepted proof of lesser indignities as sufficient grounds for divorce, permission for remarriage should be granted only when the conditions complained of were of such an extreme nature as to place the other members of the family in serious and continuing jeopardy.

Persons who have been divorced, even though innocent of wrongdoing, should pay special attention to the admonition not to marry hastily or without due consideration. Ministers asked to officiate at such weddings should assure themselves that sufficient time has elapsed and that due consideration has been had.

9. Any person who has been divorced, and who desires to be married by a member of the priesthood, should make arrangements with this minister in sufficient time to permit him to make any necessary inquiry concerning the circumstances of the divorce and to secure the approval of the branch president. If the branch president does not feel free to act, he should refer the inquiry to the next higher administrative officer of the church.

Financial Policy Reaffirmed
Adopted April 6, 1962

1035. Whereas, Since the adoption of a financial pol-

---

*This is in harmony with the basic requirements of the law and also takes note of the fact that circumstances develop and persist in certain marriages for which no remedy within that marriage seems to be discoverable, and which are so harmful in their effects on one or both of the partners to the marriage, and on their children, as to render life under those circumstances humiliating, fraught with suffering, and intolerable.

icy by the 1932 General Conference, the church has operated on the basis of that policy; and

Whereas, Adherence to this policy has made possible the establishment of firm economic and financial foundations for the church by the elimination of external debt and the setting up of substantial reserves (including the Houses of Worship Revolving Fund, Missionary Reserve Fund, Operating Reserve Fund, etc.) which have resulted in excellent morale among the membership of the church and confidence in the church on the part of those serving in various capacities, including our ministerial forces; and

Whereas, The church has experienced substantial growth in its missionary outreach, in its strengthening of stakes, districts, and congregations throughout the church which is evidenced in many ways, particularly in new houses of worship and in improvements within its institutions such as the Independence Sanitarium and Hospital and School of Nursing, Graceland College, Resthaven, and the School of the Restoration, and in all of its departments, all of which gives evidence of the wisdom of the policy and the stability of our movement; and

Whereas, We are now faced with increasing needs of our institutions, particularly Graceland College, the Independence Sanitarium and Hospital and School of Nursing, and the Herald Publishing House, and

Whereas, Presently the only outstanding indebtedness for capital expansion authorized by the World Conference is that of the bond issue of Graceland Foundation, Inc., the original amount of which was $150,000; and

Whereas, In the past it was necessary for the church to pay off debts of its institutions created by them for capital improvements, and

Whereas, There is presently a pressing need for finances to provide for the capital needs of the institutions and agencies of the church; and it is possible to obtain such additional finances through various sources, as the need justifies; therefore be it

Resolved, That the World Church in Conference assembled does hereby reaffirm the financial policy of 1932, which included the provision of the World Church operating on a basis of balanced budgets and maintaining the World Church free from debt; and be it further

Resolved, That it is the opinion of this Conference that debts of the church institutions or its agencies should be limited to a maximum consistent with their ability to repay from the sources available within the institution or agency itself and such supplementary help as may be given by way of appropriation from the World Church, and be it yet further

Resolved, That where any proposed indebtedness might become a legal obligation of the World Church, covering any debts for expansion purposes or special projects of any of the institutions or agencies of the church, approval shall first be given by the Board of Appropriations.

Unity of Restoration Movements
Adopted April 7, 1962

1036. Whereas, A resolution has been presented to this Conference by the San Francisco Bay District "to recommend to the First Presidency that appropriate steps be taken to renew discussions with the Church of Christ, Temple Lot, with reference to possible unification of that church with the Reorganized Church of Jesus Christ of Latter Day Saints," and

Whereas, A committee consisting of one each of the Presidency, Twelve, and Presiding Bishopric, each of the quorums named to select its member, has heretofore been empowered by Conference Resolution (Section 869) to consider this matter, and

Whereas, There exist, between the Reorganized Church of Jesus Christ of Latter Day Saints and certain other

Restoration movements, common roots in the miraculous events which attended the restoration of the gospel through the instrumentality of Joseph Smith, Jr., and common belief in the divine origin of the Book of Mormon maintaining continuing ties of interest between us and all organizations which trace their origin to the Restoration movement, and

Whereas, It is not the intent of this body to minimize the importance of the issues which gave rise to the decisions to walk in different paths, and the differences which do now divide us, and it is the intent of this body to express our recognition of the fact that among the organizations which have developed out of the Restoration there are those which are exhibiting moral and ethical standards which reflect creditably upon the foundational principles upon which these organizations have been developed, and

Whereas, We do declare it to be the general disposition of the Reorganized Church of Jesus Christ of Latter Day Saints to stress the affirmative aspects of our belief and to respect and to applaud all worthy achievements of individuals and of groups whose actions are influenced by Restoration ideals; now, therefore, be it

Resolved. That the Conference assembled, in harmony with the principles hereinabove expressed, does hereby reaffirm its confidence in the committee already constituted to effect the intent of this resolution and to take such affirmative action as it may deem proper in the matter of attempting to resolve such differences as may now exist between this church and such other Restoration movements.

Urban Renewal Policy
Adopted April 7, 1962

1037. *Resolved.* That since the church has limited itself in land purchase to the consolidation of areas for its future use, it is inadvisable for the church as such to engage in urban renewal land purchase programs except in cases where cooperation in connection with a limited number of our holdings is necessary for the normal development of the community.

Care of Elderly
Adopted April 7, 1962

1038. *Resolved,* That while the care of the elderly is an imperative need, we should limit our undertakings and work in this field in the foreseeable future to the resources which are available to us through the oblation fund and such contributions as may be received as offering or surplus for this purpose. This would not preclude church members from engaging in such worthy private projects where personal and financial resources were adequate to qualify them for assistance from federal funds.

Credit Unions
Adopted April 7, 1962

1039. *Resolved,* That credit unions should be considered separate and apart from the ecclesiastical and general business of the operation of the church; and that such business should therefore be engaged in by individual members of the church who provide responsible officers and agents, thus operating as a business separate from the business of the church, although it is recognized that such associations can be of assistance to individuals and groups of people who are members of the church.

Use of Surplus Funds
Adopted April 7, 1962

1040. *Resolved,* That the creation of a Revolving Fund for the promotion and development of business and industrial enterprises should come through the operation of the law of consecration of surplus funds on the part of the individual members of the church for this specific purpose, as authorized by Conference Resolution No. 977, adopted April 9, 1950; further that it would be highly inadvisable to make appropriations from tithes and offerings for the purposes set forth.

Funds for Missionary Program
Adopted April 8, 1964

1041. *Resolved,* That the Joint Council of the First Presidency, the Council of Twelve, and the Presiding Bishopric be and hereby are authorized to draw upon the Missions Abroad Capital Fund for needs which have to be met because of missionary developments and the furthering of the missionary program when, in the opinion of the Joint Council, these developments are in harmony with the missionary program and objectives of the church; it being further understood that reports of such withdrawals shall continue to be made to the General Conference, and by action of the Conference upon the recommendation of the Board of Appropriations, appropriations be made to rehabilitate the funds up to the amounts designated—namely, Missions Abroad Capital Fund, $200,000.00.

Herald House Loan
Adopted April 9, 1964

1042. The World Conference concurred in the decision of the Board of Appropriations to loan $200,000.00 to the Herald Publishing House from the Ministerial Reserve Fund in connection with the proposed Herald Publishing House plant at a suggested interest rate of 4 percent per annum in harmony with the previous Conference action on the financial policy of the church. (See GCR 1035.)

Resthaven Addition
Adopted April 9, 1964

1043. Upon the request of the Presiding Bishopric,

the Board of Appropriations and the World Conference concurred in the decision of the Presiding Bishopric that approximately $750,000.00 of the Oblation Fund be spent for an addition to Resthaven at Independence, Missouri. There are sufficient funds on hand to meet these costs and at the same time to meet other demands made upon the Oblation Fund and, with anticipated income, to meet our needs for the future.

It was further agreed that it is advisable also that consideration be given to the purchasing of sites for locations for additional facilities, such sites to be purchased as information can be obtained to assure the Bishopric that the location of such homes can meet justifiable needs and that personnel are available to administer them. (See *World Conference Bulletin,* April 10, 1964, pages 247, 293.)

Social, Economic, and Moral Problems
Adopted April 11, 1964

1045. Whereas, The members of the Church of Jesus Christ must declare and demonstrate Christian principles in relation to current social, economic, and moral problems;

Whereas, In these turbulent and rapidly changing times, the members of the church need and desire guidance concerning the Christian approach to such problems;

Whereas, Such guidance would be provided by World Conference-approved statements of principle on various subjects, including, by way of illustration only, the following:

1. What steps should members of the church take, both in the church and in society at large, to achieve our avowed policy of racial equality (GCR No. 995)?

2. Is disobedience to the civil law and authorities by our members permissible in order to achieve goals such as racial equality?

3. What is the relative responsibility of government and church in relation to the economic welfare of the individual?

4. How can members of the church maintain Christian principles of sexual morality and ethical conduct within their various cultures in these times?

. . . Therefore, be it

Resolved, That this Conference urges the First Presidency with such assistance as they may require from the quorums, councils, and orders of the church, to prepare or cause to be prepared statements of principle to submit to future World Conferences for the guidance of church members in meeting current social, economic, and moral problems, the selection of subjects and the manner of preparation of such statements to be determined by the First Presidency.

Use of Tobacco
Adopted April 11, 1964

1046. Whereas, In recent months there has been a marked increase in attention given by the public to medical and scientific studies concerning the relationship between certain diseases and the use of tobacco, and

Whereas, These studies give statistical support to the teaching of the church first stated in 1833 and emphasized by revelation or resolution in 1868, 1878, and 1887, and

Whereas, The addiction to tobacco is clearly a detriment to the physical and spiritual life of a Christian steward, although such addiction of itself is not a test of membership in the church, therefore be it

Resolved, That the Church of Jesus Christ urges its members and all men to live physically and morally in a manner that reflects the image of Christ our Savior, and further be it

Resolved, That the church reaffirms in the context of 1964 the counsel given to the church in 1833 that tobacco is not for the body and is not good for man, but is an herb to be used with judgment and skill, and further be it

Resolved, That this Conference inform the appropriate officials of our concern about and support for suitable controls over the advertising and use of tobacco and tobacco products.

Programs for Young People
Adopted April 11, 1964

1047. Whereas, The church has the unique mission of preparing for the establishment of Zion; and

Whereas, The accomplishment of this mission will require the development of a generation of church members who are equipped adequately with spiritual, moral, ethical, educational, and vocational resources to bring this monumental task to fruition; and

Whereas, The church has a consequent responsibility of assuming some leadership in making the land of America a suitable headquarters for God's kingdom on earth; and

Whereas, The decisions of the Supreme Court of the United States on religious observances in schools give further emphasis to the leadership which must be taken by the church to give young people a suitable sense of values and direction; and

Whereas, It is more desirable for young people to be guided and assisted by the church motivated by Christian principles than by paternalistic governments motivated by political considerations; now, therefore, be it

Resolved, That the World Church in Conference assembled does hereby request each appropriate department and quorum of the church and each congregation, district, and stake to give prayerful consideration and added emphasis in various aspects of the church programs to helping young people in and out of the church achieve the desire and skills to help build a perfect society under the kingship of Christ. Be it further

Resolved, That the curriculum of the church school be broadened to incorporate more emphasis on Christian morality, ethics, and behavior in addition to doctrine and church history. Be it further

Resolved, That appropriate World Church departments prepare specific recommendations, disseminate appropriate bibliographies to aid in self-preparation, and provide field training to local personnel to carry out programs to make our churches outstanding and attractive focal points for practical ministry to young people, members and nonmembers alike. Specifically, there should be provided training in the fields of recreation, personal counseling including premarital counseling, and cooperation with available community services such as the family service and other professional helps.

Resolved, That local congregations be urged to mobilize all available resources and to provide local leadership for community efforts to (1) help young people locate suitable employment, (2) help young people complete worthy and practical educational objectives, (3) prevent school dropouts prior to completion of high school, (4) provide skilled and needed counseling services, resorting to professional assistance outside the church when necessary, and (5) provide a sufficiently attractive program of wholesome recreation and social life that young people will be drawn to church-centered fellowship and thus seek what effective ministry the church is prepared to offer in other aspects of their lives.

Resolved, That in order to help overcome the reluctance of some to take advantage of available helps due to past convention and misunderstanding of the nature of counseling, that appropriate World Church departments strongly urge all young people by every practicable means available to make use of all available programs. Vocational, educational, and premarital counseling are cited for specific example and emphasis.

Television Committee
Adopted April 11, 1964

1048. Whereas, The church is continually looking for new and effective methods of presenting the gospel and recognizes the need to gear its missionary program to the situations of a modern and changing world; and

Whereas, A regularly produced and internationally distributed television series can be a successful and very special method of missionary endeavor, opening a myriad of avenues to the church's ministry; and

Whereas, It is advisable to appoint a committee to investigate the feasibility of such a series to determine the church's need, the desirability of such a series, and the expense involved therein, be it hereby

Resolved, That the First Presidency be requested to appoint a committee to thoroughly investigate the feasibility of having produced for the church a film and/or video taped television series, along with such other means by which the church can best use television, and that the committee also make recommendation for the establishment of a permanent Television Committee, and that if the committee's findings and recommendations indicate the need and desirability of a television series, that the committee recommend the procedures to be taken and develop a proposed budget, and that the findings and recommendations of the committee

Program for Unmarried Adults
Adopted April 22, 1966

1050. Whereas, We recognize that a critical need for a special ministry to unmarried adult persons exists, and

Whereas, We believe ministry to this segment of our church population presents practical and worthwhile opportunities, therefore be it

Resolved. That the First Presidency consider and implement programs of specialized ministry to meet this need, utilizing professional skills and modern technology.

Ordinations of High Priests and Bishops
Adopted April 22, 1966

(For paragraphs 2, 3, and 4 of Resolution No. 638)

1051. Nominations for ordinations to the high priesthood may be made by members of the First Presidency or the Council of Twelve, stake presidents, regional administrators, or other high priests having administrative jurisdiction. Inasmuch as high priests are especially designated as standing ministers to the church under the direct oversight of the First Presidency (Doctrine and Covenants 122:8, 9), all such nominations should be presented to the First Presidency directly or through other administrative officers for consideration and presentation to the General Conference or appropriate high council. If council approval is given, further approval shall be secured from the stake or district conference or—in unorganized areas—from the branch concerned.

Ordinations to the evangelical order, after having been recommended by the Council of Twelve and approved by the First Presidency, shall be submitted to the General

Conference or to the appropriate stake, district, or branch conference.

Ordinations to the Bishopric, which are recommended by the First Presidency, shall be presented to the General Conference or to the appropriate high council and to the stake or district conference or branch business meeting concerned.

Peace, War, and Use of Force
Adopted April 22, 1966

1052. Whereas, The World Conference of 1958 resolved that a committee be appointed by the First Presidency to study, review, and prepare a statement on peace, war, and the use of force (*General Conference Bulletin* for October 10, 1958, page 93, and October 12, 1958, page 104), and

Whereas, a report of such committee described as an interim and not a final report was adopted in 1960 (GCR 1020, *Bulletin* for April 3, 1960, page 53, and April 8, 1960, page 97) which report recommended the extension of the life of the committee to permit extended studies of such matters, and

Whereas, There have been no further interim or final reports submitted by such a committee, and

Whereas, Pending resolutions before the Conference on the subject of peace, war, and use of force reflect the concern of many members that further statements on these issues be considered, therefore be it

Resolved, That this World Conference reaffirms its concern and intent that further reports of a committee on peace, war, and the use of force be prepared and hereby refers all pending resolutions on such subjects, including the resolutions labeled "Peace, War, and the Use of Force" (Center Stake), "World Leaders and Peace" (Blue Valley Stake), and "War and Pacifism" (London, Ontario, District) to such committee for its consideration. Be it further

Resolved. That members submit their reports to the First Presidency for use in giving the members of the church guidance as they deem wise.

Utilization of Retired Members
Adopted April 22, 1966

1053. Whereas, The increasing longevity of life combined with an earlier age of retirement has released substantial numbers of church members from employment responsibilities; and

Whereas, Such retired members may make valuable contributions to the work of Christ both in their areas of residence and other areas to which they might be assigned; therefore, be it

Resolved, That this Conference looks with favor upon an investigation by the First Presidency of additional methods of making maximum utilization of the talents and time of such retired members.

Family Ministry Coordinator
Adopted April 22, 1966

1054. Whereas, The responsibility of the church toward effective family life is to bring ministry of moral uplift and spiritual enlightenment to families and individuals, and to build strong family ties through consistent ministry in the home, and

Whereas, The present problems of divorce, family disharmony, and emotional disturbance are evidences that our present program of family ministry is not providing a sufficiently strong resource to meet present needs, therefore, be it

Resolved, That we reaffirm that the basic ministerial responsibility for the spiritual and moral well-being of family life and the development of sound family relationships lies with the priesthood functioning in their several callings, and be it further

Resolved, That renewed emphasis be given to this important aspect of this distinctive ministry in the church by appointment of a Coordinator for Family Ministry for the World Church whose responsibility shall entail:

1. Working with the various departments of the church in the development of a long-range plan for family ministry and to supervise the development of a methodology with adequate materials and helps to achieve this purpose.
2. Working with stakes (and large districts when possible) in order to:
    a. Formulate a more effective program in preventative counseling leading toward stronger family relationships. This would include premarital counseling among our young people with a view toward the development of wholesome attitudes about marital life.
    b. Develop a better program of therapeutic counseling through the use of qualified personnel in the church and referral to those secular agencies which provide effective help.
3. Calling upon our membership who are engaged in related professional disciplines for advice, counsel, and evaluation of the program.
4. Reporting annually to the First Presidency with consideration being given to the printing of these reports for benefit of and information to the church.

Addition to Sanitarium and Hospital
Adopted April 23, 1966

1055. *Resolved*, That the Presiding Bishopric be

authorized, subject to approval of the Board of Appropriations, to loan an amount not to exceed $300,000.00 from the Ministerial Reserve Fund, or from other reserve funds of the church, to the Independence Sanitarium and Hospital to assist in financing the construction of a building addition currently being planned by that institution. It is understood that the terms of the loan, including the interest rate and time of repayment, will be worked out on a mutually satisfactory basis between the Board of Trustees of the Independence Sanitarium and Hospital and the Presiding Bishopric.

Television Utilization
Adopted April 23, 1966

1056. *Resolved,* That the Conference encourage the First Presidency to provide for continued inquiry into the utilization of television as a means of implementing and communicating the goals and ministry of the church.

World Conference Role in Statements of Policy
Adopted April 23, 1966

1057. Whereas, The World Conference has historically adopted statements of policy concerning issues affecting the church (see, for example, GCR 1020 on War and Peace, and GCR 995 on Racial Equality, and GCR 1025 calling for World Conference approved statements of principle on matters of current social concern),

Whereas, It is desirable to clarify the function of the World Conference with respect to the initiation and adoption of such policy statements and to facilitate the preparation of such legislation if such function is to continue,

Resolved, That the Conference request the Committee on Conference Organization and Procedures to study and report to the next Conference regarding the proper role of the World Conference with respect to such statements of policy and to study and recommend methods of implementation, including the desirability of Standing Committees of the Conference on various subjects such as social concerns and peace, war, and the use of force.

Book of Mormon Reader's Edition
Adopted April 23, 1966

1058. *Resolved,* That the "1966 Authorized Edition" as published by the Herald Publishing House be known as a reader's edition. Be it further
Resolved, That the term "1966 Authorized Edition" be blocked out of all copies of that version of the Book of Mormon now available for sale.

Ministry to Unmarried Adults
Adopted April 1, 1968

1059. Whereas, Assistance in the establishment of well-adjusted Christian families is among the great objectives of the church, therefore be it
Resolved, That the 1968 World Conference recognize that both in the church and in society there are many unmarried adults who would benefit from a ministry designed to assist them in establishing Christian, Zionic homes. To develop and implement specific and practical programs in this ministerial endeavor will require the efforts of skilled professionals and the use of modern technology. The Conference, therefore, refers this matter to the First Presidency with the suggestion that either the Committee on Ministry to Unmarried Adults continue to function and make further recommendations, or that this specialized ministry be included in the responsibility of the Family Ministry Coordinator.

Fiscal Year Change
Adopted April 2, 1968

1062. Whereas, It becomes increasingly difficult as

the church work expands to complete and adequately analyze the financial reports of the World Church for the year prior to the regular biennial Conference during the period between December 31 and the opening of World Conference inasmuch as final reports and funds are not received until several weeks after the close of the accounting year, and

Whereas, This necessitates most of the preparation of budgets being made without a complete financial statement on income and expense for the preceding year, and

Whereas, A change from the present fiscal year ending December 31 to a fiscal year ending September 30 would overcome these disadvantages, would eliminate the present practice of the church operating without a Conference-approved budget for the first three months of each Conference year, and would offer other advantages such as spreading the accounting workload more evenly over the year, and

Whereas, Such a change would appear to present no major difficulties in terms of church administration and reporting of member and financial statistics, therefore be it

Resolved, That this World Conference rescind GCR 885 and in place thereof approve the establishment of a fiscal year ending September 30, this change to be put into effect by the use of a nine-month accounting period ending September 30, 1969; and be it further

Resolved, That the Board of Appropriations is hereby authorized to readjust the 1969 budget as it shall be finally approved by this Conference to the nine-month period ending September 30, 1969, and to prepare the necessary budget for the full fiscal year October 1, 1969, to September 30, 1970.

Office Wing Addition to Auditorum
Adopted April 2, 1968

1063. Whereas, The original plans for the Auditorium provided for wings designed for use as office space for the general administration of the world church; and

Whereas, These wings have never been constructed and changes in basic design have taken place as the Auditorium construction has proceeded; and

Whereas, The need for housing quorums, councils, departments, and special ministries continues to exist and has been met by expedient use of available space, resulting in an uncoordinated and inefficient distribution of office space; and

Whereas, The problems involved in the present arrangement are compounded by urgent needs based on the church's expanding ministries for which no space in the present building is available; therefore be it

Resolved, That the World Conference does hereby authorize the development of architectural plans for and construction of an office wing addition to the Auditorium in which space can be provided for those functions which relate to the church's general administration and worldwide ministries; and be it further

Resolved, That the cost of such an addition be met by appropriations and special offerings and included among the objectives for capital fund-raising programs.

Tribute to Martin Luther King, Jr.
Adopted April 5, 1968

1064. Whereas, The shocking news of the untimely death of the Reverend Martin Luther King, Jr., by an assassin's bullet marks another sad day in American and world history, and

Whereas, His efforts for justice and the dignity of all men everywhere have been fraught with danger and opposition from many sources, although he has sought methods of nonviolent protest and crusades, and

Whereas, His efforts have been widely acclaimed and recognized through the esteemed award of the Nobel Peace Prize and other signal honors for achievements in civil rights, justice, and the dignity of all men, now therefore be it

Resolved, That the World Conference of the Reorganized Church of Jesus Christ of Latter Day Saints in Independence, Missouri, pause in tribute to the passing of this great American and world leader, Dr. Martin Luther King, Jr., for his accomplishments in civil rights, justice, and the dignity of all men, and particularly among the poor and depressed, and that we do hereby express our deepest regrets and sympathies to his widow and children in this time of bereavement. We do further share in some of the implications either directly or indirectly which have created a climate for his untimely death, and we do pledge ourselves anew to work to eradicate prejudice and bigotry in the hearts of men through Christ's message to all mankind.

Higher Education Study
Adopted April 5, 1968

1065. *Resolved,* That the church does hereby declare as one of its purposes the continuation of strong financial support of higher education to the end that as many as possible of those qualified and seeking higher education in an institution of learning related to the church may have that opportunity, and be it further

Resolved, That the Board of Trustees of Graceland College be advised that it is the intent of the Conference that the Board of Appropriations of the church shall consider budgetary support of the operational budget of Graceland on the basis of an allotment in terms of the college needs and the availability of funds, and be it further

Resolved, That capital appropriations shall continue to be made from the income of the church for developments at Lamoni as the need may indicate and subject to the availability of funds. Capital appropriations for the Lamoni campus will be used to modernize and expand facilities which now limit the achievement of the basic student body of the campus. The basic student body is that number of students which can be efficiently served by many of the present facilities of the Lamoni campus, e.g., Frederick Madison Smith Library and Floyd M. McDowell Commons, and be it further

Resolved, That members of the First Presidency direct the Commission on Education to engage competent professional services in order to conduct a long-range study as to the direction the church should go in developing institutions of higher learning and other programs related to the whole area of higher education considering present and future resources available and the need for the type of ministry which can best support the objectives of the World Church and its people, and to make recommendations to the First Presidency, Joint Council, and to the World Conference of 1970, and be it further

Resolved, That an appropriation of $40,000.00 be provided by this Conference from the general fund of the church to conduct such a study on higher education.

Graceland College Trustees
Adopted April 6, 1968

1069. *Resolved*, That the terms of office for the trustees of Graceland College which will by past custom expire four in 1970, three in 1972, and two in 1974 be changed to expire three in 1970, three in 1972, and three in 1974, and that the vacancy now in existence for a term otherwise to expire in 1970 be filled to expire in 1974.

Sanitarium and Hospital Reincorporation
Adopted April 6, 1968

1070 See APPENDIX F, page 289.

Houses of Worship Loans
Adopted April 6, 1968

1071. Whereas, The program of constructing houses of worship throughout the church continues at a rapid rate, resulting in an increasing demand for Houses of Worship Revolving Loan Funds, and

Whereas, The growing need for Houses of Worship Revolving Funds requires that such loans be retired as quickly as possible to enable a maximum number of loans being made to congregations and branches throughout the church, and

Whereas, The General Conference has previously authorized the use of $750,000.00 of the Ministerial Reserve Fund for Houses of Worship Revolving Loans at 3 percent interest, and

Whereas, It appears that the Houses of Worship Revolving Loan Fund will need to draw a substantial sum from the Ministerial Reserve Fund for revolving church construction loans, and

Whereas, It is necessary that the integrity of the Ministerial Reserve Fund be maintained by earning a reasonable rate of return on its investment to insure that its purpose will be fulfilled of assisting in defraying the costs of retired general church appointee families, and

Whereas, The interest rate charged on Houses of Worship Revolving Loans was established at 3 percent by General Conference action of 1956 (GCR No. 992), therefore be it

Resolved, That the World Conference does hereby reaffirm its authorization to loan an amount up to a maximum of $750,000.00 from the Ministerial Reserve Fund to the Houses of Worship Revolving Fund, and be it further

Resolved, That the Presiding Bishopric be authorized to establish the interest rate on the portion of the Ministerial Reserve Fund loaned to the Houses of Worship Revolving Loan Fund or to church institutions at a rate of return more nearly comparable to that being received from other invested portions of the fund, and be it further

Resolved, That the Presiding Bishopric be authorized to establish the interest rate on loans made from the Houses of Worship Revolving Fund at a level which will result in the total interest cost to borrowing congregations and branches being at least 1 percent below the prime interest rate for commercial loans at the time the loan is made, and be it further

Resolved, That this action will supersede the enactments of General Conference Resolutions 992, 1010, and 1033, and be it further

Resolved, That congregations, branches, and missions throughout the church be encouraged to retire their outstanding loans as rapidly as possible to provide necessary funds for meeting the continuing requests for Houses of Worship Revolving loans. (See GCR 1095.)

Service to Local Community
Adopted April 6, 1968

1072. Whereas, Zionic principles should be applied

in the corporate life of faithful members and the communities where they live, and

Whereas, The local church and its members must therefore become more involved in meeting and participating in the needs of society, and

Whereas, Further information is needed concerning specific techniques and programs of community participation, therefore be it

Resolved, That the World Conference request the First Presidency to provide for the dissemination of information concerning specific techniques and programs by which the local church and its members may more effectively give service and meet the needs of the community.

Gospel to Racial and Ethnic Groups
Adopted April 6, 1968

1075. Whereas, The scriptures are clear that the gospel is to be preached to all men and nations and "the voice of warning shall be unto all people, by the mouths of my disciples, whom I have chosen in these last days" (D. and C. 1:1 d), and

Whereas, General Conference Resolutions 171 and 995, adopted in 1875 and 1956 respectively, encourage our carrying the gospel to all racial and ethnic groups today, and

Whereas, This church is called forth to be the light of the world, offering a divine plan for the salvation of all men everywhere, that unity might prevail, and

Whereas, Recent changes in racial and ethnic group relations have brought many worthwhile improvements, but also have uncovered extreme militant feelings, creating tension, unrest, violence, death, and destruction which even now threaten the internal peace of several nations, and

Whereas, We believe and profess that the restored gospel is called, by its very nature, to offer the necessary ministry in times like these to replace frustration and despair with faith and hope, and to offer guidance to all races and peoples caught up in the tensions of our times, and

Whereas, Frederick M. Smith defined evangelism as "the process of getting the love of God into the hearts of men, and the lives of men into the kingdom of God," therefore be it

Resolved, That this Conference go on record as commending those who have moved out with specific programs of compassionate witness of the gospel to all racial and ethnic groups and to the Negro in particular, and be it further

Resolved, That the church at large be urged now to more adequately implement the policies and resolutions previously adopted by the World Conference, and that stakes, districts, branches, and members be called upon to reach out with a greater expression of Christian love to share this message of faith, hope, and brotherhood with all racial and ethnic groups around and among us, with emphasis upon the Negro race and the troubled areas, that this restored gospel might truly provide a pattern of Zionic brotherhood to the world.

Annotated Edition of the Book of Mormon
Adopted April 6, 1970

1076. The committee appointed following the 1968 World Conference "to study the feasibility and advisability of publishing an annotated edition of the Book of Mormon containing internal, explained literary evidences, and possibly some archaeological evidences and illustrations in order that the nonmember reader might have before him convincing scientific testimony that the Nephite record is indeed what it claims to be and that Jesus Christ is the Savior of the world" make the following report:

The chairman contacted Brother Roy Weldon, one of the major sponsors of the Conference resolution which led to the appointment of this committee, and secured an interpretation of the intent of the resolution. Brother Weldon explained that the intent of the resolution was to suggest the insertion of explanatory and illustrative materials in the present authorized edition of the Book of Mormon through a process of collating full-page tip-ins in future bindings of the book. He was especially interested in the addition of (1) archaeological photos and illustrations and (2) explanatory materials relating to the internal literary evidences of the book.

The committee discussed this approach and other alternatives. The consensus was that a fully annotated edition of the Book of Mormon would be valuable, and recommendation is made that the church move in this direction as soon as adequate manpower is available to do the research necessary for the development of such an extensive work. The committee did not, however, favor the more superficial treatment recommended in the resolution, feeling that this would not be a true annotation but an illustrative approach. Studies in archaeology and related sciences are at the present time revealing new information and new points of view at such a rapid rate that materials which might be placed in the authorized edition would soon be outdated or reinterpreted. Such a tentative arrangement of the authorized edition would tend to cheapen its value, the committee felt, since conclusions published now would need to be changed from time to time following interpretation of new evidence.

The committee did, however, recognize the value of publishing a separate booklet which would catch up the present status of research in the Book of Mormon field. The booklet should be acknowledged as a tentative and unofficial approach of the church toward a continuing search for final answers, and it should be open to change as new evidence is accumulated.

Higher Education
Adopted April 7, 1970

1079. 1. Whereas, A resolution adopted on April 9, 1960, affirmed that "the total work of the church in the field of higher education be considered as a unit"; provided for allocations to be made to the Higher Education Reserve Fund; affirmed the interest of the church in the development by Graceland College of its two-year programs, its controlled expansion into upper division studies, extension of the Graceland campus to the Independence area, and the development of a baccalaureate nursing curriculum; and requested the trustees and officers of Graceland, the School of the Restoration, and church officials to explore the extension to Independence of church-supported higher education in the fields of liberal arts and ministerial and leadership education; and

2. Whereas, A resolution adopted on April 5, 1968, reaffirmed the policy of the church to give strong support to higher education "to the end that as many as possible of those qualified and seeking higher education in an institution of learning related to the church may have that opportunity" and called for continuing budgetary and capital support to Graceland College subject to the availability of funds; and further ordered an additional study of "the direction the church should go in developing institutions of higher learning and other programs related to the whole area of higher education"; and

3. Whereas, Comprehensive reports have now been prepared by the Education Commission of the church and by a panel of consultants appointed to advise the commission, as well as by a minority of the Education Commission,

presenting alternative points of view; and

4. Whereas, Members of the First Presidency have reviewed and evaluated all these reports according to their understanding of the mission of the church and the Zionic implications of the various proposals; therefore be it

a. *Resolved*, That the church reaffirms its strong historic support of education and the liberty of inquiry essential for its conduct, which support goes back to the earliest days of the Restoration; and be it further

b. *Resolved*, That educational priority be given at the present time to developing adequate programs of Christian education and priesthood and leadership education (including education and training for full-time ministry and church service); and be it further

c. *Resolved*, That the church adopt a program of financial assistance to students in the field of higher education, a first step being the approval of the Higher Education Scholarship Fund resolution; and be it further

d. *Resolved*, That the present level of financial support to Graceland College be sustained, subject to the availability of funds, and without regard to the specific location at which the Graceland students are engaged in their studies; and be it further

e. *Resolved*, That the trustees of Graceland College be invited to explore with the church officials the advisability of the creation of a graduate department of religion, summer programs for graduate students of theology and religion, and continuing education for full-time ministers; and be it further

f. *Resolved*, That the extension of educational, experimental, research, or other programs appropriate to an institution of higher learning by Graceland College be left to the decision of members of the Board of Trustees, in terms of their judgment of the procedures required to provide quality education at the collegiate and graduate levels, the church's support being based on the budgetary policies previously indicated and to special programs for which appropriations will be sought from the Conference prior to the initiation of such programs, provided however that any funds appropriated by the World Conference to Graceland College shall not be expended to create a new undergraduate campus without the prior approval of the Conference; and be it further

g. *Resolved*, That the $100,000 contingent appropriation now held for the extension of Graceland to Independence be retained for use in the funding of ministerial education programs which may be developed in consultation among the presiding officers of the church and the board and administration of Graceland College; and be it further

h. *Resolved*, That the priesthood and leadership education and training, the area training centers, and the School of the Restoration be referred to the First Presidency for incorporation into the educational functions of the Temple; and be it further

i. *Resolved*, That the First Presidency take steps in consultation with other officials and quorums and advisory groups to expedite the creation of programs of educational ministry in relation to the Temple in anticipation of but not dependent on the full development of appropriate facilities in harmony with the provisions of Doctrine and Covenants 149; and be it further

j. *Resolved*, That the First Presidency consult with the appropriate orders, quorums, councils, and institutions in working out the necessary administrative and departmental adjustments required to implement the policies defined in this resolution; and be it further

k. *Resolved*, That church leaders at all levels and the Saints as individuals are urged to make maximum use of existing public and private educational resources insofar as they meet the needs which relate to the mission of the church and the calling to be Saints—whole persons growing in understanding, skill, and Christian virtues.

Doctrine and Covenants Format
Adopted April 7, 1970

1080. *Introduction*

The first attempt to publish the early revelations in book form was begun in November 1831. Before the work could be completed, a mob destroyed the press on July 20, 1833, and pages of the book as it had been reproduced in print up to that point were scattered through the streets. A high council held in Kirtland, September 24, 1834, authorized a second attempt. The committee selected at that time was instructed to "arrange the items of the doctrine of Jesus Christ for the government of the church." The committee consisted of Elders Joseph Smith, Jr., Oliver Cowdery, Sidney Rigdon, and Frederick G. Williams.

The quorums of the church met at Kirtland in general assembly, August 17, 1835, to take under consideration the labors of this committee. The minutes of the organization meeting and of the subsequent assembly at which the first edition of the Book of Doctrine and Covenants was presented and adopted were published in the first edition as Section 103. More recently they have appeared as Section 108A.

Additional sections were published in 1844 and in later editions of the book. Some of these were included without prior conference or quorum approval and have remained in the later editions on the basis of custom but with otherwise uncertain authority. This present edition is so arranged that the items of uncertain authority are included in a historical appendix and prefaced with introductions explaining the circumstances of publication and the reasons for placement in the appendix.

Those sections which make up the body of the book include only those which were approved by the 1835 General Assembly or by a General or World Conference of the church. The approval of the format of this edition by the 1970 World Conference specifically authorized the retention of Sections 22, 36, 100, 102, 105, and 106 which had appeared in earlier editions without Conference approval.

As a record of the revelations of God and statements of basic doctrine based upon them, we present to the Saints and to the world the Book of Doctrine and Covenants. May the Holy Spirit enlighten all who study its content.

The First Presidency

Order of the Sections

A. All sections from 1 through 98 as appearing in the 1966 edition will remain in this same order with appropriate historical introductions. This includes Sections 22 and 36, which did not appear in the 1835 edition but were first published in 1864. They also were printed in the first edition of the "Holy Scriptures, Translated and Corrected by the Spirit of Revelation by Joseph Smith, Jr.," in 1867. Their content suggests that they remain in the main body of the book and that the approval by the 1970 Conference of the proposed format will specifically authorize their inclusion.

B. Section 99 appeared as Section V in the first edition of the book. It is not a revelation but the official record of the organization of the Standing High Council and was selected for inclusion by the committee over which Joseph Smith, Jr., presided. It was approved by the 1835 General Assembly. It will remain in its present place in the book.

C. Section 100 was not included in the 1835 edition of the Doctrine and Covenants, though it had been given more than a year prior to the publication of the first edition. It first appeared in the 1844 edition. It was retained in the 1860 edition and has been published subsequently by the Reorganized Church in every edition. Its form and content suggest that it should retain its present position in the book. The approval by the 1970 Conference of the proposed format specifically includes confirmation of Section 100.

D. Section 101 was published in the 1835 edition by

authority of the General Assembly. It will be retained where it is.

E. The comments concerning Section 100 apply also to Section 102.

F. Sections 103 and 104 were included in the 1835 edition and will retain their present place in the book.

G. Sections 105 and 106 were received subsequent to the publication of the 1835 edition. They appeared in the 1844 edition and have been published by the Reorganized Church in each edition since. Their form and content suggest that they should be retained in their present position in the book. The approval of the 1970 Conference of the proposed format specifically includes confirmation of these two sections.

H. Section 107 was first printed in 1844. It contains considerable controversial material including the first references to the speculative practice of baptism for the dead, and we know of no evidence that it was ever specifically approved by a conference or assembly. Under these circumstances we recommend that it be placed in the appendix where it will be available because of its historical significance. A suitable note will refer the reader to its new location.

I. Section 108 was published in the 1835 edition as the "Appendix" by the authority of the approval of the 1835 General Assembly, and it will remain in its present position in the book.

J. Section 108A will be included in the introduction to the book, and in its present place a note will be inserted referring the reader to the new location.

K. Sections 109 and 110 are letters written by Joseph Smith while he was in hiding during a time of persecution and were never formally adopted by the church. The validity of their references to "baptism for the dead" was questioned on April 9, 1886, when the church declared that they would not be binding on the Reorganization unless they were reiterated. They have been neither reiterated nor referred to as a commandment.

Under these circumstances we recommend that these sections be included in the appendix for their historic value and that notes be included in the positions now occupied by these sections referring the reader to the appropriate pages in the appendix.

L. Sections 111 and 112 were adopted as part of the approval by the General Assembly of the first edition. These are important historical statements of basic doctrine and attitude prepared by the committee over which Joseph Smith, Jr., presided and will be retained in the body of the book in their present position.

M. Section 113 is not a revelation nor is there in it any statement of faith, doctrine, or religious belief. It was published in the 1844 edition in Nauvoo and in all subsequent editions. Its historical significance suggests that it should be retained in the book, but we recommend that it be relocated in the appendix and a suitable note be made on a page in the body of the book referring the reader to its new location.

N. Sections 114, 115, 116, and 117 were published by the authority of the 1878 General Conference. Section 118 was presented to the 1882 Conference and approved. These will be retained in their present positions in the book.

O. Sections 119, 120, and 121 are not in their proper order. Section 121 is a series of inspired answers to questions raised in the 1885 Conference and approved in 1894 for publication in the Doctrine and Covenants. Section 119 was approved at the 1887 Conference and Section 120 at the 1890 Conference. To avoid confusion these sections will retain their present numbering and order. A suitable note will be included in the preface to each to explain why they appear in nonchronological order.

P. Section 122 was approved by the General Conference of 1897 and will remain in its present position in the book.

Q. Section 123 is not a revelation. It contains the minutes of a Joint Council session in 1894. The publication of these minutes in the Doctrine and Covenants was authorized by action of the General Conference in 1895 when the body approved a report of the Council of Twelve which included this paragraph along with other items:

"*Resolved*, that in the event of an order by the conference to publish the revelation of April, 1894, in the Book of Doctrine and Covenants, we request the body to indorse and order published in connection therewith, the proceedings of the Joint Council which was provided for in the revelation." Approval in 1897 of the publication of the 1894 revelation therefore carried with it the order to publish the minutes of the council. We recommend that this section be located in the appendix with a suitable note following Section 122 referring the reader to the new location.

R. The sections from 124 onward all have been approved by Conference action and contain material presented by the president of the church as representing the Divine Will. These sections will be retained in their present order.

Appropriate historical preface will be published with each section.

Liahona Fellowship Fund
Adopted April 8, 1970

1081. Whereas, There are numerous colleges and university campuses with varying numbers of RLDS students which do not receive financial support from the World Church, therefore be it
Resolved, That a fund of $5,000.00 per year be allocated for expenditure on a per capita basis of $10.00 per student upon the approved application of an organized Liahona Fellowship to the Campus Ministry Department.

Board of Appropriations

Adopted April 10, 1970

(Replaces Resolutions No. 886 and No. 906.)

1082. Whereas, The World Conference of 1968 in G.C.R. 1074 authorized a study by the First Presidency of "the form and makeup of the Board of Appropriations for consideration of the World Conference of 1970"; and

Whereas, The World Conference has final authority and responsibility for action on budgets to support the program of the church; and

Whereas, Detailed preparation of the same must of necessity be delegated to a smaller group; therefore be it

Resolved, That a Board of Appropriations be authorized to bring to the World Conference recommended operating budgets and special appropriations for Conference action; and be it further

Resolved, That this Board of Appropriations be composed of 34 members as follows: First Presidency, 3; Presiding Bishopric, 3; Council of Twelve, 12; President of the High Priests' Quorum, 1; Senior President of the Council of Presidents of Seventy, 1; and 14 members of the Order of Bishops selected by the Order of Bishops; and be it further

Resolved, That the Board of Appropriations shall be represented in its necessary preliminary work by a committee composed as follows: one member of the First Presidency selected by the First Presidency; one member of the Council of Twelve selected by the Council of Twelve; and one member of the Presiding Bishopric selected by the Presiding Bishopric; and that in its preliminary work the committee shall be assisted by the other two members of the Presiding Bishopric as associate members and such other persons as the committee may select from time to time; the responsibility of this committee being to receive all budgetary requests, give them preliminary consideration, make necessary adjustments, and incorporate them into composite form for presentation to the Board of Appropriations for action and transmission to the World Conference, and be it further

Resolved, That the proposed budget formulated by this committee be transmitted to all members of the Board of Appropriations sufficiently in advance of a formal meeting of the said Board of Appropriations that individual study and consideration might be given; and be it further

Resolved, That the secretary of the Board of Appropriations shall file a copy of the minutes with the president of each quorum, council, and order represented on the Board.

Houses of Worship Loans

Adopted April 10, 1970

1083. Whereas, In the governmental structure of the church it is intended that stakes shall be largely autonomous units, and

Whereas, The rising costs of real estate often make it necessary to move without delay in the purchase of land and buildings, and

Whereas, Resolution No. 954 now retards the development of such autonomy and often delays the actions of stakes in doing business, therefore be it

Resolved, That this Conference look with favor on the rescinding of Resolution No. 954 as it applies to stakes, and be it further

Resolved, That all loans made by the World Church to any stake for the purpose of capital investments shall be made to the stake at large rather than to congregations within stakes.

Youth Ministries

Adopted April 10, 1970

1084. Whereas, We see a continuing and growing tendency for a significant segment of youth in the world to feel alienated from organized religion, and

Whereas, We observe many church youth from ages sixteen to twenty-five years seeking to "find" themselves and to develop a meaningful relationship between their lives and the work of the Church of Jesus Christ and his kingdom, yet each year the church loses a number of its youth to religious inactivity, therefore be it

Resolved, That the World Conference ask the First Presidency and other church leaders: (1) to reevaluate congregational and other ministry as to its relevance to the needs of youth today, (2) to initiate action and to continue to develop needed new programs, approaches, and emphases to make the Christian gospel even more meaningful in the lives of young people by setting up an Advisory Council for Youth, not only for the study of existing programs but for the recommendation of new ones; the members of the Council to be appointed by the First Presidency representing many different points of view in the youth, to give a truly representative voice to the youth in the programs in which they will be involved, (3) to take steps to train appropriate congregational personnel for youth leadership, and (4) to encourage employment, where needed, of full- or part-time regional or stake personnel for youth leadership.

Standards of Conduct

Adopted April 10, 1970

(Replaces GCR 813, 836, 924, 929, 952, and 994.)

1085. Whereas, The revelation of God in Jesus Christ involves the whole nature of man in all the various aspects of his being; and,

Whereas, Specific inspired instruction in this dispensation illuminates this principle with such affirmations as

"The worth of souls is great in the sight of God."–Doctrine and Covenants 16:3c.

"All things unto me are spiritual."—Doctrine and Covenants 28:9a.

"The spirit and the body is the soul of man."—Doctrine and Covenants 85:4a.

"Spirit and element, inseparably connected, receiveth a fullness of joy.... The elements are the tabernacle of God."—Doctrine and Covenants 90:5e, f.

"Stewardship is the response of my people to the ministry of my Son."—Doctrine and Covenants 147:5a; and,

Whereas, The concern of the Saints over the years to cultivate the level of moral and ethical conduct expressive of these principles has been incorporated into a variety of resolutions dealing with specific activities; and,

Whereas, Such resolutions inevitably omit some activities which are as important, or in some cases even more so, as those which are named, and are also subject to misunderstanding and misapplication in situations where various cultural patterns prevail; and,

Whereas, The development of persons of self-discipline based on increasingly mature judgment under the guidance of the Holy Spirit is the objective which justifies all the church's teaching in the field of personal conduct; and,

Whereas, Such personal development results from the recognition of principles and their voluntary application to life situations by the Saints in the exercise of personal agency; therefore, be it

Resolved, That it is the conviction of the church that as stewards over their temporal resources, bodies, skills, time, and social influence, it is incumbent upon members of the church to conduct themselves at all times in such manner that they use their resources constructively, promote personal health and well-being, cultivate productive skills, participate in wholesome leisure time activities, and exert an affirmative influence on their fellowmen for their mutual spiritual development and abundant life; and, be it further

Resolved, That in making such choices the Saints are admonished to avoid experimentation with or addiction to any activity or habit which is known to have an adverse effect upon health and to avoid conduct which is likely to lead others by either word or example into such activity; and, be it further

Resolved, That the conduct of the Saints of all ages in relations between the sexes should be controlled by the principle in the marriage covenant that both spouses will keep themselves "wholly for each other, and from all others" during their lives; and be it further

Resolved, That the world fellowship of the Saints, encompassing cultures where different sets of values prevail in respect to the same or similar activities, involving factors sometimes beyond the scope of knowledge and experience of persons not in the same culture, requires the Saints to refrain from passing unrighteous judgment on the conduct of members of the church in other cultures, while each one brings his own life under discipline according to the doctrine of the church and through response to the Holy Spirit.

Peace, War, and the Use of Force

Adopted April 10, 1970

1087. Whereas, Christ came into the world as the Prince of Peace, denoting God's concern for brotherhood within the human family throughout the world; and the Restoration message emphasizes the need for the "New Jerusalem" to be known as the "land of peace, called Zion," and we are commissioned to "lift up an ensign of peace, and make a proclamation for peace unto the ends of the earth"; and the official seal of the church, as a symbol of peace, should be a daily reminder of our individual and collective obligation to promote peace,

Therefore, We once again as a World Conference address ourselves to the broad subject of Peace and War and the Use of Force, as part of our continuing endeavor and growing maturity to clarify and emphasize anew our common concern on such matters which are of grave importance to the future of mankind. The following resolution represents an expansion and refinement of two previous Conference resolutions, GCR 1020 (1960) and GCR 1061 (1968).

Resolved:

I. We oppose war except as an unavoidable recourse.

The church is opposed to war and destructive violence as instruments for the settlement of internal and international differences except in those instances where all other reasonable avenues to settlement have been exhausted and resorting to force is morally unavoidable. War, like assault and murder, has its roots in the fears and frustrated lusts of humanity. War has always been characterized by unregulated violence and immoral behavior. It appears that as long as selfish interests, materialistic desire, or any forms of special privilege are valued above basic human needs, rights, and dignity, there will be armed conflict.

II. We share responsibility for world conditions.

A. The Christian ideals of turning the other cheek, returning evil with good, and doing to others as we would have them do unto us require a higher morality than is usually accepted, practiced, or appreciated. Christian love obligates us "to be in the world but not of it." It calls us to establish sufficient interrelationships with society at all levels that we may truly be "in the world," so that our witness may be effective toward bettering that society wherever we may be.

B. We recognize that human maladjustments and related evils in the social order often contribute to the development of the social, moral, and political criminal, the criminally insane, etc. These conditions call for Christian action with an extraordinary measure of love and responsibility.

C. The Christian must accept the obligation to help protect society from these criminals, in Christian love, regardless of the causes which have produced them. The Christian responsibility is twofold: to restrain in Christian love and to heal through active Christian faith and service. To neglect this stewardship would be to abdicate the Christian's God-given responsibility to love his neighbor as himself.

D. Modern society generally attempts to bring a healing ministry to the mentally ill and to the criminally insane, while seeking in non-violent ways to restrain them from hurting other members of society. It further attempts to reform and rehabilitate the criminal who may not be mentally ill, but who is nonetheless in part a result of a sinful environment. The political criminal is often disciplined in recognition of the potential threat which he represents to law and order and to the well-being of individuals and the community. Christian service is needed in all of these forms of rehabilitation.

E. Any one or all of these social ills, by extension, could be the cause of civil or international conflict. The Christian cannot ignore his responsibility for Christian service at this level any more than he should ignore his responsibility toward the individual offender.

III. We promote peace.

Christian love promotes peace through constructive and peaceful activities. The cause of peace is positively, though not exclusively, furthered in the following ways:

A. By the propagation of faith in our Lord Jesus Christ who has the power to regenerate men's souls, making them true brothers in a common love.

B. By providing equal opportunity for self-expression and recognition of equality of personal worth of the individual before God and man regardless of material, social, emotional, spiritual, or educational qualifications. This may be accomplished by cultivating a concern for those in need and encouraging Saints to qualify for and engage in those constructive professions and vocations* which contribute to meeting human needs and appreciating human dignity. These skills may be applied in both civilian and noncombatant military efforts throughout the world.

C. By upholding constitutional law which supports individual dignity and freedom, and by opposing oppression and tyranny. It is a Christian duty to participate in the voice of government, even when that participation is suppressed, and to support good and wise men in positions of leadership (Doctrine and Covenants 95:2).

D. By proclaiming loyalty to governments, consistent with the teachings of Jesus, which protect the inherent and inalienable human rights and dignity (Doctrine and Covenants 112:1-3, 5).

IV. We respect individual conscience.

The Church of Jesus Christ believes in the exercise of individual conscience and the preservation of agency. When a person freely chooses to become Christian, he attempts to live in ways consistent with the Christian ethic. The present dilemma is whether or not the cruelties of war can ever be justified within the Christian ethic. It is recognized that not all members will hold the same view. Some will feel conscientiously obligated to render full military service. Others will just as conscientiously feel obligated to object to military service. Since the church desires to maintain fellowship with all who sincerely follow the guidance of conscience, it will respect such sincere decisions.

V. We urge the control of mass destruction.

We deplore conditions in world affairs which have resulted in and from the intensified development and stockpiling of nuclear and other instruments of mass

---

*Such skills may include political science, medicine, nursing, engineering, religion, economics, agriculture, recreation, education, construction, sanitation, research, law, and social work–among others. They will also have value in such special endeavors as the Peace Corps, VISTA, Young Canadians, Older Youth Service Corps, and similar programs throughout the world.

destruction. These stand as a constant threat to the physical existence of men and nations everywhere. While we recognize that the development and use of such weapons is primarily the responsibility of heads of state and their advisers, yet it is the urgent and sobering obligation of the church and men of good will of all faiths to influence the leadership of all governments to labor for peace.

Communication between the people and their representatives in government is made difficult by disinterest and apathy on the part of the citizenry and by the alleged need for discreet control of information in the interest of national security on the part of the government. Both of these are potential threats to the preservation of an enlightened and self-determining electorate. Christian ideals will continue to make heavy demands upon both citizen and government to remain alert to assure that the citizen's voice is heard in government and that his choices are based on adequate information. The Christian citizen should labor to persuade all men to share in a responsible attitude toward the use of force, which finds its motivations rooted in love.

VI. We conclude:

It must be emphasized that peace of conscience cannot be satisfied by mere nonparticipation in war. To some extent all of us are responsible for existing social conditions. The best form of pacifism is that which removes the causes of war. These causes are removed from society by the application of the gospel of Jesus Christ in the life of the individual and of the community. To support our beliefs of the evil of war we proclaim again that we shall do all within our power to make the gospel of peace an incarnate reality. We resolve that we give ourselves wholeheartedly to the implementation of Zionic principles and the establishment of God's kingdom here on earth which, in the final analysis, is the only answer to the problem of war.

VII. We recommend:

A. See GCR 1129.

B. That a comprehensive statement of Christian service and opportunities to witness for Christ within the framework of military service be made available to church members prior to reporting for active duty.

C. That further research and discussion articles and materials be included in church periodicals and study materials.

D. That the Presidency appoint a Standing Committee on World Peace to provide for a continuing study of the role of the church in relation to war, peace, and the use of force.

E. That all members contemplating legal alternatives to military service be requested to set forth their convictions and justifications for same in writing and submit a copy to the Standing Committee on World Peace.

F. That this resolution replace GCR 1020 (1960) and GCR 1061 (1968).

Christmas Offering

Adopted April 10, 1970

1088. *Resolved,* That any monies received for the Christmas Offering be applied to the Temple Fund (GCR 846).

Office Wing Addition to the Auditorium

Adopted April 10, 1970

1089. Whereas, The 1968 World Conference authorized the development of architectural plans for the construction of an office wing addition to the Auditorium in which space can be provided for those functions which relate to the church's general administration and worldwide ministries (GCR 1063); and

Whereas, Professional studies have been made of the Temple Lot complex, and these studies have determined that the best site for the office wing is as proposed at the southwest corner of the Auditorium, and

Whereas, In harmony with the action of the 1968 World Conference, schematic architectural drawings have been developed; and

Whereas, It is feasible, if deemed expedient, to construct the office addition in stages, or units, so that the funds to meet the estimated costs of the completed building would not have to be available all at one time; and

Whereas, $50,000 was appropriated by the 1968 World Conference to the Auditorium office wing project and an additional $285,000 is available for appropriation by the 1970 World Conference to the project, making a total of $335,000 which could be available for this purpose; and

Whereas, It is the recommendation of the First Presidency and the Presiding Bishopric that no outside indebtedness be incurred for this project but that it be financed internally from assets now on hand and from appropriations which may be made for this purpose by the World Conference from accumulated capital fund offerings and from annual operating fund increases; and

Whereas, The present financial condition of the church does not, in the opinion of general church officers, justify the immediate construction of an office wing addition to the Auditorium; and

Whereas, It is the expressed intent of the general church officers to proceed with construction of the office wing as authorized by the 1968 World Conference only as the income of the church increases to the point where the necessary funds are available in the form of cash allocations and interfund loans for the capital expenditure, and that it is evident that the operational costs of such an addition can be met along with the costs of the church's program; therefore be it

Resolved, That the Conference reaffirms its support of a new headquarters building and invites contributions to the capital fund using the appropriate line on the duplex envelopes, which fund could be drawn upon for this project by Conference action; and be it further

Resolved, That when the Presiding Bishopric, in consultation with other general church officers, determine that the financial position and the income of the church is such that it is fiscally sound to begin construction of the office wing addition to the Auditorium, a financing plan for the construction costs be developed by the Presiding Bishopric for the consideration of a succeeding World Conference; and be it further

Resolved, That such a financing plan be developed by utilization of funds appropriated by the World Conference for the office addition project, an investment from cash in the real estate section of the general fund in an amount deemed feasible in relation to other needs to be met from this fund, and from loans which in the opinion of the Presiding Bishopric can be made from other funds of the church, with due respect to the integrity of such funds relating to purpose and interest earnings; and be it further

Resolved, That an advisory committee be chosen by the RLDS Society of Architects and Engineers to act as consultants to the general church officers, both as to the proposed new office wing and to any proposed remodeling and modifications of the Auditorium looking toward a more effective utilization of existing space.

Radio-Television Development Reserve Fund

Adopted April 10, 1970

1090. Whereas, The Radio Capital Account in the amount of $176,476.27 has been held in anticipation of the possible development of a church-related broadcasting facility, the likelihood of which has become quite remote; therefore be it

Resolved, That this fund be designated for Radio-Television Development Reserve Funds as a development fund for additional church radio, television, and motion picture programs, and/or purchasing capital equipment for the Broadcasting Department.

Close Communion

Adopted April 10, 1970

1092. *Resolved,* That the World Conference of 1970 ask the First Presidency to provide a clarifying statement on the subject of close Communion.

Health Ministries Day

Adopted April 10, 1970

1093. Whereas, The World Conference on October 8, 1948, adopted Resolution No. 964, recognizing the desirability of supporting the training and education of nurses as part of the development of our Zionic goals; and,

Whereas, This resolution provided for one Sunday to be designated each year in the month of April or May to be known as "Sanitarium School of Nursing Day," for the purpose of recognizing the School of Nursing, encouraging our women to enroll, and providing opportunities for contributions to be made toward meeting the cost involved in operating the School of Nursing; and,

Whereas, The Diploma School of Nursing at the Independence Sanitarium and Hospital is being expanded into a baccalaureate school as part of the curriculum of Graceland College, the complete transition to be effected by 1972; and,

Whereas, The entire field of health ministries is becoming increasingly important in the development of our Zionic goals and education in such fields is desired by many young people in the church in institutions related to or supported by the church; therefore, be it

Resolved, That the First Presidency designate one Sunday each year to be known as Health Ministries Day, the purpose being (1) to emphasize the value of physical and mental health as part of our total stewardship of life, (2) to encourage young people to qualify for and enroll in health education programs, both professional and technical, and (3) to give opportunity for contributions to be made toward meeting special and budgetary needs in church-related institutions offering health education programs and for establishing scholarships for worthy and qualified students in health education. The First Presidency will designate in advance the use to be made of these funds.

Religious Education Materials
Adopted April 11, 1970

1094. Whereas, Widespread concern now exists in the church because of statements attributed to the Department of Religious Education; therefore be it

Resolved, That this Conference reaffirm the place and need of the restored church of Jesus Christ as a latter-day work of God, and in particular,

(1) that the Restoration was divinely instituted and still has the calling to fulfill God's purpose in accordance with biblical prophecy, and

(2) that the Book of Mormon was brought forth by the "gift and power of God; . . . to the convincing of Jew and Gentile that Jesus is the Christ, the Eternal God, manifesting himself to all nations," and

(3) that Zion, the kingdom of God, applying to the social and religious needs of man in the latter days, was a primary objective in the founding of the Restoration and continues as such in the church today (129:8d), and

(4) that the principles of the gospel as contained in the Bible, Book of Mormon, and Doctrine and Covenants should be taught to all generations (42:5a), and be it further

Resolved, That this Conference urges the First Presidency to review with particularity the new curriculum and other publications of the Department of Religious Education in the light of the foregoing affirmations.

Ministerial Reserve Fund
Adopted April 11, 1970

1095. Whereas, There is an urgent need for the Ministerial Reserve Fund to be strengthened in order for it to provide a larger proportion of the cost of retiring World Conference appointee ministers of the church and thereby further relieving the General Fund operating income of this cost; and

Whereas, Sound management of the Ministerial Reserve Fund requires that a substantial portion of the fund be available for those types of investments which provide for long-term capital growth in order to meet the future demands upon the fund; and

Whereas, General Conference Resolution No. 1071 reaffirmed the authorization to use up to a maximum of $750,000 from the Ministerial Reserve Fund for houses of worship construction loans on a revolving basis without specifying a repayment date; and

Whereas, Over the years these funds have revolved with the total amount being loaned to branches and missions amounting to well in excess of $1,000,000; and

Whereas, At the present time a total of $425,000 of the Ministerial Reserve Fund is on loan to the Houses of Worship Revolving Fund; and

Whereas, It is highly desirable for the Ministerial Reserve Fund to be relieved of this $750,000 loan commitment at an early date; now therefore be it

Resolved, That the maximum amount to be loaned from the Ministerial Reserve Fund to the Houses of Worship Revolving Fund be established at $425,000.00, and be it further

Resolved, That the Presiding Bishopric be authorized to begin an orderly repayment of this loan as funds become available, either within the church or through the mobilization of capital from among church members, with these resources being applied against the Ministerial Reserve Fund loan of $425,000, with the understanding that the Ministerial Reserve Fund will be completely relieved of this obligation as soon as practicable.

Houses of Worship Revolving Fund—Missions

Adopted April 11, 1970

1096. Whereas, The Houses of Worship Revolving Fund for Missions was established in 1954 by a special appropriation; and

Whereas, Additional appropriations have been made to this fund since that time; and

Whereas, The 1954 World Conference endorsed the policy governing this fund by setting the interest rate at 1 percent and establishing the maximum loan of $7,000.00 per mission; and

Whereas, The inflationary price spiral has increased the cost of constructing houses of worship; and

Whereas, Missions are in need of larger loans than presently provided for in the policy; now therefore be it

Resolved, That the Presiding Bishopric is authorized to establish the policy governing loans to missions from the Houses of Worship Revolving Fund—Missions; and be it further

Resolved, That the Presiding Bishopric is authorized to establish the interest rate on loans made from the Houses of Worship Revolving Fund—Missions; and be it further

Resolved, That the Presiding Bishopric is authorized to establish the interest rate on loans made from the Houses of Worship Revolving Fund—Missions at a rate which will not exceed one-half of the prime interest rate for commercial loans at the time the loan is made.

Administrative Officers

Adopted April 11, 1970

(Replaces GCR 279, 580, and 581)

1097. Whereas, The basic law of the church provides for local presidencies in branches, districts, and stakes (Doctrine and Covenants 120:1, 2; 125:10); and,

Whereas, The presiding responsibilities of the First Presidency and Council of Twelve are general in nature rather than local (Doctrine and Covenants 104:11a-d, 12); and

Whereas, The members of the Council of Twelve, under assignment to various parts of the church as supervising ministers, are responsible for the general functions of the church in all jurisdictions under their charge rather than with local presidency in any one of them (Doctrine and Covenants 120:4, 6; 122:7; 133:2; 134:6); and

Whereas, Specific instruction has been given that the missionary quorums are to "be free to wait upon their ministry in gospel work, leaving the branches and districts (and stakes) where organization is effected to the care and administration of the standing ministers ... having charge of the affairs over which they are called to preside" (Doctrine and Covenants 122:7, 8); therefore, be it

Resolved, That:

1. The primary duty to preside over a conference in a branch, district, stake, or other organized field jurisdiction rests upon the presiding officer of that jurisdiction.

2. When special circumstances exist the conference concerned may ask a general officer who may be present to preside, or it may concur in the request of its local presiding officer for such general officer to preside.

3. In emergencies the presiding minister next higher in the administrative line may call and preside over a conference in any of the local organizations which constitute his jurisdiction, subject to the confirming action of the conference when it convenes.

4. Administrative decisions are to be made by each presiding minister in his jurisidiction, subject to appeal up the administrative line when there is evidence that the law has been misconstrued or abuse of authority has occurred.

Committee on Health and Nutrition
Adopted April 11, 1970

1098. Whereas, Part of man's stewardship is focused on the promotion of personal health and nutrition; and

Whereas, The church has emphasized this area, as found in the "Word of Wisdom," the *Saints' Herald,* and Conference resolutions, but presented in a random manner; and

Whereas, There is not enough information in this area being conveyed in a systematic manner to the church membership; therefore be it

Resolved, That the 1970 World Conference recommend to the First Presidency the appointment of a standing committee; and be it further

Resolved, That this committee shall be composed of professional people representing a wide range of talents and knowledge in this area; and be it further

Resolved, That this committee consistently publish, for the benefit of the worldwide church, in the *Saints' Herald* and in such other media as deemed appropriate its counsel and recommendations for better health.

Graceland College Ministry
Adopted April 11, 1970

1099. Whereas, We feel there is a lack of positive, forceful, and constructive spirit in the development of the faith and the evaluation of the ideals of the church, and

Whereas, Students of today represent leadership potential whose influence shall spread throughout the world, and

Whereas, The mission of the church requires that we point mankind to the standards of Christ and be in the world and not of it, and

Whereas, We the church have consistently supported Graceland College in financial and other ways, therefore be it

Resolved, That we express our deep concern for the spiritual nurture of the students of Graceland College and urge that the First Presidency take a more active part in its guidance.

Elder's Expenses in Regions and Stakes

Adopted April 10, 1972

1101. As a general policy the elder's expense of regional administrators and regional bishops, as well as elder's expenses for stake presidents, stake bishops, and the members of presiding quorums and their staff assistants, will be met from the tithes and general offerings of the church.

When these officers are giving ministry in the field, voluntary contributions toward their elder's expense will be accepted from field jurisdictions and individuals. This is in harmony with tradition and the provisions in the revelations that "whoso receiveth you receiveth me, and the same will feed you, and clothe you, and give you money" (D. and C. 83:16a). Such offerings are accounted for through the monthly elder's expense reports to the Presiding Bishopric.

Missions Abroad Education Fund

Amended April 12, 1972
(Substitute for GCR No. 1060)

1102. Whereas, The expansion of the church into missions abroad, the consequent need for developing nationals as leaders in the church, and the ever increasing need for persons from missions abroad to receive education at institutions other than those sponsored by the church make it urgent that we broaden the base of assistance to students in missions abroad; therefore be it

Resolved, That this World Conference authorize the establishment of the Missions Abroad Education Fund for assisting persons in missions abroad in achieving an education on any level that is found to be appropriate under the circumstances of the students' respective countries, and which contributes to the achievement of the purpose of this resolution. Be it further

Resolved, That the First Presidency, president of the Council of Twelve, and the Presiding Bishopric appoint a Missions Abroad Education Fund Committee which shall receive applications from persons living in missions abroad who desire assistance to further their education, it being understood that such education should be pursued in the country of the student's residence except as specifically approved otherwise. The committee shall select those who should receive assistance on the basis of their need, ability to profit from the education which they propose, and the increased value which the education of these persons may bring to the church. Be it further

Resolved, That the committee may also recommend the terms of repayment of money borrowed from the Missions Abroad Education Fund, and in cases where the committee feels that the nature of the need and the benefit to the church make it advisable to give assistance in the form of a grant, it shall, with the concurrence of the minister in charge of the field in which the student lives, so recommend to the First Presidency and the Presiding Bishopric. Be it further

Resolved, That assistance from the Missions Abroad Education Fund shall be available for students who attend Graceland College and those who attend other institutions of education.

Sustaining of General Officers

Adopted April 12, 1972

1103. The vote shall be individually on the members of the First Presidency, the Council of Twelve, the Presiding Bishopric, the Presiding Evangelist, the Presidents of Seventy, and the Church Secretary, with the other quorums and orders being voted on as quorums and orders.

Time for Election of Delegates

Adopted April 12, 1972

1106. Whereas, There has been increasing concern regarding improving the legislative process of the World Conference; and

Whereas, There has been increasing concern on the part of many delegates regarding the possibility of improving their preparation for their legislative responsibilities; and

Whereas, Time is needed for the delegates to prepare for their legislative responsibility; therefore be it

Resolved, That World Conference delegates and alternates be elected in time for the lists of delegates and alternates to be in the hands of the Credentials Committee not later than forty-five days prior to the convening of the World Conference.

Superannuated Seventy

Adopted April 12, 1972

1107. Whereas, GCR No. 579 reads, "That a Seventy when superannuated is thereby released from his quorum," and

Whereas, The Seventy under appointment will be superannuated hereafter at age 65 instead of age 70, and

Whereas, It is not the desire of our council or of the church that a Seventy be released from his quorum at age 65; therefore be it

Resolved, That GCR No. 579 be rescinded.

Health Ministries Commission

Adopted April 13, 1972

1109. Whereas, The ministry of the church in response to the teachings of the Lord Jesus Christ is directed toward physical as well as spiritual needs; and

Whereas, Opportunities for such ministry are becoming more widespread and are increasing in scope and complexity throughout the international church; and

Whereas, A growing number of professional people in health services are participating in church-related programs; and

Whereas, Health ministries have evangelistic and pastoral as well as physical values; and

Whereas, Health education in relation to the total stewardship of life can be encouraged at a higher level of awareness; and

Whereas, Coordination of health ministries should lead to greater efficiency and broadened opportunities for such services through program policies and procedures; therefore be it

Resolved, That the Conference looks with favor upon the creation of a Health Ministries Commission under the direction of a commissioner who reports to the First Presidency and works in harmony with other general officers, field jurisdictions, and church-related institutions in the pursuit of objectives such as indicated in the preambles and others which may be defined as further investigation shows to be wise; be it further

Resolved, That the selection of personnel for the Health Ministries Commission be undertaken with due regard to the other pressing needs of the church for leadership personnel; and be it further

Resolved, That the Presiding Bishopric, in consultation with the First Presidency and other appropriate officers, be authorized and requested to explore possible sources of funding for the work of the Commission, with the understanding that any such arrangement will be incorporated into the regular accounting and budgetary procedures of the church.

Headquarters Office Building

Adopted April 15, 1972

1113. Whereas, On April 9, 1970, the World Conference adopted a resolution concerning the headquarters office needs which

1. Affirmed the support of the Conference for a new headquarters building;

2. Provided for capital fund contributions to assist in financing such a building;

3. Requested the Presiding Bishopric to recommend a financing plan to a succeeding World Conference;

4 Provided for the use of special appropriations, cash in the real estate section of the general fund, and possible loans from other funds with due respect to the integrity of such funds;

5. Requested consultation with an advisory committee of the church Society of Architects and Engineers; and

Whereas, Further study and consultation have resulted in proposals by the Committee of the Society of Architects and Engineers, which proposals have been explored with the Joint Council of First Presidency, Council of Twelve, and Presiding Bishopric, resulting in the submission to the Conference of the following recommendations, based on the committee's report and on master plan studies now being developed for the headquarters area; and

Whereas, It becomes increasingly difficult to provide appropriate housing for related official functions now located within the Auditorium; and

Whereas, Some headquarters functions are now located in other facilities which can be transferred into the Auditorium, provided some space within the building can be freed by relocating the presiding quorums; and

Whereas, No permanent solution of the office space problems appears to be feasible by further major remodeling of the interior of the Auditorium; and

Whereas, Provision of permanent facilities for headquarters offices should be undertaken in harmony with master planning for the Temple area; therefore be it

Resolved, That master planning for the headquarters area be continued, with a view toward the selection of specific sites for the Temple, general office facilities, and facilities for appropriate supporting agencies and institutions; and be it further

Resolved, That a moratorium be placed on further additions to the Auditorium until the master plan is adopted; and be it further

Resolved, That a target date of no later than 1980 be set for the beginning of construction on a general office building as determined by the master plan and with a financing plan approved by a World Conference previous to the start of construction; and be it further

Resolved, That in the interim the presiding quorums be relocated in the Central Professional Building which is presently under construction by a development corporation for the church on the site of the former Battery Block and Herald Publishing House offices and plant at West Lexington and Osage Streets; and be it further

Resolved, That other headquarters functions now outside the Auditorium be consolidated within the Auditorium by the reallocation of available space; and be it further

Resolved, That up to $100,000.00 of the special appropriations designated for headquarters offices be made available for capital expenditures for space preparation and for office rental during the fiscal years 1973 and 1974, with rental costs beyond fiscal year 1974 being included in the regular operational budgets.

Ministries to Primitive Cultures

Adopted April 15, 1972

1114. The High Priests' Quorum recommends that the Conference not attempt to legislate on the subject matter of proposed resolutions A-2 and A-9, but rather let the principles of Doctrine and Covenants Section 150 and other relevant scripture (such as Doctrine and Covenants 17:7; 104:11a-j, 12, 37; and 120:4) guide the responsible officers, quorums, and councils concerned.

Doctrine and Covenants Section 107

Adopted April 15, 1972

1115. Whereas, The 1970 World Conference passed a resolution to place in the historical appendage sections selected by the First Presidency; and

Whereas, Material was distributed in 1968 that clarified the points and reasons for exclusion from the main body of the Doctrine and Covenants these selected sections; and

Whereas, It is clearly understood that the 1844 edition

printed by John Taylor removed the section known by us as 108; and

Whereas, This section, known as the General Assembly section, gave to us basic procedure of accepting revelation; and

Whereas, This section and others did not receive this acceptance; therefore be it

Resolved, That Section 107 could not in good judgment be placed back in the Doctrine and Covenants without prophetic reevaluation and Quorum approval; and be it further

Resolved, That any section placed in the historical appendage by the 1970 Conference must come before the president of the church and be considered as a document under the accepted procedure before it can be placed back in the main body of the Doctrine and Covenants.

Opportunities for Women

Adopted April 15, 1972

1116. Whereas, Restoration scriptures are replete with references to the equality of all in the eyes of God (D. and C. 1:6a, 38:4c, 17:4a, b, 119:8b; II Nephi 11:114-115; Genesis 1:29, 6:9 I.V., Galatians 3:27-29) and to the desirability of God's people reflecting that spirit of equality (D. and C. 38:5d; Mosiah 11:153, 13:54; James 2:1-9); and

Whereas, For its own sake and the sake of the world, the church has seen fit to declare in World Conference resolutions its belief in and support of the principle of the equality of all as basic to its Zionic philosophy (Resolutions 171, 963, 1032); and

Whereas, The present age is witnessing a worldwide struggle in which women are seeking the same equality that the church cherishes in scripture and resolution; therefore be it

Resolved, That the church reaffirm its belief in the principle of equality as applying also to women; and be it further

Resolved, That all those in administrative positions within the church be encouraged to appoint, hire, and nominate more women for positions not scripturally requiring priesthood so that women, who constitute over half of the church membership, may be more adequately and equally represented in the administrative decision-making of the church.

Book of Mormon Education

Adopted April 15, 1972

1117. Whereas, The Book of Mormon contains the fullness of the gospel (Doctrine and Covenants 26:2a, 42:5a, and 113:3b, c); and

Whereas, It was given to us for instruction (Doctrine and Covenants 32:3d); and

Whereas, It gives us a promise that no other book of scripture gives (Moroni 10:3-7); and

Whereas, The Book of Mormon and the restoration of the gospel are divinely related; be it therefore

Resolved, That the World Conference of 1972 request the First Presidency to direct the Department of Christian Education to prepare written materials and visual aids that teach the Book of Mormon to all age groups in the church school; and be it further

Resolved, That men and women in the church who have long years of experience in teaching and preaching the Book of Mormon be used in preparation of these materials.

Women's Ministry Commission
Adopted April 1, 1974
(Replaces GCR 987 and 1049)

1118. Whereas, Women's Ministry is a continuing concern of the church and is facilitated at all levels of church administration by structures which provide for wide participation by women, and

Whereas, The Division and Commission type organization under which major staff functions of the First Presidency are presently administered provide for participation by all persons, therefore be it

Resolved, That the function of Women's Ministry shall be assigned to the appropriate division of the World Church.

Health Ministries Commissioner—
Sanitarium Corporation
Adopted April 1, 1974
(Replaces GCR 1015 and 1017—See GCR 1070 and 1120)

1119. Whereas, Resolution 1015, adopted October 12, 1958, provides for a General Church Medical Council to provide health ministries and counsel to the church; and

Whereas, Resolution 1017, adopted April 7, 1960, provides that the chairman of the General Church Medical Council is designated as the "Church Physician" for the purpose of "qualifying as a member of the Board of Trustees of the Independence Sanitarium and Hospital"; and

Whereas, Resolution 1109, adopted April 13, 1972, authorized the creation of a Health Ministries Commission under the direction of a commissioner who reports to the First Presidency and carries on functions similar to those anticipated in Resolutions 1015 and 1017; therefore, be it

Resolved, That Resolutions 1015 and 1017 be rescinded; and, be it further

Resolved, That the Commissioner of Health Ministries be recognized as a member of the Independence Sanitarium and Hospital Corporation under the terms of the current Articles of Incorporation.

Independence Sanitarium and Hospital Corporate Membership
Adopted April 1, 1974

1120. See APPENDIX F, page 289.

Church Mission and World Witness
Adopted April 1, 1974

1121. Whereas, The church's mission is to fulfill the commission of its Lord to go into all the world and make disciples of all nations (Matthew 28:18, 19); and

Whereas, The church's mission is to provide ministry of reconciliation as it witnesses of the revelation of God in Christ, embodying the hope and love of God for all people (II Nephi 13:29); and

Whereas, In recent years the leading councils of the church have tirelessly labored to create that helping and healing climate and the means by which the church might more fully magnify that mission (Doctrine and Covenants 49:5); and

Whereas, The leading councils have enunciated basic objectives of the church, first in 1966 and more lately in 1973, and have made continuing efforts to fulfill the universal commission of this church as commanded by Christ so that the living gospel of our Lord Jesus Christ can be relevant and meaningful in the lives of people in this land and in missions abroad; and

Whereas, We recognize the relevancy of these objectives for all people of all nations; therefore be it

Resolved, That we sincerely reaffirm our continuous appreciation to the leading councils of this church for their patient efforts as they work together to help us as people of God to more fully understand the evangelistic mission of this church to all nations; and be it further

Resolved, That we unanimously voice our intent to support and uphold our leading councils more diligently in our prayers, and in our Christian witness and mission, and we sincerely encourage them in their quest for ever more effective ways to strengthen us through the living Christ so that all people of all nations can be united together for the cause of Zion.

Christian Education Curricula
Adopted April 4, 1974

1122. Whereas, Through the Scriptures, both ancient and modern, God continues to invite all people to come unto him through the fullness of his restored gospel; and

Whereas, The doctrines of the Church of Jesus Christ are founded on principles revealed in the Inspired Version of the Holy Scriptures, the Book of Mormon, and the Book of Doctrine and Covenants; and

Whereas, These Scriptures reveal a gospel which is unchanging in principle but demanding of an ever expanding understanding and interpretation (Doctrine and Covenants 147:7); and

Whereas, Any curriculum of materials for Christian education at a given time is by nature incomplete and not fully expressive of the prophetically interpreted gospel; and

Whereas, Continual improvement in Christian education materials and techniques is essential to meet the needs of a growing church in a changing world; and

Whereas, A great strength of the church is the wide diversity and rich variety of talents and insights within its people, and in conjunction the church must minister to persons with a wide diversity of backgrounds, understandings, resources, and needs, and must provide a variety of educational materials to meet this diversity adequately; and

Whereas, The culture under which we live is ever changing, but the nature of persons and the commandments of God governing the conduct and relationship between God and persons as enunciated by Jesus Christ remain unchanged; therefore be it

Resolved, That his gospel, as revealed in the life of Christ and as recorded in the Three Standard Books, be used and identified as the central resource material for all church school curricula; and be it further

Resolved, That the First Presidency be requested to commission the appropriate officers and departments to provide such variety of instructional materials as to meet as adequately as possible the diversified needs within the church for educational resources and to continually supplement, revise, and replace current materials as required to improve the presentation of traditional as well as emerging insights dealing with the central message and distinctive principles of the Restoration; and be it further

Resolved, **That the *Saints Herald* and other available avenues be used** to communicate with the church at frequent intervals regarding development of materials and techniques for encouraging persons to center their lives in Christ through the process of Christian education.

Missionary Ministry in Twos
Adopted April 4, 1974

1123. Whereas, The Lord set a pattern for the sending forth of his missionary ministry when he sent the first apostles by twos to preach repentance to the people (Mark 6:9-13 I.V., Mark 6:7-12 K.J.V.); and

Whereas, He repeated this pattern when he launched the seventy on his missionary work (Luke 10:1-17); and

Whereas, This pattern was followed by the early apostles of the New Testament Church (Acts 3:1-4; 8:14; 11:25-26; 12:25; 13:2-4; 13:43-46; 14:17; 15:2, 12, 27, 32; 16:19, 25; I Corinthians 1:1; II Corinthians 1:1; Philippians 1:1; Colossians 1:1; Philemon 1:1); and

Whereas, The Lord restored this principle as a basic law to the church in Doctrine and Covenants 42:1 and 2, ". . . again I say unto you, Hearken and hear and obey the law which I shall give unto you; for verily I say . . . ye shall go forth in the power of my Spirit, preaching my gospel, two by two, in my name, lifting up your voices as with the voice of a trump, declaring my word like unto angels of God"; and

Whereas, The Lord repeated this pattern and principle in Doctrine and Covenants 52:3; 60:3; 61:6; 62:2; 115:1; 135:4; and

Whereas, The church has departed from the practice of this divine principle and pattern; therefore be it

Resolved, That the church reaffirm its faith in this divine pattern and principle that was repeatedly given by our Lord; and be it further

Resolved, That "the authorities of the church whose duty it is to appoint men to missionary tasks should remember the previously given instructions to send out by twos" (Doctrine and Covenants 135:4) in order to receive the spiritual power as promised in Doctrine and Covenants 135:3.

World Scouting
Adopted April 4, 1974

(Replaces GCR 812)

1124. Whereas, The youth of our church need a program of character building, citizenship training, and physical and mental fitness development; and

Whereas, World Scouting endeavors to serve these purposes through its program in the nations where it is established; and

Whereas, The Scouting movement offers its program to institutions, groups, and churches for their use; and

Whereas, The ministry to youth in Scouting in the World Church requires good, competent leadership and would benefit from World Church direction; therefore be it

Resolved, That the Saints Church go on record as supportive of the World Scouting movement as a resource for missions, regions, and stakes in the development of a program for youth; and be it further

Resolved, That the presiding ministers be encouraged by this body to use the membership of the church in providing this ministry to youth; and be it further

Resolved, That the First Presidency authorize an appropriate World Church officer to coordinate the work of Scouting in the church; and be it further

Resolved, That this World Church officer be charged with the responsibility of developing a distinctive emblem which can be awarded to the Scout who fulfills the requirements of our God and Country program.

Conference Organization for Elders and Aaronic Priesthood
Adopted April 5, 1974

1125. The voting members of the mass meeting of the elders when organized at the World Conference shall consist of those elders holding ex officio status under the terms of Rule IV, paragraph 22, and, in addition, those other elders present who are delegates.

The voting members of the mass meeting of the Aaronic priesthood when organized at the World Conference shall consist of those members of the Aaronic priesthood holding ex officio status under the terms of Rule IV, paragraph 22, and, in addition, those other members of the Aaronic priesthood present who are delegates.

The mass meeting of the elders shall have a president pro tem and a secretary appointed by the First Presidency. It shall be authorized to transmit legislation to the World Conference which has the affirmative support of a majority of the voting members.

The mass meeting of the Aaronic priesthood shall have a president pro tem and a secretary appointed by the Presiding Bishopric. It shall be authorized to transmit to the World Conference legislation which has the affirmative support of a majority of the voting members.

Temple School of Zion
Adopted April 5, 1974
(Replaces GCR 998)

1126. Whereas, The education and training of the Saints and the priesthood early in the Restoration movement was under such programs as the School of the Prophets and similarly named movements; and

Whereas, These functions were described in the early revelations as having a relationship to facilities designed for this purpose, one of which was dedicated in 1836 and is now known as the Kirtland Temple; and

Whereas, Ministerial and leadership education and training have been implemented under a variety of short-term institutes, seminars, conferences, and conventions, as well as courses offered in religious studies at Graceland College; and

Whereas, The School of the Restoration was organized to give more specific attention to ministerial education and leadership training in the fields of theology, church history, scriptures, and church administration; and

Whereas, In 1968 the church was directed by revelation to make preparation for the construction of a facility especially designed for this and related purposes and referred to as the "Temple in the Center Place," and which was subsequently described as a facility for instructional opportunities for ministerial education and leadership training; therefore be it

Resolved, That the functions of the School of the Restoration now be redefined under the general purposes described in the document entitled "The Temple School of Zion"; and be it further

Resolved, That all of the assets and liabilities, equipment, supplies, programs, and other materials both tangible and intangible which are the property of the School of the Restoration be transferred to the Temple School of Zion at a time when this transfer can be accomplished without disruption of certain activities heretofore begun by the School of the Restoration.

* * * * * * *

General Purposes

1. General theological education for all members interested in higher education in the fields of study described in Doctrine and Covenants 85:36 (not all courses implied by this description are necessarily to be offered in the Temple School of Zion, but arrangements with other institutions may enrich a curriculum which gives primary attention to general theology, historical studies in the field of religion, psychology of religion, sociology of religion, church administration, stewardship economics, leadership development, office-centered ministries, and the Scriptures).

2. Ministerial training for specific offices in the Melchisedec priesthood as related to instructions in Doctrine and Covenants 142:4; 149:4, 5; 149A:6.

3. Ministerial training for specific offices in the Aaronic priesthood as related to instructions in Doctrine and Covenants 150:4.

4. Problem-solving seminars and consultations for quorums of high priests, elders, priests, teachers, and deacons.

5. Resources and training in basic ministries for priesthood and membership: evangelism, pastoral care, counseling, communications.

6. Exploratory theology seminars for church leaders in the spirit of the commandment to "seek learning by study, and also by faith."

7. Opportunities for intercultural enrichment by experiences in the Temple's Court of World Culture and specific exposure of representatives of various cultures to the life-styles and heritage of other cultures.

Basic Structure

1. The policy-making body for the school is the First Presidency.

2. A consulting Advisory Board is composed of repre-

sentatives of the official quorums and staff specialists of the World Church and of the academic community.

3. The director or president of the school is appointed by the First Presidency.

4. Assistants to the president may be assigned as needed by the First Presidency for Melchisedec priesthood and general religious education and leadership training.

5. Assistants may also be assigned by the Presiding Bishopric, in consultation with the First Presidency, for Aaronic priesthood training to implement Doctrine and Covenants 104:8 and 150:4.

6. Faculty may be recruited from among the general quorums of the church, from among volunteers having the necessary personal and academic qualifications, and—as needs require and resources permit—a core faculty of full-time instructors.

7. The president of the school will coordinate the training of Melchisedec priesthood, Aaronic priesthood, and general religious education and leadership training.

8. Instruction and related activities involving temple ministries may center in the Temple in Zion, with extensions into the field by various programs and procedures found to be responsive to needs and feasible in relation to personnel and fiscal resources.

Higher Education Scholarship Fund
Adopted April 5, 1974

1127. Rescinds GCR 1078, and transfers assets to the Higher Education Reserve Fund.

Church Expansion
Adopted April 6, 1974

1128. Whereas, The principle of incarnation involves

the expression of eternal values in tangible forms and substances; and

Whereas, This principle has particular meaning in the Restoration as stated in the inspired word that "the spirit and the body is the soul of man" (Doctrine and Covenants 85:4); and

Whereas, There are many ministries of reconciliation and new life implied in the principle of stewardship and our mission to go into all the world; and

Whereas, The World Church budget is the appropriate financial structure to support this most important program of expansion into all the world; therefore be it

Resolved, That this World Conference reaffirm the conviction that the expansion of the church in new places (under direction of the Council of Twelve, Doctrine and Covenants 16:5b, c; 125:12) is of high priority in the program of the church; and be it further

Resolved, That the Board of Appropriations and World Conference be directed to consider, beginning with the fiscal year 1976-77, identifying a significant proportion of the World Church budget with programs of reconciliation and church extension looking toward the opening and the sustaining of the work in new fields.

Legal Alternatives to Military Service
Adopted April 6, 1974

(Substitute for GCR 1087, Article VII-A)

1129. That adequate information and counseling with respect to various legal alternatives to military service be made available by the World Church through the chairman of the Committee on Ministry to Armed Forces Personnel to all church members upon request prior to their registration for conscription and that counseling resources be made available to them throughout their period of obligation. Further, that the names of all those requesting such information be filed with the chairman of the standing Committee on World Peace and the Office of Youth Ministries.

Task Force on Aging
Adopted April 6, 1974

1130. Whereas, Persons over 60 years of age are an increasing proportion of the membership (19.9 percent in 1969); and

Whereas, These persons are a valuable resource to the church, bringing wisdom, training, dedication, and experience to their tasks; and

Whereas, These persons contribute financially to the program of the church (32.2 percent of the tithing paid in 1969); and

Whereas, These persons do have particular needs and concerns because of the adjustments and changes in life-style which aging may require; and

Whereas, All persons need to understand the developmental stages of life and the aging process; and

Whereas, All persons are of worth and need the assurance of a continuing caring fellowship that will provide for their ministry; and

Whereas, This concern has been voiced in previous Conferences (GCR 1038, GCR 1053) without specific means of implementation; therefore be it

Resolved, That a Task Force on Aging be appointed by the First Presidency and be charged with the responsibility to investigate structure, program, and funding that will provide for

1. Research in the process of aging, and the resources and needs that exist among those over 60 years of age.

2. Resources for (a) the general membership, (b) those who minister to the aged: family members, counselors, priesthood, the congregation, (c) the aged.

3. Programs of ministry to and by those over 60 years of age; and be it further

Resolved, That the First Presidency report to the 1976 World Conference on the program of ministry to the aging.

Book of Mormon to Heritage People
Approved April 6, 1974

1131. Whereas, One of the early directions of the Lord to the church was to take the Book of Mormon to its heritage people (Section 3:6 and also the preface to the Book of Mormon); and

Whereas, They are to have a primary role in establishing the New Jerusalem (III Nephi 10:1-4); therefore be it

Resolved, That this Conference go on record recognizing the commission to take the Book of Mormon to its heritage people as one of the church's primary commissions; and be it further

Resolved, That members of the Joint Council be encouraged to increase their effort in making men and means available for the fulfillment of this divine commission.

Ministry of Reconciliation
Approved April 6, 1974

1132. Whereas, The love of the Lord Jesus Christ

reaches out to all persons in need; and

Whereas, The Lord Jesus Christ illustrated the redemptive love of God in the parable of the prodigal son; and

Whereas, There often exists in the lands in which the church is established the problem of persons evading military service; and

Whereas, Such persons are often imprisoned or forced into exile from their homelands; and

Whereas, Bitterness among the citizens of such lands prevents the redemptive love of God from healing the wounds which separate families, friends, and fellow citizens; therefore be it

Resolved, That the membership of the church be encouraged to advocate and work toward such reconciliation, when able to do so in good conscience, so that all men might have love toward one another and be free to come to Christ.

Budgeting Policy and Operating Reserve Fund
Adopted March 29, 1976

1133. Whereas, A resolution was presented to the 1970 World Conference which provided that future annual operating budgets will not exceed the World Church income as related generally to the tithes and general offerings received from the previous budgetary year; and

Whereas, The World Conference referred this resolution to the Presiding Bishopric and the Board of Appropriations which resulted in the Board of Appropriations adopting a policy which stated "that a budgetary policy be adopted which provides that the General Fund operating budget will not exceed the tithes and general offering income of the preceding fiscal year" and further provided that the implementation of the policy would be undertaken over a "reasonable transitional period" which was interpreted to mean "as soon as possible so as not to do damage to the church program"; and

Whereas, Since it is the current practice for the church to meet in World Conference every other year it becomes necessary to project the program and General Fund operating budgets well in advance of the ending of the previous fiscal years and requires that an estimate of tithes and general offering income be utilized in formulating the budget for each of the new fiscal years; and

Whereas, It is not possible to precisely estimate the tithes and general offering income for a given year; and

Whereas, The Operating Reserve Fund was established (GCR 948, April 6, 1944) to "provide for adjustments in operating costs on an annual basis"; therefore be it

Resolved, That the Presiding Bishopric be authorized to make withdrawals from the Operating Reserve Fund in amounts as recommended by the Presiding Bishopric and approved by the First Presidency and the Board of Appropriations as a supplement to the General Fund income at times when the actual tithes and general offering income for the current year falls substantially below the budgetary requirements for such year to a point where, in the judgment of the First Presidency, significant damage may be done to the continuity of the program and ministry of the church; and be it further

Resolved, That such withdrawals from the Operating Reserve Fund will be made only in times of economic stress after appropriate steps have been taken to effect necessary economies in the church operation including such adjustments and reductions in the budget that will enable the program to proceed with reasonable effectiveness without severely impairing the onward progress of the church; and be it further

Resolved, That any amounts withdrawn from the Operating Reserve Fund will be restored by appropriate action of subsequent World Conference as soon as the church achieves sufficient net General Fund income to enable this to be accomplished; and be it further

Resolved, That this action supersedes GCR 1007.

Missionary Development Section of the Budget

Adopted March 29, 1976

1134. Whereas, The church has been commanded to go into all nations (Matthew 28:18, 19); and

Whereas, The financial support for this ministry is inherent in many aspects of the budget and the special funds of the church; and

Whereas, Opportunities for significant ministries of outreach and expansion result from unforeseen developments in human relationships throughout the world, for which the direction of the Holy Spirit prompts responses sometimes requiring financial resources in addition to those already allocated to existing ministerial programs; and

Whereas, Action of the 1974 World Conference emphasized that the expansion of the church into new places under the direction of the Council of Twelve is of high priority; and

Whereas, The 1974 World Conference directed the Board of Appropriations and the World Conference to "consider . . . identifying a significant proportion of the World Church budget with programs of reconciliation and church extension looking toward the opening and the sustaining of the work in new fields" (GCR 1128); therefore be it

Resolved, That the Missionary Reserve Fund shall be phased out and its residual assets be transferred to the Missionary Development section of the budget; and be it further

Resolved, That the Missionary Development section of the budget shall be phased into the budget ceiling policy under current procedures by which the total budget is developed as soon as possible and no later than the budget for fiscal year 1980-81, and that during the phasing period funding from net cash shall be sufficient to assure that a significant proportion of the World Church budget be reflected in this section; and be it further

Resolved, That programs and financial projects for expansion of missionary work to be administered under the direction of the Council of Twelve and funded from the Missionary Development section of the budget shall be approved according to policies and procedures established by the Joint Council of First Presidency, Council of Twelve, and Presiding Bishopric. These policies and procedures shall be publicized from time to time to permit members and jurisdictions of the church to have access to the means of initiating and evaluating programs which contribute to the achievement of the church's missionary objectives; and be it further

Resolved, That this resolution supersedes those resolutions or parts thereof having to do with the Missionary Reserve Fund (948, 1035, 1041).

Higher Education Reserve Fund
Adopted March 29, 1976

1135. Whereas, Resolutions adopted in relation to the church's interest in higher education have included the creation of the Higher Education Reserve Fund to which appropriations have been made from time to time; and

Whereas, The purpose of the Higher Education Reserve Fund has been designated in general terms "in order to meet such inter-Conference needs as may arise"; and

Whereas, Specific needs for partial support to the administrative and program costs for ministry to college people on various campuses are met through General Fund budgetary allocations as funds are available; and

Whereas, Needs arise which are not specifically covered by the budget due to the contingent nature of the circumstances, but the satisfaction of which contributes in important ways to the church's ministry and leadership development; and

Whereas, The education of full-time ministerial personnel has been conducted under the provisions of the Missionary Reserve Fund (GCR 948, 1041) which is being phased out according to the provisions of another proposed resolution (GCR 1134); therefore be it

Resolved, That the Higher Education Reserve Fund be used in harmony with the procedures described in Resolution 1024 (April 9, 1960), that is, by action of the Joint Council of First Presidency, Council of Twelve, and Presiding Bishopric, to meet such needs as

1. Education and training for the full-time ministerial personnel of the church in fields of study related to their ministry.

2. Student part-time employment in relation to church life and the enriched participation of such students as committed members of the church.

3. Employment on full time but limited terms of interns in church life and ministry as part of their professional education and training.

4. Other ministries and activities which serve the interests of the church and the persons concerned when unusual opportunities and needs occur in the realm of higher education; and be it further

Resolved, That the provisions of this resolution extend and clarify GCR 1024 but do not replace it.

Audio-Visual Library
Adopted March 30, 1976

1136. Whereas, It is widely recognized that audio-visual materials comprise outstanding aids to the educational process on all levels of instruction; and

Whereas, Need exists within the church to supplement materials and resources; and

Whereas, The Audio-Visual Department came into being through Conference action in 1952; the lending library was introduced under this department in response to the needs for rental and distribution of materials unique to the Restoration; it continued in operation until March 15, 1969, when it was discontinued, but was subsequently reopened May 1, 1969, due to many requests indicating a real need for the type of material handled by the library; and

Whereas, The library services were again discontinued December 31, 1974; and

Whereas, The major portion of the lending library still remains intact (i.e., films, filmstrips, records, etc.) with only some equipment having been sold; and

Whereas, This lending library has provided a vital service—the only one of its kind available with materials peculiar to the Restoration movement; and

Whereas, Its significantly low-cost policy has afforded many congregations and branches the opportunity to use its materials; and

Whereas, Many of its resources have been used as focal points for effective evangelistic endeavors; and

Whereas, At this time it is imperative and timely that the church recommit itself to the Audio-Visual Lending Library; therefore be it

Resolved, That the church reestablish in full the Audio-

Visual Lending Library; that is, all services previously provided be reinstated and promoted (such as *Herald* advertisement, etc.) among the membership and that a budget for the sum of not less than $60,000 be allocated for operation and acquisition. (This is to be divided $30,000 for fiscal year 1977 and $30,000 for fiscal year 1978.)

Mexico Church Properties
Adopted March 31, 1976

1137. Whereas, The church has, over the years, invested sums of money in the sovereign country of Mexico for church buildings, improvements, and furnishings; and

Whereas, The constitution of the sovereign country of Mexico (Section 1, Article 27) provides that (paraphrasing) all religious associations known as churches, whatever be their creed or denomination, do not have the power to acquire and possess real estate and that all such property becomes the property of the nation; and

Whereas, To permit the Reorganized Church of Jesus Christ of Latter Day Saints to continue to be a church of high regard and good standing in the sovereign country of Mexico it would be in the best interest of the church to permit the Presiding Bishopric, as trustees of said church properties, to take such action as may be necessary for the church to comply with the constitution and local laws of the sovereign country of Mexico; therefore be it

Resolved, By the Reorganized Church of Jesus Christ of Latter Day Saints in World Conference assembled this thirty-first day of March, 1976, that the Presiding Bishopric be hereby authorized to take such necessary legal action in the sovereign country of Mexico in order to continue the high regard and good standing of the church and to fully comply with the constitution and local laws of said country which will include, among other legal acts, the deeding of various church properties in Mexico to the sovereign government of Mexico and to take such other necessary and proper church administrative actions according to accepted legal and accounting practices.

Selection of Graceland College Trustees
Adopted April 1, 1976

1140. Whereas, The Board of Trustees of Graceland College is elected by the World Conference by such means as the Conference may direct; and

Whereas, The preservation of the principle of common consent in the work of the World Conference is a basic principle of church government; and

Whereas, The effectiveness of this process is increased by the members of the Conference being made fully aware of all available and valid information; and

Whereas, The selection of trustees should be made by members of the Conference based on the awareness of the particular areas of expertise needed on the board, as well as the understanding of the qualifications of the persons nominated; and

Whereas, The personal commitment of the prospective trustee is an important factor in his/her service; therefore be it

Resolved, That the First Presidency be requested to appoint a trustee nominating committee, composed of knowledgeable persons, not less than one year prior to each World Conference, consisting of five members whose duty it is to provide recommendations to the succeeding World Conference which include a clarification of the areas of expertise needed on the Board of Trustees; and be it further

Resolved, That said nominating committee shall be urged to consult with the First Presidency, other members of the presiding quorums, the Board of Trustees, the Alumni Association, Graceland Student Government, and any other interested groups or persons at their discretion in explorations necessary to determine the existing and needed strengths of the board in filling expiring terms or vacancies; and be it further

Resolved, That a report of their findings be submitted to the First Presidency at least one month prior to the convening of the World Conference, and that such report shall contain at least two names for each vacancy to be filled by the action of the Conference; and be it further

Resolved, That this procedure shall in no way deny the right of nomination either by the First Presidency or other members of the World Conference.

Ordination of Women

Adopted April 1, 1976

1141. Whereas, Resolution 564, adopted April 18, 1905, is no longer responsive to the needs of the church; and

Whereas, A limited number of recommendations for women to be ordained to the priesthood have been submitted through administrative channels; and

Whereas, We are restricted from processing these under the provisions of Resolution 564 arrived at by common consent; and

Whereas, After research, consultation, and prayerful consideration of many factors, we find no ultimate theological reason why women, if it were thought wise to do so, could not hold priesthood; and

Whereas, Acceptability by those to whom ministry is offered is a significant factor and to some extent would be determined by existing cultural and sociological conditions; therefore be it

Resolved, That Resolution 564 be rescinded; and be it further

Resolved, That consideration of the ordination of women be deferred until it appears in the judgment of the First Presidency that the church, by common consent, is ready to accept such ministry.

(The Conference ordered an explanatory letter of the First Presidency to be published, and this was printed on pages 265-266 of the 1976 *Conference Bulletin*.)

Integration in Church Activities
Adopted April 2, 1976

1142. Whereas, Each person is unique in his or her own gifts; and

Whereas, There is a need for greater understanding of each other's calling; and

Whereas, There is need to share ideas and views for the enhancement of the work entrusted to all; therefore be it

Resolved, That this legislative body of the Reorganized Church of Jesus Christ of Latter Day Saints continue to encourage the creation of ways for the integration of all persons where feasible in the congregations, district, stake, regional, and World Church activities.

Task Force on Single Life-style
Adopted April 2, 1976

1143. Whereas, The Church of Jesus Christ is concerned with the worth and ultimate value of all persons, and

Whereas, It is the calling and responsibility of the church to minister to the needs of its members; and

Whereas, An increasing number of church members are

living a single life-style with particular needs and concerns; therefore be it

Resolved, That a World Church Task Force on Single Life-style be appointed to explore specific needs and concerns of single persons within the church and to develop means by which effective ministry can be given by and for single persons; and be it further

Resolved, That the Task Force on Single Life-style have adequate representation of a variety of single persons (e.g., widowed, divorced, etc.); and be it further

Resolved, That a report be made to the 1978 World Conference on the recommendations made by the Single Life-style Task Force.

Name of the Church
Adopted April 3, 1976

1144. Whereas, We are incorporated in several countries under the official name of "The Reorganized Church of Jesus Christ of Latter Day Saints"; and

Whereas, GCR 1000 provides that "we do not circumscribe the press or our own members in selecting short phrases to identify the church, except that we shall always be alert to be sure that any such terms do actually identify the church as a distinctive body apart from others"; and

Whereas, Many problems attach to the effort to apply a single decision based on English and on the North American history of the church to other languages, nations, and cultures; and

Whereas, Repeated actions, resulting in reversals of direction and emphasis, lead only to greater confusion; therefore be it

Resolved, That all resolutions pertaining to the name of the church be rescinded (GCR 1000, 1022, 1067, 1077, 1112); and be it further

Resolved, That the church be identified locally by such terms as may be responsive to the time and place and circumstances; and be it further

Resolved, That the English language name of the church whenever it is used officially and legally be "The Reorganized Church of Jesus Christ of Latter Day Saints."

Development of Christian Education Materials

Adopted April 3, 1976

1145. Whereas, The Office of Christian Education has a vital role to play in providing useful and meaningful education and resource materials in the Restoration Church; and

Whereas, The Bible, Book of Mormon, and Doctrine and Covenants provide sound bases for teaching the principles of the gospel, the word of God, and the distinctives of the church; and

Whereas, The new curriculum has been initiated and used throughout segments of the church for some time; and

Whereas, Portions of the new curriculum have been found to enrich the educational experience, and church background of persons in contact with it; and

Whereas, Some segments of the curriculum have been found, by some, to be lacking in sufficient scriptural, doctrinal helps, Restoration concepts, and emphases; therefore be it

Resolved, That the Reorganized Church of Jesus Christ of Latter Day Saints adhere to the Three Standard Books as the fundamental nucleus for teaching the word of God and the distinctives of the church; and be it further

Resolved, That the Conference recognize the Office of Christian Education for their positive and honest efforts to provide the church with usable and appropriate educational materials; and be it further

Resolved, That the Conference encourage the Office of Christian Education to continue its efforts to revise, develop, and create materials that will more directly provide concrete resources of doctrinal, scriptural, and historical heritage; and be it further

Resolved, That the Office of Christian Education make these materials available for use by the church as soon as practicable; and be it further

Resolved, That this resolution not be construed as censuring the Office of Christian Education; and be it further

Resolved, That the reaffirmation of Conference Resolutions 918 and 919 be endorsed to serve as guidelines for all church officials in preparing Christian Education materials; and be it further

Resolved, That persons serving in the Office of Christian Education include in their efforts the development of material for non-English speaking church jurisdictions.

General Fund Income Projection Policy

Adopted April 3, 1978

1146. Whereas, GCR 1133 outlines the basic budget policy and philosophy for establishing the General Fund Operating Budget which states, "That the Board of Appropriations will continue to submit to the World Conference, for its consideration, budgets prepared under the prevailing procedures for the two fiscal years following the World Conference, based on the best estimate of the fiscal year tithes and general offering income previous to each of the fiscal years for which budgets are presented"; and

Whereas, There are income sources to the General Fund in addition to tithes and general offerings, such as bequests and General Fund investment earnings; and

Whereas, It is desirable to provide optimum financial support for program budget growth while still providing institutional increase for World Conference appropriation to meet certain needs for capital expenditure, special fund(s) and project(s); and

Whereas, Historically slightly less than the approved budget is fully expended on an annual basis; and

Whereas, There is a need to provide flexibility in the basic budget policy in order to recognize other sources of General Fund income as they may develop, and to utilize unexpended budget dollars to offset short-term declines in income to sustain budget growth; therefore, be it

Resolved, That the Board of Appropriations will continue to submit to the World Conference for its consideration budgets prepared under the then prevailing procedures for the two fiscal years following the World Conference, based on the best estimate of the fiscal year's tithes, general offering, and appropriate income projections to the General Fund from other sources, prior to each of the fiscal years for which budgets are presented, thus maintaining in principle the provision for institutional increase; and be it further

Resolved, That every effort shall be made to sustain program continuity during temporary periods of declining fluctuations in income growth in order to allow a careful evaluation of trend factors, recognizing that such efforts may result in a temporary deviation from the "prior year's income base" for budget purposes; and be it further

Resolved, That the unexpended portion of each year's approved General Fund Budget (not to exceed net income) shall be transferred to a contingency section of the Operating Reserve Fund until there is accumulated a maximum of 10 percent of the then current year's operating budget, to be used by the Presiding Bishopric to meet "shortfalls" caused by a temporary decline in growth rate in actual vs. projected yearly income in order to support and stabilize planned program budget growth; it being understood that should the contingency section be inadequate, the provisions of GCR 1133 with regard to the Board of Appropriations and the Operating Reserve Fund will then apply; and be it further

Resolved, That when funds in the contingency section of the Operating Reserve Fund exceed 10 percent of the then current year's budget, such excess funds shall be transferred to the basic Operating Reserve Fund until the equivalent of six months budget is reached; thereafter any such excess funds would be made available for special appropriation; and be it further

Resolved, That this action supplements GCR 1133, except that the first and second enacting paragraphs of GCR 1133 shall now be superseded by this action.

Committee for Archaeological Research

Adopted April 4, 1978

1147. Rescinds GCR 950, and commends and encourages all students and scholars in the field of scriptural archaeology to pursue their studies individually and in teams as it may suit their circumstances.

World Hunger

Adopted April 7, 1978

1148. Whereas, The covenant members of the body of Christ are commissioned by their Lord to be concerned for the well-being of all persons in the world (Luke 4:18, Matthew 25:36, John 6:35, Mosiah 2:43, Jacob 2:24, and Doctrine and Covenants 151:9: "You who are my disciples must be found continuing in the forefront of those organizations and movements which are recognizing the worth of persons and are committed to bringing the ministry of my Son to bear on their lives"); and

Whereas, The majority of the world's people are poor and there is mounting evidence of global starvation-level hunger involving more than one billion persons (40 percent of whom are estimated to be children); and

Whereas, There has always been an empathetic concern expressed as a dimension of stewardship shared by the Saints; therefore be it

Resolved, That the Reorganized Church of Jesus

Christ of Latter Day Saints in World Conference action express its concern about this critical human need by developing a specific emphasis within our celebration of worship; and be it further

Resolved, That the First Presidency, in consultation with other World Church officers, be encouraged to develop ministries based on the "repression of unnecessary wants" in the spirit of fasting; and be it further

Resolved, That the World Church be requested to facilitate the accumulation of funds resulting from the discipline of fasting and provide for the distribution of such accumulated funds through the selection of church-related and/or other agencies to best accomplish a saintly response to the concern for world hunger, giving consideration, where appropriate, to our brothers and sisters; and be it further

Resolved, That the First Presidency develop by January 1, 1979, in consultation with other World Church officers and advisers of their choosing, a program which will facilitate opportunities for those interested and motivated to participate in additional ways beyond the fasting discipline and to add these moneys to the support of ministries directed toward the problems of world hunger and excessive population.

Ham Radio Call Signs

Adopted April 8, 1978

1149. Whereas, Certain organization stations in the Amateur Radio Service have consistently carried call signs for many years, which call signs are identified with those stations; and

Whereas, The call sign WØYO is identified with the Amateur Radio Club at Graceland College, which has been in continuous operation since 1915; and

Whereas, The call signs of many such organizations represent an identifiable focal point about which rally a number of worthwhile national and worldwide net operations in the amateur radio fellowship; and

Whereas, An example of the latter is WØSHQ, the call sign of the headquarters station of the Association of Saints Church Radio Amateurs, affiliated with the Reorganized Church of Jesus Christ of Latter Day Saints, about which operate amateur traffic networks totaling some fifty hours weekly; and

Whereas, In some instances the very call sign's acronyms bear significance, such as WØrld Saints HeadQuarters (WØSHQ); and

Whereas, The net control stations with their recognizably distinct call signs are an important function in gathering together the amateur fellowship in far-flung lands and isolated missions around the world; and

Whereas, The Federal Communications Commission in Docket 21135, Part 97, is proposing to eliminate all organizational call signs as presently issued in the Amateur Radio Service; therefore be it

Resolved, That we petition the Federal Communications Commission to allow those organizational stations so desiring to retain their present call signs when they expire, upon proper application for renewal.

Utilization of Unordained Men

Adopted April 8, 1978

1150. Whereas, We as a church have a need to more effectively utilize the talents and abilities of unordained men; and

Whereas, There is a need for the better utilization of these men at both the World Church and local levels; therefore be it

Resolved, That this Conference recommend to the Presidency that a study be made of ways and means to more effectively use this vital resource of the church at all jurisdictional levels; and be it further

Resolved, That a progress report of this study be made to the 1980 World Conference.

Redemptive Ministry

Adopted April 8, 1978

1151. Whereas, The ministry of the church is both a redeeming and a nurturing ministry—nurturing in that it teaches principles, doctrines, and the kingdom way of life; redemptive in that the church is called to "heal the brokenhearted...preach deliverance to the captives...to set at liberty them that are bruised" (Luke 4:18 and D. and C. 151:9); and

Whereas, The brokenness occurring in the lives of people continues to increase in the midst of society, bringing with it increased alienation, i.e., alcoholics, offenders and their families, drug abusers, persons hurt by marital conflict or divorce, children in distress, emotionally troubled and mentally ill people, unwed mothers, chronically financially distressed people, homosexuals, youthful dropouts, and other social outcasts and their families; and

Whereas, The people of God are increasingly concerned that the Restoration speak to these needs without delay; therefore be it

Resolved, That this Conference affirm its concern for those evangelistic and redemptive ministries which would nurture the wholeness of all persons in a manner designed of God; and be it further

Resolved, That the First Presidency prepare a report to the Conference of 1980, which would include the following:

1. An inventory and description of existing redemptive ministries now occurring

    a. within the church with particular emphasis on ministry to the broken and bruised; and

    b. with an evaluation of what is occurring outside the church.

2. An evaluation of the successes and failures of existing ministries identifying the key ingredients of the successful.

3. An assessment of the Restoration's mission in the 1980s in this urgent area of outreach.

Vocational Education

Adopted April 8, 1978

1152. Whereas, The church recognizes as outlined in the report from the special task force appointed by the First Presidency, the value of vocational education (see World Church Task Force on Vocational

Education, World Conference *Bulletin*, pages 214-216); and

Whereas, The church has for many years invested large amounts of resources to minister to its youth participating in higher education through sponsorship of Graceland College and campus programs in other areas, and such support apparently recognizes the church's responsibility to provide a religious environment conducive to spiritual growth on the campuses involved even though such programs duplicate academic services available elsewhere; and

Whereas, A large segment of church youth have educational interest met more advantageously by vocational education; therefore be it

Resolved, That the church needs to be consistent in its spiritual concerns for those seeking higher education at *academic level* and for those seeking higher education at *vocational level*; and be it further

Resolved, That this Conference request the First Presidency to appoint a committee of persons who have been and/or are involved in vocational education to present to the World Conference of 1980 a possible approach to vocational education; such as providing a school where the same kind of spiritual environment strived for at Graceland could be provided or the possible development of significant vocational programs at Graceland or Park; and be it further

Resolved, That such report contain projected cost, federal assistance available, and enrollment possibilities among church young people.

Missions Abroad Education Fund

Adopted April 7, 1980

(Replaces GCR 1102)

1153. Whereas, The expansion of the church into regions abroad, the consequent need for developing local personnel as leaders in the church, and the ever increasing need for persons from regions abroad to receive education make it urgent that we broaden the base of assistance to students in regions abroad; therefore be it

Resolved, That this World Conference authorize the establishment of the Missions Abroad Education Fund to assist persons in regions abroad to achieve an education on any level that is found to be appropriate under the circumstances in the students' respective countries. It is understood that such education should be pursued in the country of the student's residence except as specifically approved otherwise. Those who should receive assistance shall be selected on the basis of their need, ability to profit from the education which they propose, and the increased value which the education of these persons may bring to the church. Be it further

Resolved, That the Council of Twelve shall recommend a policy for the administration of the program to the Joint Council of the First Presidency, Council of Twelve, and Presiding Bishopric for their approval, and the Council of Twelve shall be responsible for the administration of the program according to that policy. Be it further

Resolved, That the Saints are encouraged to continue to support this fund from their personal and collective contributions, not excluding special appropriations to the fund by the World Conference.

Park College Relationship
Adopted April 7, 1980

1154. Whereas, The First Presidency have received the reports of the Select Committee on the Church and Higher Education and of the Committee on Vocational Education Study; and

Whereas, Consideration has been given to the substance of the reports as advice and counsel to the First Presidency; and

Whereas, Some of the recommendations made by the committees require legislative action by the World Conference for proper implementation; and

Whereas, The First Presidency do intend to appoint a Higher Education Advisory Board which will include members capable of representing the field of vocational education, which board will function to coordinate all of the church's interests in post-secondary education, thereby relieving the Graceland College Board of the responsibilities described in paragraph 4e of World Conference Resolution 1079; therefore be it

Resolved, That paragraph 4e of World Conference Resolution 1079 be rescinded and the remaining subparagraphs reenumerated, it being understood that the functions of Graceland College's Independence Center are within the provisions of paragraph 4g of this resolution which remains unchanged; and be it further

Resolved, That the World Conference approve a continuation of the current relationship between Park College and the Reorganized Church of Jesus Christ of Latter Day Saints for a period of two years until the World Conference of 1982; and be it further

Resolved, That for its consideration in the 1982 World Conference the Conference be provided with:
1. An externally audited financial statement for Park College, and
2. Opinions of legal counsel regarding any recommended permanent affiliation, including

a. A description of the legal obligations of both parties of the affiliation, and
b. A description of operational relationships between the church and the college.

World Conference Legislation
Adopted April 10, 1980

1155. Whereas, The World Conference is becoming truly a world representative of the church; and

Whereas, Many of the legislative items could become parochial in nature; and

Whereas, Many of the legislative items are duplicative; and

Whereas, The time for legislative assembly has probably reached its maximum; therefore be it

Resolved, That the First Presidency appoint a Resolution Committee whose purpose will be to assist persons in the preparation of legislative items for the World Conference prior to their submission to national, regional, stake, or district conferences and to review items approved by such conferences or other groups prior to submission to the World Conference to insure that legislative proposals are understandably written, not in conflict with the Rules of Order, implementable and otherwise appropriate for consideration by the World Conference.

Robert's Rules of Order
Adopted April 10, 1980
(Replaces GCR 1091)

1156. Whereas, *Robert's Rules of Order* has been proven as an effective tool in conducting legislative assemblies for the past 100 years; and

Whereas, Some legislative assemblies have passed special rules to govern their own special situations; and

Whereas, There are distinctive legislative processes in the Reorganized Church of Jesus Christ of Latter Day Saints; and

Whereas, The Reorganized Church of Jesus Christ of Latter Day Saints is a worldwide organization; and

Whereas, The rules contained in *Robert's Rules of Order* are unknown in many nations and subsequently are exceptionally difficult to apply in legislative assemblies in these nations; therefore be it

Resolved, That *Robert's Rules of Order* be continued as the standard for the legislative assembly of the World Conference, and be it further

Resolved, That the First Presidency appoint a special committee to study and formulate special rules which would be beneficial to the World Conference; and be it further

Resolved, That in nations where the rules contained in *Robert's Rules of Order* are generally known, these rules shall be used as a guide for parliamentary procedure in conducting the business of the church at all levels in these nations; and be it further

Resolved, That in nations where the rules contained in *Robert's Rules of Order* are not known, appropriate rules shall be used as guide for parliamentary procedure, for conducting the business of the church in these nations, which are in harmony with the circumstances present in these countries with the provision that these rules shall be in agreement with the democratic principles of the church; and be it further

Resolved, That this action supersedes GCR 1091.

Participation in Interdenominational Christian Ministries
Adopted April 10, 1980

1157. Whereas, The Reorganized Church of Jesus Christ of Latter Day Saints is called to be "in the forefront of those organizations and movements which are recognizing the worth of persons and are committed to bringing the ministry of my Son to bear on their lives"; and

Whereas, Many interdenominational Christian ministries exist which do recognize the worth of persons and which are committed to bringing the ministry of Jesus Christ to bear on their lives; and

Whereas, There are many members of the church who have developed a deep conviction that the call to "establish the cause of Zion" requires the full participation of the church in community, national, and international affairs as disciples of the Lord Jesus, leavening and enabling the whole world to become his kingdom; and

Whereas, The church has many significant theological insights and much practical experience to share with other Christians; and

Whereas, The strength and voice of the church should be added to those of other Christian organizations and movements when they are engaged in ministries which are consistent with our own ministries and beliefs; and

Whereas, The beliefs and values of the church are more than strong enough to withstand interaction with the beliefs of other Christians, though possibly different from our own; and

Whereas, There is concern in some quarters of the church that participation in interdenominational Christian ministries would require the church to alter or abandon its traditional beliefs and practices and/or would result in a serious drain upon the church's resources of time, money, and personnel; therefore be it

Resolved, That the World Conference hereby endorses the participation of the World Church in interdenominational Christian ministries where such participation does not require the World Church to (1) alter or abandon any of the traditional beliefs and practices of the church, (2) endorse any creeds or theological positions which are inconsistent with any of the traditional beliefs and practices of the church, or (3) commit a disproportionate share of the church's resources of time, money, or personnel; and be it further

Resolved, That the World Conference hereby affirms the right of each field jurisdiction to determine the nature of its own participation in interdenominational Christian ministries and to determine the level of commitment of its resources of time, money, and personnel where such participation does not require any field jurisdiction to (1) alter or abandon any of the traditional beliefs and practices of the church, or (2) endorse any creeds or theological positions which are inconsistent with any of the traditional beliefs and practices of the church.

Ministerial Silences and Appeals
Adopted April 11, 1980
(Replaces GCR 1110)

1158. Whereas, Persons are called of God to function as ordained ministers of the gospel, and

Whereas, The call to priesthood is subject to recognized administrative procedures of the church; and

Whereas, The church is charged with maintaining the highest standards of conduct of the ministers who represent it; and

Whereas, There continues to be a need to clearly outline the reasons for which a minister may be silenced and to outline the procedure to be followed in silencing; and

Whereas, The interests of Christian justice would be best served if supervising administrative officers had available to them a concise description of silenceable offenses and the procedures to be followed; and

Whereas, The minister involved has the right to adequate notice, the right to be heard in his own defense, and the right to be informed of the procedure involved; therefore be it

Resolved, That the following standards and principles be adopted to govern the silencing of priesthood.

1. Ministers are charged with the personal responsibility of maintaining the highest standards of Christian conduct.

2. Grounds for silencing may include but not be limited to any one or more of the following:

    a. Conviction of a felony or other serious crime.

    b. Conduct constituting moral turpitude.

    c. Willful disregard of church law, administration, or

the properly exercised authority of a supervising administrative officer.

d. Willful failure to function in the office or calling for a continuous period exceeding two years in length.

e. Willful failure to preserve or maintain a shared confidence.

f. Voluntary silence or surrender of priesthood license.

g. Misuse or abuse of priesthood privileges.

h. Such other disregard for the standards of Christian conduct as may result in loss of power to minister effectively.

3. Silencing is an administrative action which does not affect membership status and is not within the jurisdiction of the civil or church courts.

4. The minister to be silenced shall be given written notice of the silence, including a concise statement describing one or more grounds for silencing and the facts supporting each ground, written description of the appeal process, the right to be heard at the appellate level, the right to present relevant evidence at the appellate level to support his position, and the right to appeal on grounds that a substantial error was committed.

5. A minister may function in his office and calling until the right to function is suspended by silence, by excommunication, or by termination of his membership in the church.

6. Upon receiving notice of his silence, the silenced minister shall refrain from functioning in his office until the silence has been terminated. The pendency of an appeal shall not suspend the operation of the silence, unless so ordered by the appellate officer.

7. It is the obligation of the supervising administrative officer to attempt redemptive ministry with the minister to be silenced. The silence action is not invalidated, however, by failure to achieve redemptive ministry, and it cannot be considered a prerequisite to silence.

8. A silenced minister has the right to appeal the silence to the next higher supervising administrative officer within sixty days after receiving notice of the silence or notice of the denial

of an appeal. The appellate officer shall, without unreasonable delay, review the silence to see that it is both procedurally and substantively correct. The silenced minister may—by letter, in person, or through an appropriately appointed church representative—present his evidence to the appellate officer. After hearing and reviewing all of the evidence, the appellate officer shall, without unreasonable delay, notify both the silenced minister and the supervising administrative officer who imposed silence whether or not the silence is upheld and the specific reasons therefor.

9. Either the silenced minister or supervisory administrative officer may appeal a ruling adverse to his position until all levels of appeal are exhausted. The decision of the highest supervisory administrative officer shall be final. In the event the original silence is imposed by the First Presidency, the silenced minister's right to appeal is governed by Doctrine and Covenants 104 and 122.

10. A silencing action shall not be barred by lapse of time except as follows:

   a. Failure of the silencing officer to act within a reasonable time after gaining knowledge of the grounds for silence may be procedural grounds on appeal for dismissal of the silence.

   b. In no event shall a silencing action be commenced later than five years after the commission of a silenceable offense; and be it further

Resolved, That the First Presidency publish without unreasonable delay descriptive guidelines for enforcement and implementation of this resolution, including definitions of the terms used herein; and be it further

Resolved, That this resolution shall supersede GCR 1110 and shall govern all future silencing procedures; however, the validity of any silencing procedure heretofore taken shall not be affected.

Committee on Relations with the Church of Christ (Temple Lot)
Adopted April 11, 1980
(Replaces GCR 869)

1159. The First Presidency will appoint a committee of appropriate church officers to continue conferring with the Church of Christ on matters of mutual interest and concern.

Initiation of Conference Legislation
Adopted April 11, 1980
(Replaces GCR 1105)

1160. Whereas, Matters brought before the World Conference should have the support of a substantial number of delegates; therefore be it

Resolved, That proposed legislation shall come before the World Conference upon the approval of a conference of a region, stake, metropole, national church, tribal church, district, or branch within a Developmental Area; or of a quorum, council, or order of the World Church; or of a standing committee of the World Conference, or over the signatures of at least 100 members of the World Conference; and be it further

Resolved, That legislation proposed by 100 signatories shall be submitted in writing at last eighteen hours before the deadline for introduction of new business in order to provide opportunity for the Credentials Committee to certify the signatories to be members of the World Conference.

Human Freedom and Injustice
Adopted April 11, 1980

1161. Whereas, The Sesquicentennial Celebration affirms our continual call to mission as a world church; and the gospel affirms basic principles of freedom and justice for all nations, cultures, and people (Romans 1:14-16; Psalm 82:1-4;

Isaiah 58:6-10; Jeremiah 22:13-17; II Nephi 11:113-116; IV Nephi 1:3; Jacob 2:27; Mosiah 1:49; Galatians 3:28; Acts 10:34-35; Doctrine and Covenants 77:1f; 151:9); and

Whereas, The personal ministries of Jesus consistently expressed a commitment to justice, freedom, and human dignity (John 17, Matthew 25:31-47); and

Whereas, There is a global concern about the continuing existence of injustice, inequity, and loss of freedom; therefore be it

Resolved, That we, the members of the Reorganized Church of Jesus Christ of Latter Day Saints, affirm our commitment to uphold the sanctity of every person as a divine gift from God; and be it further

Resolved, That we consider it the requirement of the gospel to proclaim justice; and be it further

Resolved, That as a World Church we call on national governments to increase their efforts to secure conditions of peace, justice, and liberty, and invite them to support international agencies which so seek to do; and be it further

Resolved, That this Conference calls us to unite in a common commitment to pray and work for the elimination of all inhumane conditions which nations and peoples heap upon the poor, the dispossessed, the imprisoned, and those who suffer other social conditions which limit freedom, such as discrimination by reason of tribe or race, age or sex, and to promote peace, justice, freedom, and respect for personal dignity.

Youth Ministries Day
Adopted April 12, 1980

1162. Whereas, Each child and youth is precious in the Lord's sight; and

Whereas, The church provides several programs of ministry with children and youth to guide their growth in the church; and

Whereas, The church in the United States and Canada

participates with other denominations in observing Boy Scout Sunday to recognize the participation of boys and the commitment of adult leaders in the Boy Scout program; and

Whereas, Comparable opportunities for recognition may not be available in other nations or to girls and boys who participate in other church-sponsored programs (i.e., Skylarks, Orioles, O-teens, Zioneers, Zion's League, World Community, children's choirs); and

Whereas, Such recognition can be a positive influence on children and youth, expressing to them the continued support and guidance of the church on their behalf; therefore be it

Resolved, That each pastoral unit be encouraged to observe an annual Youth Ministries Day on a Sunday deemed most appropriate by the pastoral unit; and be it further

Resolved, That this observance be for the purpose of giving recognition to the participation and contribution of children, youth, and adult leaders in those programs of youth ministry offered by the pastoral unit; and be it further

Resolved, That resources to assist in the planning of a Youth Ministries Day be provided in the *Leaders Handbook* and other appropriate publications.

Seventy Quorum Releases
Adopted April 12, 1980
(Replaces GCR 996)

1163. Whereas, Release from the office of Seventy (apart from priesthood silence) allows continued priesthood function as an elder; therefore be it

Resolved, That the following reasons be recognized for honorable and/or just release from the office of Seventy and be substituted for GCR 996.

Honorable release from the Seventy may take place due to
1. Health disabilities
2. Advanced age
3. Personal request

Circumstances which require just release of men from the Seventy are
1. Ministerial silence
2. Willful neglect of ministerial duties through
    a. persistent rejection of apostolic assignment,
    b. abstention from Quorum participation for two successive World Conference periods,
    c. failure to report to the Quorum President for two successive Conference periods.

APPENDIX A

Articles of Incorporation of The Reorganized Church of Jesus Christ of Latter Day Saints (1872)

Articles of Association adopted by "The Reorganized Church of Jesus Christ of Latter Day Saints," at a general meeting of the members of said church, held at Plano, in the county of Kendall, in the state of Illinois, on the twenty-first day of October, A.D. 1872.

Article 1. The name of this association and organization shall be "The Reorganized Church of Jesus Christ of Latter Day Saints," and shall be incorporated under the laws of Illinois, under and by that name.

The church adheres to the doctrines and tenets of the original "Church of Jesus Christ of Latter Day Saints," as organized by Joseph Smith (the martyr), now deceased, on the sixth day of April, A.D. 1830, as the same has been reorganized by Joseph Smith, now of Plano, Illinois, with the advice and assistance of Jason W. Briggs, Zenas H. Gurley, Sen., William Marks, Sen., Israel L. Rogers, Isaac Sheen, and many others. The church government consists of:

1. A First Presidency—consisting of a President and two counselors.
2. A Quorum of the Twelve (a traveling High Council).
3. A "Standing High Council" of the church; and at each "stake" a similar subordinate "standing high council"—consisting of twelve chosen for that purpose.
4. A High Priests' quorum.
5. One or more quorums of Seventy, not exceeding seven.

6. Quorums of elders.
7. Bishops, consisting of a Presiding Bishop, and associate or local bishops—said bishops having temporal jurisdiction subject to the general direction of the church, and higher church authorities.
8. Quorums of priests.
9. Quorums of teachers.
10. Quorums of deacons.

Until otherwise provided, the Reorganized Church at Plano, Illinois, shall be the principal or central church. All others shall be "stakes" or "branches," but all subject to the same church government subordinate to this organization and constituting a part thereof.[1]

A "branch" may be organized at any time, or place, by the concurrence of six or more resident members in good standing, of said Reorganized Church, one of whom must be an elder, priest, teacher, or deacon.

A stake is a large branch, organized into a "stake" at the direction of a General Conference of the church; and Plano, Kendall County, Illinois, shall be the principal place of business of said corporation.[2]

Said Reorganized Church and its stakes and branches are in all respects subject to the doctrines and tenets of the said original, and reorganization, in this article mentioned.

Article 2. The Presiding Bishop and his Counselors, shall be the Trustees of the Church, and perform all the duties contemplated by an act, entitled *"An act concerning corporations,"* approved April 18, 1872, and in force in Illinois, July 1, 1872, a majority of whom may perform any act under said law, or contemplated by this organization.

Article 3. This organization shall publish, print, circulate, sell or give away religious, school, and missionary books, papers, tracts, and periodicals, such as said church shall deem necessary or useful to the promotion of religion and morality; and for that purpose may purchase, or own such printing presses, types, cases, and material as shall be necessary to conduct such publication, binding, and circulation of books and published matter aforesaid; and said publication business shall be under the immediate control and management of a Committee of Publication, to be nominated by the Presiding Bishop and confirmed or approved by the church, at any general annual or semiannual conference; but the title of the property to be in the corporation, and all suits relating thereto must be in the corporate name.

Article 4. This corporation may purchase and hold or receive donations, or in any other legal way, procure, receive and hold the title of any real or personal property for the use of said church, its stakes, and branches, the title of all of which, whether purchased, donated or otherwise legally obtained, or received, and wherever the same shall be located, whether procured by the General Church or any stake or branch, shall be taken to the corporation and in the corporate name of said Reorganized Church; and said corporation shall hold the same for the use of said church, its stakes and branches; and said corporation may sell and convey the same, or any part thereof, applying the proceeds to the use aforesaid.

Article 5. This church corporation shall have a corporate seal, all conveyances shall be signed by the Presiding Bishop, as such trustee, and sealed with the seal of said corporation.

These Articles of Association constitute the Bylaws of said corporation, until revised or amended. Said Bylaws or Articles of Association may be revised or amended at any General Conference of the church, by a two-thirds majority vote of the members of said church present and voting at such Conference. Notice of such amendment shall be given in the church paper at least two months before action can be had on such proposed change.

The principal place of business of said corporation may be changed, from Plano aforesaid to any other place, by the direction of the Quorum of the First Presidency, the Bishop and Counselors, and the Publishing Committee. Upon such change being made, a certified copy of the affidavit of organization of this corporation, together with a similar affidavit of the action of said church reorganizing said corporation, and naming such new principal place of business, shall be filed in the office of the Recorder of Deeds of the county in which such new principal place of business is located. Such change of principal place of business shall not change or affect the rights of said corporation, but only the location of its principal office or place of business. Said corporation may establish subordinate places of business at any time and in any place; but all shall be subject to the control of the general office. Said corporation may appoint agents at any time and place to act in behalf of said corporation. Said corporation may sue and be sued, defend and be defended, in all courts and places—but all shall be done in said corporate name.

Article 6. All property now held or owned by said church, in the name of any person or persons, as trustees or otherwise, including the publication establishment at Plano, Illinois, shall vest in said corporation. And all persons holding such property in trust for said church are hereby directed and required to transfer and convey the same to said corporation as the property of said church. And said corporation shall by operation of law succeed to all property now owned by said church or held for its use, and may sue for and recover the same in the name of said corporation.

Article 7. The term of office of said trustees shall be as follows, viz: of the trustee, who is the Presiding Bishop of the church, during his good behavior, and while he remains such Presiding Bishop. Of the other trustees, who are the counselors of said Presiding Bishop, during their good behavior—not extending beyond the term of office of said Presiding Bishop as such trustee; except as hereinafter provided. Upon the death, resignation, or removal from office of said Presiding Bishop, the office of the other trustees shall become vacant, upon the appointment of another Presiding Bishop, who shall be the successor as Bishop, and his assuming the office of such trustee—and thereupon such new Presiding Bishop and his counselors shall be the trustees of said corporation; it being understood that no person can be trustee of said corporation except the Presiding Bishop of said church and his counselors. Said trustees, or either of them, may be removed by said church for cause, the same as any other church officer.

---

1. By proper action of Conference, Independence, Missouri, was made the legal headquarters of the church in 1920.
2. Since removed to Independence, Missouri.

APPENDIX B

Articles of Incorporation of The Reorganized Church of Jesus Christ of Latter Day Saints

(A reincorporation)

Whereas, The Reorganized Church of Jesus Christ of Latter Day Saints was organized as a corporation not for profit on the twentieth day of June, A.D. 1891, as evidenced by its Articles of Incorporation filed and recorded in Book 59, at page 427 of the records in the office of the Recorder of Deeds of Decatur County, Iowa, at Leon, and has ever since exercised corporate functions; and

Whereas, By the terms of said articles said corporation is about to expire; and

Whereas, At a regular General Conference of said church held at Independence, Missouri, on the eleventh day of April, A.D. 1940, the trustees of said corporation were authorized and directed to reincorporate said corporation;[1]

Now, Therefore, We, the undersigned, of full age, being the present and acting trustees and other members of the said church association, a majority of whom are residents and citizens of the state of Iowa, hereby reincorporate said corporation under the provisions of Title XIX, Chapter 394, of the Code of Iowa of 1939, dealing with Corporations Not for Pecuniary Profit and acts amendatory thereof, and hereby taken unto the reincorporation all the powers and privileges granted by the laws of the state of Iowa; and we do hereby ordain and adopt Articles of Incorporation as follows:

1. The name of the corporation shall be *Reorganized Church of Jesus Christ of Latter Day Saints.*

2. The principal place of business of the corporation shall be Lamoni, Decatur County, Iowa.

3. The corporation is affiliated with the international unincorporated association known as the Reorganized Church of Jesus Christ of Latter Day Saints, with headquarters at Independence, Missouri.

4. The purpose of the corporation shall be to take title to property, real and personal, by gift, purchase, devise, or bequest, for purposes appropriate to its creation, and to hold, manage, control, lease, mortgage, sell, and convey the same for the benefit of said church association.

5. The affairs and management of the corporation shall be conducted by a board of three trustees consisting ex officio of the Presiding Bishop of said unincorporated association and his two counselors, known as the Presiding Bishopric of said church, a majority of whom may do any of the acts and things provided under the laws of the state of Iowa respecting such corporations.

6. The Board of Trustees for the time being shall consist of G. Leslie DeLapp, Presiding Bishop, and Clarence A. Skinner and Henry L. Livingston, Counselors, constituting the present Presiding Bishopric of said association.

7. The members of the corporation shall consist of the undersigned; and their successors shall from time to time be designated by resolution of the General Conference of the unincorporated association.

8. No member of the corporation or of the unincorporated association shall receive any profit or dividend from the corporation, and the property of the members of the corporation shall be at all times exempt from corporate debt or liability.

9. The corporation shall continue for a term of fifty (50) years.

10. These articles may be amended by a vote of a majority of the members of the corporation at any regular meeting or at a special meeting called for that purpose.

In witness whereof, we have hereunto affixed our sig-

natures this twentieth day of June, A.D. 1941
In the presence of:

C. L. Olson	Israel A. Smith	Martin A. Hynden
Frederick M. Smith	A. Neal Deaver	
G. Leslie DeLapp	Verne L. Deskin	
Clarence A. Skinner	Daniel B. Sorden	
Henry L. Livingston	George N. Briggs	
Stephen Robinson	David M. Vredenburg	

Amendment Adopted April 11, 1970

Whereas, The Articles of Incorporation of the church in the state of Iowa provide that the members of the corporation for legal purposes shall be designated by resolution of the General Conference of the unincorporated association of the church; and

Whereas, Several members no longer reside in Iowa or are deceased, and it is desirable to update the membership of the Iowa Corporation; now therefore be it

Resolved, That the following persons shall be members of the Iowa Corporation of the church:

W. Wallace Smith	Merle Spence
Aaron B. Coonce	Charles W. White
Verne L. Deskin	Harold W. Cackler
Robert B. Hynden	Francis E. Hansen
Jerry C. Runkle	Walter N. Johnson

---

1. Whereas, The church was incorporated June 6, 1891, in the state of Iowa for a period of fifty years, which period will expire in the year 1941; and

Whereas, The General Conference by resolution adopted April 14, 1926, appearing on pages 4087-8 of the 1926 Conference Minutes set forth clearly the relationship between the respective scopes of the church as a corporate body and as an unincorporated association; and

Whereas, It is desirable to reincorporate the church in the state of Iowa in harmony with said resolution; therefore, be it

Resolved, That the Presiding Bishopric be and they are hereby authorized to renew the incorporation of the church in the state of Iowa in harmony with the aforesaid resolution of 1926, and to take whatever legal steps are necessary to effect such reincorporation. (Adopted April 11, 1940).

APPENDIX C

Incorporations: Canada, etc.

Adopted April 5, 1952

Whereas, The General Conference of 1926 adopted a resolution in regard to the legal form of the church organization which reads in part as follows:[1] "Be it

Resolved, By the Reorganized Church of Jesus Christ of Latter Day Saints in General Conference assembled this fourteenth day of April, 1926, that this church organization is and of necessity must be an unincorporated association generally throughout the world; and that where the church has been or is incorporated under local laws such corporations have been and are maintained for the purpose of exercising corporate rights and functions within such jurisdictions, and only such powers as may be exercised under the comity of states in other jurisdictions," and

Whereas, It has been found helpful in matters of titleholding to continue the Illinois corporation of the church which was formed in 1872, in the state of Illinois, and which has a perpetual charter, and also to reincorporate the Iowa incorporation in 1941 at the expiration of the fifty-year period for which it was organized in 1891, by authority of the General Conference of 1940; and

Whereas, The Presiding Bishop and his counselors are named as the trustees in the Illinois incorporation of the church in 1872 and the Iowa incorporation of 1891 and the reincorporation of 1941, and are also named as the trustees of the unincorporated association in harmony with the resolution of April 14, 1926, above referred to, which reads as follows: "Be it also further

"*Resolved,* That the Presiding Bishop and/or his counselors, or either of them as trustee or trustees, shall have the authority and right to accept, take hold, mortgage, and convey title to property, either real or personal or mixed, and wheresoever situated which the church as an unincorporated association may lawfully take and hold, and to which it may assert title and ownership, and from any source whatsoever, either by deed or conveyance or by last will and testament."

Whereas, In harmony with the foregoing the titles to church properties in states, where the church is not incorporated or registered as an Iowa or Illinois corporation, have been taken in the name of the Presiding Bishop as trustee in trust for the church, which requires, however, that when one Bishop succeeds another it is necessary or advisable in most jurisdictions to have a deed executed by the retiring Bishop in favor of his successor; and

Whereas, From a legal and business point of view it would be more convenient to have the titles to church properties held in the name of a corporation rather than in the name of the Presiding Bishop as trustee in trust for the church, particularly in those states where the church owns a large number of properties, and by virtue of the recent change in the Missouri State Constitution the previous limitations of ownership of property in Missouri by a Missouri religious corporation were removed; and

Whereas, In Canada certain questions have also been raised on title and income tax matters by virtue of the fact that the church is not incorporated in Canada at the present time, and it would be helpful to have the temporal aspect of the church work which is under the jurisdiction of the Presiding Bishopric to be incorporated in Canada; now, therefore be it

Resolved, By the Reorganized Church of Jesus Christ of Latter Day Saints in General Conference assembled this fifth day of April, 1952, that the Presiding Bishopric be and they are hereby authorized to incorporate the temporal aspects of the work of the church in such of the provinces of Canada as are deemed advisable, and also in the state of Missouri and in such other states of the United States as will be convenient and advisable; it being understood that the Presiding Bishopric shall be the trustees or directors of any such corporations formed, and that such state or provincial corporations shall continue to be affiliated with and a part of the international unincorporated association of the church under which legal form it operates generally throughout the world. Be it further

Resolved, That wherever practicable and as soon as advisable the titles to all church properties located in the various states and the District of Columbia and provinces where the church is incorporated or registered to do business as a corporation, shall be conveyed to such corporation. Be it also

Resolved, That the intention of this resolution is not in any sense to change the aforesaid resolution of April 14, 1926, but simply to authorize the Presiding Bishopric to use the corporate form of organization for carrying on the temporal work of the church in those jurisdictions where corporate rights and functions may be exercised under the laws of such jurisdiction.

---

1. See General Conference Resolution 866.

APPENDIX D

Australasian Incorporation

Adopted April 7, 1938

Whereas, The title to church property in the Australasian Mission consisting of the respective states of the Commonwealth of Australia and the Dominion of New Zealand has heretofore been held in the names of various individuals because of which difficult legal problems have arisen from time to time, and

Whereas, The taking of title to church property in the name of the Presiding Bishop as Trustee in Trust for the use and benefit of the church, as provided in previous General Conference Resolutions, may also create other legal problems, it may be found practicable to incorporate the temporal arm of the church under the laws of the respective States of the Commonwealth of Australia and the Dominion of New Zealand for the purpose of holding title to real estate or to use some other form of holding title within the laws of the said respective States of the Commonwealth of Australia and the Dominion of New Zealand in order to overcome the legal problems heretofore referred to, Wherefore be it

Resolved, That the First Presidency and the Presiding Bishopric be, and are, hereby empowered to take such steps as in their judgment are necessary to incorporate the temporal arm of the church in the respective States of the Commonwealth of Australia and the Dominion of New Zealand for the purpose of holding title to real estate in said areas or to effect some other form or plan of holding title to church real estate in said areas, all of which must conform and be in accordance with the laws of the respective States of the Commonwealth of Australia and the Dominion of New Zealand in which any change or changes may be made.

Adopted April 31, 1952

Whereas, The General Conference of the Reorganized Church of Jesus Christ of Latter Day Saints on April 7, 1938, adopted a resolution authorizing the First Presidency and the Presiding Bishopric to take such steps as are necessary to incorporate the church in the respective states of the Commonwealth of Australia and the Dominion of New Zealand for the purpose of holding title to real estate in said areas; and

Whereas, In taking these necessary steps, some uncertainty has arisen in respect to the authority of the Board of Trustees of said proposed incorporation, as to whether the Board of Trustees as such would have power to supersede locally elected committees and officers in the management of their affairs, and it is the desire of this General Conference to clarify this point; therefore be it and it is hereby

Resolved, That the said Board of Trustees when officially constituted in connection with the corporation in any of the States of the Commonwealth of Australia or the Dominion of New Zealand is hereby directed that local management of branch, mission, and district projects be left to their respectively elected officers and committees, and that the purpose of setting up the said incorporation under the direction of its Board of Trustees is to take title to church properties, and have power relating thereto in the matter of buying, selling, or transferring in harmony with the decision of the proper church bodies concerned.

278

APPENDIX E

Articles of Incorporation of Graceland College

A REINCORPORATION

As Amended April, 1952

Heretofore, on the ninth day of April, A.D. 1895, the General Conference of the Reorganized Church of Jesus Christ of Latter Day Saints in session assembled at Independence, Jackson County, Missouri, did authorize the establishment of Graceland College; and pursuant to such action Articles of Incorporation of Graceland College were, on the sixth day of June, A.D. 1895, duly filed for record in the office of the Recorder of Decatur County, Iowa, and recorded in Book 86 on pages 240 to 246, inclusive; and since the corporate period of Graceland College is about to expire

Now Therefore, Pursuant to authority granted by the General Conference of the Reorganized Church of Jesus Christ of Latter Day Saints in session in the city of Independence, Jackson County, Missouri, on the seventh day of April, A.D. 1944,

We, whose names are hereunto subscribed, do hereby become associated for the purpose of reincorporating GRACELAND COLLEGE, under and by virtue of TITLE XIX CHAPTER 394, of the CODE OF IOWA, 1939, and acts amendatory thereto, if any, continuing to assume and to have all the powers, rights and privileges granted such bodies corporate in the state of Iowa; and to that end we do hereby adopt the following Articles of Incorporation, in substitution for the Articles of Incorporation of Graceland College now in full force and effect and in extension of the term of corporate existence thereof, to-wit:

Article I—Name of Corporation

The name of this corporation shall be GRACELAND COLLEGE.

Article II—Place of Business

The principal place of business of this corporation shall be in LAMONI, DECATUR COUNTY, IOWA.

Article III—Purposes of Organization

The general purposes and objectives of this corporation shall be:

Section 1. To maintain Graceland College as an established institution of higher learning and to provide basic general education of accredited collegiate quality.

Section 2. To provide courses of study in religion and Christian philosophy; to establish, on the college level, other courses of study of a preprofessional or semiprofessional character; to conduct conferences, clinics, classes, and discussions on any lawful subject; and to do any and all things customarily done by such organizations, without limitation or hindrance.

Section 3. To develop a fellowship of students whose lives are activated by the ideals and principles of Christian living; to engender in the student a sound philosophy of life based upon social co-operation; and to provide a social and recreational program and environment that will create a desire on the part of the student to participate in the community life of which he is a part.

Section 4. The facilities, opportunities, and fellowship of Graceland College shall be available to and for the benefit of all persons who meet requirements for admission currently in force, regardless of race, sex, religion, or politics.

Article IV—Duration - Powers

Section 1. For a period of fifty years from the date of filing of a certified copy of these Articles of Incorporation in the office of the Secretary of State of Iowa and/or in the office of the Recorder of the County of Decatur, State of Iowa, this corporation shall have perpetual succession in a Board of Trustees, shall have a common seal, and may sue and be sued in its own name.

Section 2. This corporation may buy, hold, own, transfer, sell, and otherwise dispose of real or personal property; may accept, hold, control, invest, transfer, and otherwise dispose of or use gifts, devises, and bequests of real and personal property; may establish funds, endowments, foundations, and investments incidental to the carrying out of the purposes of its organization.

Section 3. This corporation, through and by its Board of Trustees, shall have power to confer such degrees and grant such certificates as its accreditation by recognized accrediting agencies may justify, and as may be customary usage of similar corporations.

Section 4. This corporation shall have power to do all things which are necessary or convenient, or which are incidental to or in connection with the carrying out of the purposes of its organization.

Article V—Management

Section 1. The affairs of this corporation shall be managed by a board of trustees consisting of nine members who shall, respectively, be elected for six-year terms by the General Conference of the Reorganized Church of Jesus Christ of Latter Day Saints, which election shall be held according to the rules of procedure of said church.

Section 2. Until their successors are duly elected and qualified, the following named persons constitute the membership of the Board of Trustees of Graceland Collgee, their terms of office expiring as shown, to-wit:*

J. F. Garver, Lamoni, Iowa   Terms expires April 25, 1946
F. M. McDowell, Independence, Mo.
                            Term expires April 25, 1946
Lonzo Jones, Warrensburg, Mo.
                            Term expires April 25, 1948
Mrs. B. F. Moats, Kansas City, Mo.
                            Term expires April 25, 1948
Howard Andersen, Independence, Mo.
                            Term expires April 25, 1948
Charles F. Grabske, Independence, Mo.
                            Term expires April 25, 1950
Verne L. Deskin, Lamoni, Iowa
                            Term expires April 25, 1950

Section 3. The remaining members of the Board of Trustees shall have power to fill any vacancies in the membership of their board until the meeting of the General Conference of the Reorganized Church of Jesus Christ of Latter Day Saints next following such vacancy or vacancies.

Section 4. The officers of the Board of Trustees shall consist of a chairman, a vice-chairman, and a secretary. Other officers may be provided as needed. Officers shall hold office, at the pleasure of the Board, for one year, or until their successors are duly elected by the Board.

---

*Trustees, June 30, 1974, are

William A. Piedimonte	Term expires 1976
Donald E. Manuel	Term expires 1976
Malcolm L. Ritchie	Term expires 1976
Deam H. Ferris	Term expires 1978
Daniel E. Waite	Term expires 1978
Mrs. Ruth Bradley	Term expires 1978
Linden E. Wheeler	Term expires 1980
Donald D. Landon	Term expires 1980
Aleta Runkle	Term expires 1980

Until their successors are duly elected and qualified, the following named persons constitute the respective officers of the Board, to-wit:†

Chairman .... J. F. Garver
Vice-Chairman .... F. M. McDowell
Secretary .... Verne L. Deskin

Section 5. At their annual meeting the Board of Trustees shall elect a chairman, vice-chairman, and secretary, and other officers as needed, and provide for the election or appointment of standing and/or special committees.

The Board shall also provide for the selection of the administrative officers, instructors, agents, assistants or other helpers necessary to the purposes of the organization, and shall fix their compensation. Until the next annual meeting of the Board of Trustees of this corporation or until their successors are duly selected and qualified, the following named shall be officers of this corporation, to-wit:‡

President .... George N. Briggs, Lamoni, Iowa
Business Manager .... A. Neal Deaver, Lamoni, Iowa
Treasurer .... A. Neal Deaver, Lamoni, Iowa

Article VI—Meetings

Section 1. Election of the members of the Board of Trustees to fill any vacancy and/or to succeed those whose terms expire concurrently with the assembly of the General Conference of the Reorganized Church of Jesus Christ of Latter Day Saints shall be conducted at the times ap-

---

†Officers of the Board, June 30, 1960, are
Chairman..Earl T. Higdon
Vice-Chairman..L. F. P. Curry
Secretary...Verne L. Deskin
‡Officers of the corporation, June 30, 1960, are
President..Harvey Grice, Lamoni, Iowa
Vice-President-Treasurer................James W. White, Lamoni, Iowa

pointed for the holding of such General Conference, according to the rules of said church, and the delegates to said General Conference shall constitute the voting body for this purpose.

Section 2. The annual meeting of the corporation and of the Board of Trustees shall be held on the twenty-fifth day of April in each year, except if said date be a legal holiday the meeting shall be held on the business day next following. If no quorum is present on the day set for the annual meeting of the Board, the meeting shall be held upon call of the chairman or vice-chairman after giving at least five days notice in writing to each board member.

Section 3. Other and special meetings of the Board may be held upon call of the chairman or vice-chairman or any four of the other members of the Board. Unless notice of the other and special meetings of the Board is waived, at least five days' written notice of such shall be given, which notice shall state the time and place of the proposed meeting and the general nature of the business to be considered.

Section 4. A majority of the membership of the Board shall constitute a quorum for the transaction of all business.

Article VII—Conveyances, etc.

All conveyances, mortgages, assignments, releases, contracts for purchase and sale of real estate, and contracts for construction of buildings shall be signed by the chairman or vice chairman of the Board of Trustees and attested by the secretary, and the seal of the corporation affixed after such shall have been duly authorized by majority vote of the trustees.

Article VIII—Bylaws

The Board of Trustees shall have power to make, adopt, and enforce bylaws or other rules and regulations, not inconsistent with these articles, for their own government and for the government of the corporation, and they may modify or alter them from time to time as may be necessary.

Article IX—Exemptions

The private property of the individual members of this corporation and of the officers and members of the Board of Trustees shall be exempt from liability for any and all corporate debts.

Article X—Dissolution

This corporation may be dissolved by a three-fourths vote of the delegates present at any regular meeting of the General Conference of the Reorganized Church of Jesus Christ of Latter Day Saints, or at any special session thereof called for that purpose, provided that ninety days' notice of said meeting stating the time, place, and such purpose shall be given by publication in the official paper of said church and in some other paper in general circulation in Decatur County, Iowa.

Article XI—Reversion

If for any cause whatsoever this corporation is dissolved, all properties thereof, whether real, personal, or mixed, or of whatsoever nature or description, shall revert to and become the absolute and unqualified properties of the Reorganized Church of Jesus Christ of Latter Day Saints.

Article XII—Amendments

These articles, except Article IX, may be amended at any business session of the General Conference of the Reorganized Church of Jesus Christ of Latter Day Saints, provided that notice of such proposed amendment shall be given by publication in the official paper of said church at least sixty days prior to the convening of such General Conference.

The Undersigned, jointly and severally, do hereby certify that, pursuant to proper notice, the foregoing Articles of Incorporation of Graceland College were duly adopted by resolution of the General Conference of the Reorganized Church of Jesus Christ of Latter Day Saints on the seventh day of April, A.D. 1944, in the city of Independence, County of Jackson, State of Missouri; and that the undersigned are, by said resolution, authorized and empowered to execute and acknowledge these Articles of Incorporation on behalf of GRACELAND COLLEGE. In testimony of all of which witness our signatures this seventh day of April, A.D. 1944.

    (Signatures)   (Addresses)
H. P. Andersen, Independence, Missouri
Verne L. Deskin, Lamoni, Iowa
J. F. Garver, Lamoni, Iowa
Charles F. Grabske, Independence, Missouri
Lonzo Jones, Warrensburg, Missouri
F. M. McDowell, Independence, Missouri
(Mrs. B. F.) Mary W. Moats, 40 East 53rd Terrace,
                                        Kansas City 2, Missouri
George N. Briggs, Lamoni, Iowa
A. Neal Deaver, Lamoni, Iowa
Edmund J. Gleazer, Jr., Lamoni, Iowa
Lewis E. Landsberg, Lamoni, Iowa

State of Iowa   SS.
County of Decatur

Before me on this twenty-ninth day of April, A.D. 1944, personally appeared Verne L. Deskin, J. F. Garver, Lonzo Jones, George N. Briggs, A. Neal Deaver, Edmund J. Gleazer, Jr., and Lewis E. Landsberg, who, being by me duly sworn, did state that they are the persons who executed the foregoing ARTICLES OF INCORPORATION of GRACELAND COLLEGE; and that the statements contained in the certificate bearing their signatures are true; and they acknowledged that they voluntarily executed the same on behalf of the said GRACELAND COLLEGE.

In testimony of which, witness my hand and official seal this twenty-ninth day of April, 1944.

S/by   CLARA L. ALLEN
Notary Public in and for Decatur County, Iowa
My commission expires July 4, 1945

State of Missouri SS.
County of Jackson

Before me on this fifth day of May, A.D. 1944, personally appeared Howard Andersen, Charles F. Grabske, F. M. McDowell, and Mrs. Mary W. Moats, who, being by me duly sworn, did state that they are the persons who executed the foregoing ARTICLES OF INCORPORATION of GRACELAND COLLEGE; and that the statements contained in the certificate bearing their signatures are true; and they acknowledged that they voluntarily executed the same on behalf of the said GRACELAND COLLEGE.

In testimony of which, witness my hand and official seal this fifth day of May, 1944.

S/by   C. L. OLSON
Notary Public in and for Jackson County, Missouri
My commission expires Oct. 30, 1944

CERTIFICATE

State of Missouri SS.
County of Jackson

We, S/BY FREDERICK M. SMITH and S/BY O. W. NEWTON, being first duly sworn, depose and state that we are, respectively, the chairman and secretary of the 1944 General Conference of the Reorganized Church of Jesus Christ of Latter Day Saints; that we have custody of the records of the business transacted at said General Conference; and that there is attached to this certificate a true copy of the ARTICLES OF INCORPORATION of GRACELAND COLLEGE as they were ratified, confirmed, approved, and adopted by majority vote of the delegates present at said General Conference on the seventh day of April, A.D. 1944, in the city of Independence, Missouri

In testimony of which we hereunto subscribe our names and affix the official seal of said church.

S/by   FREDERICK M. SMITH, Chairman
S/by   O. W. NEWTON, Secretary

On this twenty-fourth day of April, A.D. 1944, before me, a Notary Public in and for Jackson County, Missouri, appeared Frederick M. Smith and O. W. Newton, who being duly sworn did state that they are respectively the chairman and secretary named in and who executed the foregoing certificate on behalf of said church; and that the statements therein contained are true.

S/by   C. L. OLSON
Notary Public, Jackson County, Missouri

CERTIFICATE

Regarding the Articles of Incorporation recently approved by the General Conference of the church, it was moved by Mr. Deskin and Mrs. Moats and carried, as follows: Be it

Resolved, That the Board of Trustees of Graceland College do hereby ratify, confirm, approve, and adopt the Articles of Incorporation of Graceland College as they were also done by the General Conference of the Reorganized Church of Jesus Christ of Latter Day Saints on the seventh day of April, A.D. 1944, and as hereafter appear, and we do authorize and empower the chairman and secretary of this Board to do all things necessary to place the same on record.

(There follows a copy of the Articles of Incorporation identical with that to which this certificate is attached.)

I hereby certify that I am the secretary of the Board of Trustees of Graceland College and that I have custody of the records thereof, and that the foregoing is a true copy of a portion of the minutes of a meeting of said Board held at Lamoni, Iowa, on the thirtieth day of April, 1944, at which the full Board was present and voted unanimously in favor of said resolution.

        S/by   VERNE L. DESKIN
                      Secretary

Office of the Secretary of State
Des Moines, Iowa

This instrument recorded in Book 1-F, page 740, June 4, 1945. Expires June 6, 1995, Cert. No. 1203, Receipt No. 1321. Filed by Verne L. Deskin, Esq., Lamoni, Iowa. Filing Fee, $5.00. Recording Fee, $3.00. Wayne M. Ropes, Secretary of State
                1516

State of Iowa   SS.
County of Decatur

Filed of Record on the seventh day of June, 1945, at 9:00 o'clock A.M. and recorded in Book 2, pages 89-92.
        S/by   LLOYD H. BLACK Recorder

.... Deputy

APPENDIX F

Articles of Incorporation
Independence Sanitarium and Hospital

Incorporated September 24, 1909
Amended August 9, 1930

Reincorporated under 1953 Missouri
"The General Not for Profit Corporation
Law," April 6, 1968, as amended
April 1, 1974.

Whereas, The present Articles of Incorporation of the Independence Sanitarium and Hospital provide for a board of trustees which ex officio consists of the three members of the First Presidency, the three members of the Presiding Bishopric, the chairman of the Church Medical Council, the mayor of the city of Independence, and the eastern judge of the Jackson County Court; and

Whereas, From a legal point of view, the said persons fulfill a dual capacity, that of members of the corporation as well as trustees of the corporation, and for various reasons it seems advisable to form two separate groups in the corporation known as the Independence Sanitarium and Hospital, one to consist of the members of the corporation, and the other group to consist of the trustees who shall be elected by the members of the corporation; and

Whereas, The burdens of administering the Independence Sanitarium and Hospital by the present trustees have in the past years become considerable in addition to their other various responsibilities, and it would be to the benefit of the hospital, the church, and the community if other personnel could be selected to carry the responsibilities of trustees, who would be selected by the members and not necessarily hold other ex officio responsibilities; and

Whereas, In 1953 the Missouri Legislature adopted "The General Not for Profit Corporation Law" which was a very substantial improvement over the previous law which required such corporations to be organized under special order of the circuit court known as a "Pro Forma Decree," by which method the Independence Sanitarium and Hospital was originally incorporated in 1909 and its articles amended in 1930 following appropriate action previously taken by the World Conference of the church; and

Whereas, It would be to the best interests of the Independence Sanitarium and Hospital to accept the benefits of the new General Not for Profit Corporation Law and amend its articles and take such legal action as necessary in order to avail itself of these provisions and to make a general review and rewriting of all articles in order to bring them completely up-to-date; now therefore be it

Resolved, That the Reorganized Church of Jesus Christ of Latter Day Saints in World Conference assembled does hereby authorize the present trustees of the Independence Sanitarium and Hospital to amend and rewrite the Articles of Incorporation and to take advantage of the provisions of the General Not for Profit Corporation Law of Missouri, adopted in 1953, under which there shall be established a body of members of the corporation to consist ex officio of the three members of the First Presidency, the three members of the Presiding Bishopric, the chairman of the Medical Council, the mayor of the city of Independence, and the eastern judge of the Jackson County Court; it being understood that said group of members of the corporation shall have the authority to elect the trustees and to create a board of trustees in whatever number they deem advisable and to select them from individuals who will be in a position to serve the hospital in such capacity, and to further amend and rewrite the Articles of Incorporation to bring them up-to-date and to include all provisions that in their judgment will be for the best interests of the hospital, the church, and the community.

APPENDIX G

Church Court Procedure

(Adopted April 7, 1954, as Resolution 983, and amended in paragraph 69 by Resolution 991 and in paragraph 8 by Resolution 1018)

I. Court Actions

1. Actions between members.
2. Actions brought by the church against members, or members asking for withdrawal from the church.
3. Style of cause in commencing church actions Place of membership of defendant to be stated.

II. Limitations of Actions

4. Member actions which may be denied hearing; and conditions warranting hearing.
5. Time limitation to file "Member Action."
6. Time and place of filing "Church Action."
7. Limitation of filing of "Church Action" if not filed in reasonable time after notification.

III. Parties to Actions

8. Persons who may prosecute or defend court actions.
9. The name in which "Member Actions" must be brought.
10. The joinder of parties, plaintiffs, and defendants.
11. Who may be a party plaintiff. The age of parties.
12. The barring of actions against insane persons,

and the manner of bringing actions for insane persons.

IV. Jurisdiction of Parties

13. The procedure in filing "Member Actions."
14. The procedure in filing member action if the office is vacant or if the officer refuses or neglects to act or is disqualified.
15. The procedure in filing against a general church officer.

V. Prior Labor Required

16. Labor by one offended and by church officers endeavoring to effect a reconciliation prior to filing Court Action.
17. Court Actions filed after labor performed.
18. Manner in which nonresident members may be labored with.
19. Manner in which members may be expelled from church, or have their names removed from the church records.

VI. The Complaint and Service

20. What the complaint consists of.
21. The manner of setting up each cause of action.
22. The content of the complaint or petition.
23. How the complaint may be served on the defendant.

VII. Commitment to Court

24. The procedure in appointing the court and notifying the parties to the action.
25. The officers who may appoint elder's courts.
26. Duties of the officer appointing the courts.
27. Restrictions on the officer appointing the court and on the members of the court.

VIII. Objections to Hearing

28. Agreements by which action may be dismissed.
29. Parties who may file objections; the procedure in dealing with them.
30. Objections which may be filed by the defendant.
31. Time for filing objections.

IX. Pleadings of Parties

32. Effect of defendant filing no pleading.
33. The kind of pleading a defendant may file prior to hearing.
34. When the defendant may file a cross complaint.
35. What the defendant's answer and cross complaint must contain.
36. Effect of plaintiff's failure to file reply to defendant's answer.
37. Additional pleadings allowed to be filed until issues made.
38. When motions to make more definite and certain may be filed.
39. Legal effect of pleadings filed in the case.

X. Appearance at Hearing

40. Power of court to grant continuances.
41. Appearances in person or by counsel.
42. Duty of court to hear case at appointed time, if defendant is duly served but fails to appear.
43. Duty of court to dismiss case if plaintiff fails to appear, and to proceed to hear defendant's cross complaint, if one is filed.
44. Duty of court if both plaintiff and defendant fail to appear without proper excuse.

XI. Jurisdiction of Courts

45. Courts of original, special, and appeal jurisdiction defined.
46. Elders' court defined.
47. Bishop's court defined.
48. Stake high council defined.
49. Standing High Council defined
50. Power of First Presidency to appoint court where there is no standing court, or local administrative officer to appoint a court.

XII. Incidental Duties of Court

51. The officer who shall preside over the court.
52. Duties of the court before naming time and place of court hearing.
53. Duties of the chairman of the court while presiding.
54. How the clerk of the court shall be chosen, and the duties of the clerk. Power of court to appoint stenographic assistance.

XIII. Notice of Court Hearing

55. On whom and when notices of court hearings shall be served.
56. How notices shall be executed and served on the parties.

XIV. Requirements of Witnesses

57. Power of court to subpoena witnesses.
58. Limitation as to when nonmembers may be used as witnesses.
59. Power of court to discipline witnesses during hearing.
60. Limitation as to witnesses testifying.

XV. Rules of Evidence

61. Rules governing the hearing of the testimony.
62. Limited use of affidavits or ex parte statement in writing.
63. Testimony which may be or must be excluded by court.
64. Matters on which no testimony shall be required.
65. Documents which may be offered in evidence.

XVI. Depositions

66. The right to take and use depositions.
67. The right of the adverse party to be present when taking depositions, and also take cross-interrogatories.
68. The procedure in using depositions.

XVII. Final Judgment

69. Power of the court to hear and decide the issues, and to render final judgment.
70. What the judgment of the court shall state, and power of the court to fix penalties for noncompliance.
71. Who may render the decision of the court.
72. Power of court to suspend judgment.
73. Where the court shall transmit judgment as soon as rendered.

XVIII. New Trial or Rehearing

74. Ground on which plaintiff or defendant shall be denied new trial or an appeal to a higher court.
75. The right of a party to an appeal, and time for giving notice of appeal.

76. Grounds for new trial or rehearing and how stated.

XIX. Procedure in Appeal

77. Necessity of person appealing to file required notice of appeal with court and serve a copy on adverse party.
78. When and how appeal may be perfected.
79. Appeals from elders' court.
80. Appeals from bishop's court.
81. Appeals from stake high council.

XX. Appellate Court Procedure

82. Procedure in transmitting court papers and documents to appellate courts.
83. The power of the appellate court to determine matters appealed.
84. Power of court to fix time and place of hearing.

XXI. Duties of Administrative Officers

85. Duties of administrative officers in transmitting court decision.
86. Procedure on receiving notice of appeal.
87. Procedure when no notice of appeal is filed within time allowed.

XXII. Inherent Powers of Standing High Council

88. Right to supervise lower and inferior courts.
89. Right to interpret the laws of the church.

XXIII. Enacting Clause

90. Enacting clause.

CHURCH COURT PROCEDURE

I. Court Actions

1. There may be but one form of court action between members in this church, called a "Member Action." The member complaining shall be called the plaintiff and the adverse member the defendant.

2. Between the church and a member there may be two forms of action: One shall be known as a "Church Action," in which the church is the plaintiff and the adverse party the defendant. The other shall be called a "Withdrawal Action," in which a member files an application requesting severance of membership.

3. Church actions shall be brought in the name of the Reorganized Church of Jesus Christ of Latter Day Saints, plaintiff, *versus* the member complained of, defendant, and shall state the branch or other jurisdiction where the defendant holds membership.

II. Limitation of Actions

4. Member action shall be denied against a member whose whereabouts is unknown or who was not duly notified thereof, unless he waives notice or willfully evades service thereof. The court shall accept evidence of such waiver or evasion as sufficient notice to the accused.

5. Member action shall be unlawful unless filed within one year from the time of alleged acts complained of. Notwithstanding the foregoing, action may be filed at any time within sixty (60) days after such acts become known to plaintiff. If the whereabouts of the defendant is unknown, the action may be filed at any time after he may be found within one year.

6. In cases of crime, church action may be filed at any time either where the alleged act was committed or where the defendant may be found.

7. Church action shall not be barred by lapse of time, but the failure of officers to act for an undue period of time after being notified of alleged wrongful conduct of the defendant may be urged and accepted as grounds for dismissal of the action, subject to the right of appeal.

III. Parties to Actions

8. Members may prosecute or defend their own actions in person or by counsel selected from the membership of the church, except that where the possible penalty is expulsion from the church, and no counsel has been retained by the defendant, the court shall appoint such counsel. In all other cases where no counsel has been retained, the court may at its discretion appoint such counsel.

In the event that either plaintiff or defendant does not personally appear at the trial, but some church member appears as counsel for such absent party, other than someone appointed by the court, such counsel shall present to the court a written authorization signed by the party he represents.

9. Every member action shall be prosecuted in the name of the member alleged to be wronged or injured by the defendant.

10. Members having an interest in the cause of action may be joined as plaintiffs or as defendants, when justice or equity is thus served, and said joinder is subject to the discretion of the trial court having original jurisdiction, subject to appeal.

11. Any member regardless of age may be a party plaintiff to any action in which an interest is claimed. Children under eighteen years of age may appear by next friend or guardian.

12. No action shall be brought against an insane person in any church court, and no action shall be brought

on behalf of any insane person except by his legally appointed guardian or by the church.

IV. Jurisdiction of Parties

13. Actions between members of the same branch shall be by complaint filed with the branch president. If such president does not hold the Melchisedec priesthood he shall at once transmit the complaint to the next higher officer having jurisdiction over him. Members of different branches of the same district or stake shall file complaints with the president of the district or stake. Members of different districts or stakes in the same mission shall file complaints with the minister in charge of said mission. Members of different missions shall file complaints with the First Presidency.

14. If a vacancy exists in the specified office, or if the officer refuses or neglects to act, or is disqualified in any case, complaint may be filed with the next higher officer having jurisdiction. No complaint shall be dismissed because of failure to file with the proper officer, but in that case it shall be transferred to the officer having jurisdiction of the parties.

15. Complaints against a general officer of the church shall be filed with the First Presidency and shall be heard by the Standing High Council of the church, except when the action is against one of the First Presidency it shall be filed with the Presiding Bishopric. The above shall not apply to any officer who had ceased to act as such prior to the time of alleged misconduct complained of or who in writing waives his right of original jurisdiction of said council.

V. Prior Labor Required

16. Prior to any court action full and consistent labor must be performed according to the laws and rules of

the church. The offended party shall seek the offender and an opportunity to state the offense between themselves alone, and shall endeavor to effect a reconciliation in the spirit of fairness and brotherhood. If such effort shall fail, the one offended shall take with him an officer of the church or a member, as may be practicable, but in no case shall it be a party in interest, and shall again seek an adjustment of the matter, stating it before the witness in the presence only of said offender.

17. After the full performance of labor as hereinbefore provided, if such labor or effort be without avail, the proper officer if a church action, or the one offended if a member action, may file complaint with the administrative officer having jurisdiction of both parties.

18. Members inaccessible to labor in person may be labored with by registered mail with return receipt. In such cases the request of the defendant for postponement of court action, if for good reasons, may be granted. If a member shall persistently refuse to receive or hear or shall evade those who attempt proper labor, such attempt upon proper showing may be accepted by the court as sufficient labor.

19. No member shall be expelled from the church or have his name removed from the church records except after court action. A member who requests orally or in writing to withdraw from the church or who unites with a church of another faith, and who persists after due labor has been performed, on advice of the court, shall be permitted to withdraw his membership and have his name removed from the church records; except that if unchristian conduct is charged in the action, the court may render judgment accordingly.

VI. The Complaint and Service

20. The complaint, petition, is the first pleading of the plaintiff. It should contain: First, the names of the

parties to the action, specified as plaintiffs and defendants, and the court having jurisdiction of the parties; second, a plain and concise statement of facts, without unnecessary repetition, which if true would constitute unchristian conduct of the defendant, and in member actions plaintiff must allege that such conduct wronged or injured the plaintiff; third, the time and place of each offense stated as far as justice requires; fourth, the time and place required labor was performed; and fifth, an allegation that the accused had failed to make restitution or reconciliation.

21. Each cause of action shall be set out separately in the petition, numbered consecutively, and denominated as Count I, Count II, Count III, etc.; but shall contain no threat, insinuation, or evidence, and no accusation except a brief and concise statement of the offense complained of.

22. The complaint shall include all grievances of the plaintiff against the defendant which require adjustment, and shall unite in one petition all grievances which the plaintiff has in common against all defendants named. Any grievance which is not against all of the defendants shall be stated in a separate action.

23. Service shall be made upon the defendant by handing him or her a copy of the complaint, if practicable, or by leaving it at his last known address with a member of the family over fifteen years of age, or it may be sent by registered mail, requesting a return receipt signed by addressee only.

VII. Commitment to Court

24. When a lawful complaint is filed with the proper officer he shall without delay transmit it to the presiding officer of the court having original jurisdiction of the parties; or if there be no such court he shall appoint an elders' court and transmit the complaint to the first-

named member thereof and shall include therewith the names and addresses of all parties to the action.

25. Elders' courts may be appointed by administrative officers holding the Melchisedec priesthood who are presidents of missions, stakes, districts, or branches; or they may be appointed at the direction of district or stake [conference] if within a district or stake, and if in organized territory by the missionary in charge having jurisdiction of the parties.

26. The officer who appoints the court shall serve written notice thereof upon all members of the court and upon all the parties to the action. The case is thereafter entirely within the control of the court until its final judgment has been rendered and transmitted to the officer who appointed the court.

27. No officer who appoints a court and no member of any court may be a party in interest or may act as counsel or witness in the action before said court or any court of appeal therefrom.

VIII. Objections to Hearing

28. By agreement of both parties and with the approval of the court, an action may be dismissed either before or during the hearing, or at any time before judgment is rendered.

29. Either party to an action may file with the officer who appointed the court an objection to any member of the court, stating the reasons therefor. If his objection is overruled he shall proceed to trial, unless he shall have, within five (5) days before said hearing, appealed to the next higher administrative officer. A copy of said appeal shall be filed with the court as to which one or more members thereof objection was raised. Such objections may be made on grounds of prejudice, personal interest in the action, or previously expressed opinion in the matter concerned, and the evidence there-

of should be submitted to the administrative officer without delay. These objections may be made against any member of any church court, and, if sustained, another shall be substituted for the one so released. The stake presidency shall rule on objections to any stake high councilman, and the First Presidency shall rule on objections to any Standing High Council member, which rulings shall be conclusive upon all the parties.

30. The defendant may file written objections to the complaint on any of the following grounds: (1) That the required labor has not been performed; (2) that the court has no jurisdiction of the defendant; (3) that the action is barred by limitations of law; (4) that the alleged facts even if true do not constitute unchristian conduct; (5) that a like action for the same cause is pending, or that it has been adjudged, or that it has been dismissed, or that it has been finally adjusted between the parties; (6) that parties are made plaintiff or defendant who are unnecessary to a determination of the matter.

31. Objections to the complaint should be filed promptly so that if sustained by the court an amended complaint may be filed prior to the trial. All rulings of any court on objections, except a court of last resort, may be appealed by the adverse party.

IX. Pleadings of Parties

32. If the defendant appears at the set time and place without filing any pleading and proceeds to trial, he will be deemed to have waived objections to the members of the court and the complaint, but objections to the jurisdiction of the court may be made in writing at any time before final judgment is rendered.

33. The defendant at any time before or at the time of trial may make partial or full confession; or he may present a demurrer or answer to the complaint prior to

the hearing. If no written answer is filed it will be assumed that the defendant denies all material allegations of the complaint.

34. The defendant may file with his answer a cross complaint against the plaintiff if the cross complaint grows out of the same transactions set forth in the complaint; or he may file with his answer a cross complaint that does not grow out of the same transactions, if in the discretion of the court it will not cause undue delay or prejudice the issues of the original complaint, provided all church rules of action have been observed.

35. If the defendant files an answer it shall be in plain and concise language and without repetition. He shall admit that part which is true, and deny the allegations which are false. If he believes all the allegations are false, he may file a general denial without specifically denying each and every allegation in plaintiff's complaint. New matter set up as a defense in a cross complaint or counterclaim shall be in addition to the defendant's answer denying in whole or in part the allegations of plaintiff's petition, and follow the answer in the same pleading and become a part of it.

36. If the plaintiff files no objection or reply to the defendant's answer he will be presumed to have denied any new matter set up therein.

37. The court shall allow additional pleadings to be filed until the issues shall have been determined, whereupon the parties shall be notified in writing of the time and place of the hearing.

38. Either party may file a motion to make more definite and certain the pleadings of the adverse party, and the court shall allow such amendments thereof as will clarify without changing the scope or purport of the complaint or defense of it, until the issues become certain. By leave of court, formal defects may be cor-

rected at any time prior to or during the hearing of the case.

39. Pleadings shall be signed by the parties or by their counsel, and the allegations thereof shall be binding upon the parties making them. However, as to form pleadings shall be liberally construed.

X. Appearance at Hearing

40. Parties shall appear and prosecute or defend at the time and place stated by the court in the notice; but for good cause shown, the court or its chairman may grant continuances.

41. Either party to a complaint may appear in person, or by counsel properly certified to the court, but a member and his counsel may not both present argument before the court in the same cause. It shall be optional with the party in interest which shall address the court.

42. If after due notice of the hearing the defendant fails to appear, the court shall proceed to hear the cause of the plaintiff, and render judgment on the evidence presented. It is within the power of the court to appoint counsel for the defendant if occasion and justice so demand.

43. If after due notice of the hearing the plaintiff should fail to appear, the court may dismiss the action, or it may hear the evidence of the defendant and render judgment thereon, and if the defendant has filed a cross complaint the court shall render judgment on the evidence presented. The court may appoint counsel for the plaintiff if occasion and justice so demand.

44. If after due notice of the hearing, both parties fail to appear without proper excuse, the cause may be dismissed as to both parties.

XI. Jurisdiction of Courts

45. The courts of the church before which causes of actions are first heard are known as courts of original jurisdiction. Courts to which appeals may be taken are known as appellate courts or courts of appeal. A court which is appointed and organized for hearing one or more particular causes and which is dissolved when final judgment has been rendered thereon is known as a special or temporary court; but a court which after being established continues to maintain jurisdiction over the church, a stake, or a district is known as a standing court.

46. An elders' court is a temporary court, and consists of two or more, usually three, elders of the Melchisedec priesthood appointed by an administrative officer to be held within his own jurisdiction to hear and determine one or more causes which have been filed with him. Such courts are courts of original jurisdiction—trial courts. Appeal therefrom is to a bishop's court.

47. A bishop's court is a standing court, and consists of a bishop and one or two bishops or elders as counselors. Such courts have original jurisdiction in stakes, districts, or other subdivisions of the church. From their decisions appeal may be made to the stake high council, if in its jurisdiction, but otherwise to the Standing High Council of the church. The bishop's court is also a court of appeal from the decision of an elders' court in districts and unorganized territories.

48. A stake high council consists of twelve high priests under the presidency of the stake, and from its decision appeal may be made to the Standing High Council of the church. It constitutes a standing court of appeal from a bishop's court in the same jurisdiction, and is also a council of original jurisdiction in certain general or official matters within the stake.

49. The Standing High Council is the highest appellate council or court of the church. It has original jurisdiction when complaint is made against a General Church officer in accordance with the provisions hereinbefore stated, and may exercise original jurisdiction in any case when no other court having jurisdiction exists and justice so requires. It is presided over by the First Presidency of the church.

50. When there is no court having jurisdiction of both parties to an action and there is no local administrative officer having jurisdiction to appoint such a court, the First Presidency may, in its discretion, appoint a special bishop's court or an elders' court to hear the cause.

XII. Incidental Duties of Court

51. The first-named member of an elders' court appointed to hear a cause shall preside at its meetings until a permanent chairman has been chosen. A bishop's court shall be presided over by a bishop.

52. Before appointing the time and place of hearing, the court shall see that the complaint is properly drawn, including a statement of required labor, and the addresses of parties.

53. The chairman of the court shall open all sessions at the time and place appointed, preside over and direct the proceedings, decide on the admissibility of evidence, and maintain order and decorum. All church courts shall be conducted in a solemn and orderly manner and all sessions thereof be opened with prayer.

54. The court shall choose a clerk, either a member of the court or any suitable person not a party in interest. The clerk shall record all proceedings of the court, including its rulings and final judgment, the names and abstract of testimony of the witnesses, and shall mark for identification all documents submitted to the court.

The court may appoint a stenographer to report any or all testimony given before the court. The notes so made or a transcript thereof shall become a part of the record of the case.

XIII. Notice of Court Hearing

55. The court shall serve on all parties to the action written notice of the time and place of hearing, allowing sufficient time for them to receive said notice and present themselves at the time and place stated.

56. All notices of hearings shall be signed by the court or its presiding officer, and may be delivered by a church officer to each party or at his usual place of address to a member of the family more than fifteen years of age, or may be sent by registered mail, requesting a return receipt signed by addressee only.

XIV. Requirements of Witnesses

57. Church courts have the right to require the attendance of any church member at its hearings, either as a party to the cause or as a witness, and any member who after due notice refuses or fails to appear, unless excused by the court, may be dealt with for unchristian conduct.

58. Persons not members of the church may not attend court hearings except as witnesses in cases where evidence cannot be secured from church members, and only when no enmity is known to exist on their part toward the adverse party or the church, and only when admitted by ruling of the court.

59. A disorderly witness who persistently refuses to heed the admonitions of the court may be excluded therefrom until he or she offers redress or apology and promises to observe the required decorum. The court should, if practicable, exclude all witnesses from the hearing except when they are testifying.

60. A witness is required to answer truthfully all questions of the court or of counsel, except questions excluded by ruling of the court; but a wife or husband not legally separated is not compelled to testify against the other.

XV. Rules of Evidence

61. The court shall impartially hear both parties, their counsel, and the testimony of all witnesses who appear; but no witness shall be heard without the adverse party having the right to be present and cross-examine him, if he so desires.

62. Affidavits or ex parte statements in writing are inadmissible as proper testimony in any cause before a court, unless consented to by opposing party. A witness may to a limited extent refresh his memory by a writing, if necessary, but cannot make a written statement in lieu of his testimony in court.

63. Irrelevant, immaterial, misleading, or other matter of too conjectural and remote connection should be excluded by the court. Hearsay testimony shall not be accepted as evidence, but direct testimony of voluntary admissions of guilt by the accused may be received. Private opinions of a witness shall be excluded, but the opinion of a qualified expert on a matter in dispute may be admitted by the court.

64. No testimony shall be required as to matters of which the court may take judicial notice, nor to support testimony not denied.

65. Public records, quasi public documents, certified and authenticated copies (the originals of which are not procurable), necessary physical representations, and all original papers involved in a case may be admitted in evidence.

XVI. Depositions

66. Depositions may be taken by the court or by a duly appointed commissioner for the jurisdiction where the required witnesses are. The procedure in taking testimony by deposition is similar to that for witnesses in court. Such testimony may be either by oral depositions or on written interrogatories as shall be specified in the notice to the adverse party.

67. Sufficient notice must be given of the taking of a deposition to permit the adverse party to be present and cross-examine the witness if he so desires. If the testimony is to be taken upon written interrogatories, a copy of the same must be placed in the hands of the adverse party or his counsel in sufficient time for him to file cross-interrogatories.

68. When taking depositions, the objections of the opposing party or his counsel shall be duly recorded as a part of the record of the deposition, subject to review by the court which shall hear the cause. The record of the proceedings and of the testimony in full shall be certified to the court by the officer before whom the deposition is taken.

XVII. Final Judgment

69. All courts of the church have full power to hear and decide the issues involved in the cases submitted to them in accordance with the provisions heretofore set out, and their final decisions shall have all the authority, power, and effect of a branch, district, stake, or mission conference action of the jurisdiction of the parties concerned. In cases of expulsion from the church the judgment of the court is final and conclusive, but must be presented to the church (a properly constituted unit of church organization, such as a branch, district, stake, or mission, having jurisdiction of the person involved) in conformity with the law for removal of names from the

church record. "And the elders shall lay the case before the church, and the church shall lift up their hands against him or her" (D. and C. 42:22).

The above statement is imperative and mandatory, not discretionary. When a duly appointed church court has found a member guilty of an offense which makes that member subject to expulsion from the church, after the time for filing an appeal has expired, or the appeal has been heard and overruled by the appellate court, the finding of the trial court becomes final and the member is disfranchised and cut off from the church. Inasmuch as the one thus disfranchised is a member of a certain branch, district, stake, or mission, the members of this unit of church organization wherein he or she may have membership must thereafter by lifting up their hands remove his or her name from the membership of the church wherever located.

In the event that the members of such branch or other unit of church organization shall under these circumstances fail to lift up their hands against the person involved in the aforesaid judgment of the court, the administrative officer in charge of that unit of church organization shall certify the matter to the next larger unit, such as for example from a branch to a district, and in the event of failure of the appropriate district, stake, or mission conference to act in the matter, or of branches in unorganized territory, the matter shall then be certified to the General Conference or Standing High Council of the church for the necessary action on behalf of the church. (This section was revised by action of the 1956 General Conference.)

70. The judgment of the court shall state whether or not the complaint is sustained, and shall make a declaration as to each separate count thereof, as for instance: "Counts I and III are sustained, but Count II is not sustained." The court may make such requirements as

justice and the law of the church require, and may assess such penalties for noncompliance therewith as may rightly and lawfully be enforced by church authority.

71. The decision of a majority of the members comprising the court shall be the judgment of the court and shall be so rendered. A minority may offer a separate statement of views, if convinced that injustice would otherwise result.

72. The church law for certain offenses prescribes expulsion. Where expulsion is not compulsory the erring member should be given ample time and Christlike encouragement for repentance, and the court may decide whether suspension of his membership until repentance be shown would be likely to yield better results than expulsion.

73. When the court has rendered final judgment, it shall without delay transmit the same with a complete record of the proceedings to the officer who committed the case to such court. Copies of the judgment shall also be transmitted to the parties in the case, and said judgment shall be and remain in force and effect until it is reversed or overruled by another court of competent jurisdiction.

XVIII. New Trial or Rehearing

74. If without proper excuse the plaintiff neglected to appear at the hearing of his complaint, he shall be denied a new trial of the cause or an appeal from a decision of the court thereon. Likewise, if without good excuse the defendant permitted judgment against him by default, a new trial or an appeal shall not be granted to him.

75. If any party who has been diligent in his cause is dissatisfied with the decision of the court, he may move for a new trial or rehearing of the case at the time, and, if the motion is denied by the court, he may

give notice of appeal at the time, or within thirty (30) days, if he so desires. Notice of appeal given at the time should appear as a part of the record in the case.

76. Grounds for a new trial or rehearing must be clearly stated and filed with the court within thirty (30) days after filing notice of appeal, and a copy shall be served on the adverse party.

A motion for a new trial may be filed with the court: if error of law in the record of the court is alleged; if the court had been petitioned to compel attendance of a witness who refused to appear; if mover's counsel had withdrawn from the case at or near time of trial and other counsel was not available; if the judgment ignores the weight of vital evidence; if newly discovered evidence is found which the party could not have obtained before; or if fraud is alleged.

XIX. Procedure in Appeal

77. Subject to the rules and exceptions hereinbefore stated, any party to a cause may appeal from the judgment rendered by a court thereon. Notice of appeal may be filed with said court at the time judgment is rendered, or at any time within thirty (30) days thereafter with the officer who appointed the court, and copies of such notice must also be served on the court and on the adverse party.

78. Appeals may be made and perfected at the time of filing notice thereof, but otherwise they shall be perfected within thirty (30) days thereafter, unless extension of time has been granted by the court of appeal. Grounds for appeal shall be clearly stated in writing and signed by the appellant.

79. Appeal from an elders' court shall be made to a bishop's court in the same jurisdiction, if such there be; otherwise an appeal shall be made to the First Presidency to appoint such a court.

80. Appeal from a bishop's court shall be made to the stake high council, if in a stake, but if outside of stake organization the appeal shall be to the Standing High Council of the church. Appeals shall be filed with the presidency of the council to which the appeal is made.

81. Appeal from a stake high council shall be made to the Standing High Council of the church, and shall be filed with the First Presidency.

XX. Appellate Court Procedure

82. On the filing of the notice of an appeal, the court which heard the cause shall transmit all records and documents in the case to the court of appeal. If the documents and papers have been lodged with some administrative officer, he shall, upon receiving notice of the appeal, forward same to the court to which the case has been appealed.

83. Upon receiving an appeal, the appellate court shall determine the procedure and shall grant or deny the petition, or order a rehearing before the former court or a new court within the same jurisdiction, as the case may require.

84. The court to which appeal is taken shall fix the time and place of the appellate hearing, if granted, and shall notify all parties in interest in ample time for them to appear.

XXI. Duties of Administrative Officers

85. Upon receiving the records and an authorized copy of the final judgment of the court, the administrative officer who committed the case thereto shall report the judgment of the court to the branch, district, stake, or mission having jurisdiction; but he shall hold such court

records until a notice of appeal has been filed, if less than thirty (30) days after judgment has been rendered.

86. Upon receiving notice of an appeal lawfully made, the administrative officer having jurisdiction shall promptly transmit all records of the case appealed to the proper officer of the appellate court to which said case is appealed.

87. In case the administrative officer holding the records of a court does not receive notice of an appeal from its final judgment within the time allowed for such appeal, he shall transmit such records to the office of the First Presidency to be permanently filed therein.

XXII. Inherent Powers of Standing High Council

88. The Standing High Council shall regulate and supervise all lower courts.

89. The Standing High Council shall construe and interpret all laws of the church relating to church court procedure. If the Council should determine that the law governing court procedure fails to cover a given situation, it may by its own ruling supply the deficiency in order that justice may be done to all parties involved, and such Council ruling shall be effective until General Conference legislates on the matter; but in no event shall an adverse action by the Conference be retroactive so as to nullify the judgment of the Council or affect the rights of the parties in any case adjudicated by the Council prior to such General Conference action.

XXIII. Enacting Clause

90. "All rules, enactments, and customs of the church not in harmony with the provisions and requirements set forth in the foregoing sections and paragraphs are hereby declared inoperative and void."

GLOSSARY INDEX DEFINING WORDS AND PHRASES IN CHURCH COURT PROCEDURE

1. **MEMBER ACTION** is an action in which one member of the church files a complaint against another member.
2. **CHURCH ACTION** is an action in which the church through one of its administrative officers, such as branch, district, or stake president or a General Church officer, for and on behalf of the church, files a complaint against a member of the church or a member of the priesthood.
3. **WITHDRAWAL ACTION** is an action in which a member of the church files with an administrative officer a request for withdrawal of membership from the church.
4. **ADMISSION OR CONFESSION** is a voluntary oral statement or written pleading filed, admitting part or all of the facts to be true as alleged or charged in the complaint or cross complaint, or other pleading.
5. **AFFIDAVITS** are voluntary statements in writing made under oath before a notary public, or other public official authorized to so officiate.
6. **APPEARANCE** is the formal proceeding by which a defendant submits himself to the jurisdiction of the court; or the actual coming into court for a special hearing or trial by either plaintiff or defendant in person or by attorney or by both.
7. **ANSWER** is the pleading filed by the defendant admitting or denying the facts alleged in the plaintiff's complaint and setting forth the facts as believed by defendant.
8. **COMMITMENT TO COURT** is the proper transmittal of all papers filed with an administrative officer to the court having jurisdiction of the cause of action and the parties, plaintiff and defendant, or from one court to another.
9. **CONTINUANCE** is the granting by the court of a request made by the plaintiff or defendant for further time to plead in any action, or for a change of the date of the hearing of the action.
10. **COUNSEL** is the person designated by one of the parties to the action, or by the court, to represent the party before the court. Either party may choose to act as his own counsel before the court.
11. **COUNTS** in a complaint or action are the various causes of action the plaintiff or complainant has against defendant

or member, each being designated separately as Count I, Count II, etc.

12. COUNTERCLAIM is a pleading filed by the defendant in a member action asking relief of some sort.

13. CROSS COMPLAINT is a pleading filed by the defendant in a member action against the plaintiff asking for relief.

14. DEFENDANT is the member against whom the complaint is filed, and is sometimes called "the accused."

15. A DEMURRER is an objection made by one party to his opponent's pleading, alleging that, even if the facts as stated in the pleading are true, yet under the law no case has been made against the party objecting, therefore no answer to same is necessary.

16. A DEPOSITION is the testimony of a witness taken by agreement of the parties to an action or by order of the court on the application of one of the parties before a notary public or a commissioner appointed by the court. In the latter case, notice to take deposition must be served on the opposing party. The deposition may be read in court if the deposing witness is not available to testify in person, or it may be used to impeach his oral testimony. The opposing party must agree to the taking of the deposition or be notified of the taking and permitted to cross-examine the witness if he so desires.

17. EX PARTE STATEMENTS are those statements made by one of the parties to an action, or by someone in his behalf, not in the presence of the opposing party.

18. A GUARDIAN is a person appointed by a court having civil power to appoint, to handle the affairs of some other person who is by law incompetent to manage his or her affairs, such as infants or persons who are mentally or otherwise incapable of managing their own affairs.

19. IRRELEVANT, IMMATERIAL, AND MISLEADING STATEMENTS are statements made which have little or no connection with, or which if true would in no way affect the action, or which would tend to give the court the wrong impression of the material facts presented or to be presented.

20. JURISDICTION is the right and power to act within the office or place.
    (a) The court as an institution must have specified territorial jurisdiction, and jurisdiction of the action brought before it.

(b) The court hearing the action must be duly appointed as such and have jurisdiction of the parties to the action by the proper service of the cause of action upon the parties with due notice of time and place of the hearing.

21. LABOR is the endeavor required by the church of the complaining member to bring about reconciliation of the parties, or a settlement of their dispute, before filing the complaint or action against the other member.

22. LIMITATION OF ACTION is the effective time within which a member of the church may file a complaint against a member of the church, or a member of the priesthood.

23. A MEMBER is one who has become affiliated with the church through baptism by immersion and confirmation by a duly ordained minister of the church having authority to perform the ordinance.

24. The PETITION is the formal complaint filed by the plaintiff.

25. The PLAINTIFF is the member filing the complaint.

26. SERVICE in a court action is the notification to the opposing party in the action of the filing of certain documents in court, and the delivery to him of a copy of same, and at times it is the notice to appear in court as a party to the action or as a witness in the action before the court.

27. PERSONAL SERVICE is the delivery, in person, of a document or notice to one of the parties to an action, or to a witness, or by registered mail, requesting a return receipt signed by addressee only.

28. PUBLICATION SERVICE is the notification in an established newspaper in the community where the action is filed, notifying the person sought to be served of the nature of the action brought and the date of the hearing on same before the court. This type of service can only be resorted to where the party sought to be served cannot be found and personal service cannot be made. At the present time there is no provision for publication service in the Church Court Procedure.

29. UNCHRISTIAN CONDUCT is such conduct on the part of a member for which he or she on proper proof before a court of competent jurisdiction may be expelled from membership in the church.

Index

Subject	Resolution No. or *Rules of Order* Par.	Page
Abstinence from intoxicating drinks and tobacco	92	37
Abstract doctrines not a test of fellowship	222	42
Abuse, *Saints' Herald* editorial policy to avoid	298	45
Acts valid till silenced, elders (in transgression)	90	37
Administration of Appointees	862	82
Administration of Sacrament dignified	894	92
Administration, purpose of church	849	73
Administration ... rights of body are safeguarded in, church	11	13
Administrative functions	10	12
Administrative Officers, field presiding responsibilities	1097	208
Administrators, regional	10	12
Adultery and readmittance, expulsion for second offense of — for	864	85
Adultery and remarriage; marriage, divorce after	272	44
Adultery as evidence, witnesses of	343	48
Adultery, file written confessions of	713	63
Advertisements in church publications	725	65
Advertising and use of tobacco	1046	1964, p. 172
Affirm basic doctrines	861	80
Affirmative message, appointees and ministers with	854	76
Agenda, branch business meeting	58	31
Agenda, district conference	49	28
Aging, Task force on	1130	230
Agreements of working harmony with Church of Christ;	783	66
rescinded	858	76
Agriculture colonization for Zion	940	110
Allowances and elders' expenses, printing of appointee family	1006	144
Allowances and inheritances, appointee	1001	139
Amend rules and orders	60	34
Annual statements of tithing and offerings, printing lists and	878	91
Apostles, presidency to counsel and direct	386	50

Appeals, ministerial silences and	1158	258
Appoint persons of any race	995	137
Appointee allowances and inheritances	1001	139
Appointee elders' expense reports	804	70
Appointee family allowances and elders' expenses, printing	1006	144
Appointees and ministers with affirmative message	854	76
Appointees in stakes, minister in charge to direct	551	57
Appointees, missionary in charge to move	367	49
Appointees not to use tobacco nor strong drink	463	54
Appointees opposing the church	862	82
Appointees, retiring and superannuating	560	58
Appointees, selecting, training, placement, and financing of	949	114
Appointees to create missionary opportunities	897	93
Appointees to strengthen faith of church	298	45
Appointment of church architect	784	69
Appointment of stake officers	551	57
Appointments submitted to General Conference	839	71
Appropriations meeting, call Board of	1007	145
Associations as trustees, Presiding Bishopric create business	907	94
Archaeological Research Committee	1147	247
Architect, appointment of church	784	69
Architects, employment and use of	986	134
Assemblies, conferences and	15-21	16
Assemblies, Conferences are legislative	15	16
Assembly, General	17	16
Assistance, worldwide worthy	1019	147
Assisting young people, program for	1047	166
Associations make financial report, departments and	901	93
Atherton, Lamoni, and Ozarks; Stewardship projects at	917	97
Audio-Visual Library	1136	237
Auditorium, construction fund	948	112
Auditorium, office wing addition to	1063, 1089, 1113	176, 202, 214
Australia and New Zealand, incorporation of church in	—	276
Authorities, General Conference a body of spiritual	61	37
Authority; Bible, Book of Mormon, Doctrine and Covenants, standard of	215, 222	41, 42

Authority, the reality and extent of priesthood	8	11
Authorized publications, church responsible only for	368	49
Avenging enemies, cursing and	308	46
Avoid advancing speculative theories	222	42
Baptism, eight years old for	552	57
Baptism for the dead	308	46
Baptism, procedure in ordinance of	212	41
Baptism, requirement for candidate for	705	62
Baptism, words to be used	48	37
Baptized, ordinations void when rebaptized	329	48
Basis of representation	24	18
Bible, Book of Mormon, Doctrine and Covenants, standard of authority	215, 222	41, 42
Bible, indorse Inspired Version of	214	41
Binding on Reorganization, Local commandments not	282	44
Bishop and counselors are trustees, Presiding	866	87
	—	266, 270
	—	273, 274
Bishop to hold seal and sign conveyances, Presiding	—	266
Bishop, Stake	41	24
Bishopric and Order of Bishops	788	69
Bishopric create business associations as trustees, Presiding	907	94
Bishopric, Stake Bishopric, Order of Bishops, Presiding	710	63
Bishopric to see finances are used rightly, Presiding	915	96
Bishops, Bishopric and Order of	788	69
Bishops, evangelists, high priests, ordination of	1051	169
Bishops having temporal jurisdiction	—	274, 276
Bishops; High Councils; courts, elders	14	14
Bishops, ordination and release of	982	132
Bishops, Presiding Bishopric, Stake Bishopric, Order of	10, 710	12, 63
Bishops, Regional	10	12
Bishops, release of evangelists and	884	91
Blessing of bread and wine at sacrament	172	39
Blessing to children under eight, ordinance of	701	61
Board of Appropriations meeting, Call	1007	145
Board of Appropriations, 34 members and committee	1082	192
Board of Publication to manage Committee	—	267

Bond issue, authorize Graceland College	1004	143
Book of Mormon, annotated edition	1076	182
Book of Mormon, authorize Readers' Version of	1002, 1058	141, 174
Book of Mormon, Doctrine and Covenants standard of authority; Bible	215, 222	41, 42
Book of Mormon education	1117	218
Book of Mormon into Spanish, Translation of	970	123
Book of Mormon language, committee on clarity of	993	136
Book of Rules and Resolutions, revision	—	34
Branch business meetings	52-58	29-31
Branch business meetings, when held	55	30
Branch business meetings, agenda for	58	31
Branch business meetings, quorum	56	30
Branches, multiple—metropolitan, business meetings	55	30
Branch officers	51	29
Branch or district where residing, members responsible to	594	59
Branch president	10	12
Branch program, cradle roll and religious education in	872	89
Branches	50-58	29
Branches and districts conducted by rules in law	59	32
Branches, high priests to preside over	111	38
Branches, members locate near	895	92
Branches, organization of	50	29
Branches organized on basis of administration, not race	995	137
Branches, stakes and		266
Bread and wine at sacrament, blessing of	172	39
Broadcasting and station, radio	960	120
Broadcasting station, radio	971	124
Budget, church subdivision to operate on approved	1008	145
Budget, World Church, significant proportion identified with programs of reconciliation, church extension	1128	228
Budgeting policy	1133	232
Building and purchasing of churches, lands, and investments	903	94
Building Commission authorized, General Church	1027	151
Building fund from surplus, establish church	863	84

Building specifications, church	974	126
Bureau of research and service for Zion	997	138
Business Associations	907	94
Business from surplus, fund for development of	1040	162
Business meeting, agenda for branch	58	31
Business meeting, quorum at branch	56	30
Business meetings, branch	50-58	29-31
Called by, special conferences	20	17
Calling and ordination of high priests	638	60
Calling and ordaining of priesthood, procedures in	988	134
Canada, incorporation of church in	—	273
Candidate for baptism, requirement for	705	62
Capital Fund authorized, Missions Abroad	1041	163
Care of the elderly	1038, 1130	162, 230
Central Missouri and Center Stakes, reorganization of	1030	153
Certificates of stewardship	722	64
Certification of delegates	26	19
Charges, officer to decide validity of	743	65
Children under eight, ordinance of blessing	701	61
Christ, Agreements of working harmony with Church of	783	66
Christ, Agreements of working harmony with Church of, rescinded	858	76
Christ, church is exponent of doctrine of	718	64
Christ committee, Church of	1159	261
Christ to give commandments	308	46
Christian Education, new curriculum, new materials	1094, 1117, 1122, 1145	205, 218, 221, 243
Christmas offering for Temple Fund	1088	201
Church activities, report on General	985	134
Church administration, purpose of	849	73
Church administration . . . rights of body are safeguarded in	11	13
Church and reunion ground purchases and improvements	954	118
Church, appointees opposing the	862	82
Church architect, appointment of	784	69
Church, as defined, the	6	11
Church Building Commission authorized, General	1027	151
Church building fund from surplus, establish	863	84
Church building, Lamoni	948	113

Church building specifications	974	126
Church continues to function, the	5	10
Church Court procedure	983, 991, 1018	292
Church expansion, a significant proportion of church budget identified with	1128	228
Church flag	887	92
Church, government of the	849, 861	73, 80
Church, higher education in the	1024	148
Church historian to appoint district historians	498	56
Church in Australia and New Zealand, incorporation of	—	276
Church in Canada, incorporation of	—	273
Church includes, government of the	9	12
Church in Iowa, incorporation of	—	270
Church institutions and agencies, indebtedness of	1035	158
Church insurance	800	70
Church is exponent of doctrine of Christ	718	64
Church literature in libraries, placement of	1026	150
Church members, Standards of Conduct	1085	194
Church Mission and World Witness	1121	220
Church of Christ, agreements of working harmony	783	66
Church of Christ, agreements of working harmony, rescinded	858	76
Church of Christ committee	1159	261
Church of Christ committee to work for unity	1036	160
Church of Jesus Christ, the	1	9
Church, organization, purpose, and membership	1-5	9
Church—Presidency is leading quorum—presides over	386	50
Church publications, advertisements in	725	65
Church, purposes for offices in	386	50
Church responsible only for authorized publications	368	49
Church secretary	115, 411	38, 53
Church subdivisions to operate on approved budget	1008	145
Church . . . through priesthood, government of	7	10
Churches, lands and investments; building and purchasing of	903	94
Close Communion	91, 1092	37, 204
College (See Graceland College)		
College Day	558	57

College Fund, Graceland	948	113
College people, Committee on Ministry to	1024	148
Colonization for Zion, agriculture	940	110
Commandments, Christ to give	308	46
Commandments not binding on Reorganization, local	282	44
Commission authorized, General Church building	1027	151
Commission authorized, Health Ministries	1109	213
Commission authorized, Women's Ministry	1118	219
Committee authorized, General Conference organization	1025	150
Committee (Board) of Publication to manage	—	267
Committee, Church of Christ	1159	261
Committee of Board of Appropriations	1082	192
Committee on clarity of Book of Mormon language	993	136
Committee on Health and Nutrition	1098	209
Committee on Ministry to College People	1024	148
Committee on Name of the Church	1067, 1077	185, 191-193
Committee on use of television authorized	1048	168
Committee on World Peace	1052, 1087, 1129	170, 196, 229
Committee to study equality	1032	155
Committee to work for unity, Church of Christ	1036	160
Common consent	834, 849	71, 73
Community, service to local	1072	180
Conducted, by rules in law, branches and districts	59	32
Conference (See General, District, Stake)		
Conference, agenda district	49	28
Conference, appointments submitted to General	839	71
Conference, chief legislative body, General	15, 861	16, 80
Conference credentials committee, General	617	60
Conference, delegate district	29	20
Conference delegates elected not appointed, General	936	110
Conference, Delegates to General	23	18
Conference, ex officio member of General	22	18
Conference, General	16	16
Conference legislation, initiation of proposed	1155	255
Conference, object in	854	76
Conference Organization and Procedures Committee study and report	1057	173

Conference Organization Committee authorized, General	1025	150
Conference, quorums report to General	666	61
Conference role in statements of policy	1057	173
Conference, time and place for General	808	70
Conferences and assemblies	15-21	16
Conferences and reunions, dates and locations	873	90
Conferences are legislative assemblies	15	16
Conferences, . . . called by, special	20	17
Conferences, district	46	27
Conferences, preside at district	47	27
Conferences, stake	43	25
Conferences, stake and district	19	16
Confessions of adultery, file written	713	63
Conform to law, writers, editors	379	50
Consecration	308	46
Consecration and use of surplus in storehouse treasury	977	128
Consent, common	834, 849	71, 73
Coordinator for Family Ministry	1054, 1059	171, 174
Corporate Membership, Sanitarium and Hospital	1120	289
Corporation to hold property	—	267
Council of Twelve as judicial body (Quorum)	280	44
Council, stake high	40	24
Council to interpret law, Standing High	864	85
Counsel and direct apostles, Presidency to	386	50
Counselors of quorums to be ordained, presidents and	109	38
Court procedure, church	—	292
Courts; elders', bishops', high councils	14	14
Cradle roll and religious education in branch program	872	89
Created one blood and one race, men	963	120
Credentials Committee, General Conference	617	60
Credit unions	1039	162
Curriculum, new Religious Education	1094, 1117, 1122, 1145	205, 218, 221, 243
Cursing and avenging enemies	308	46
Dates and locations for conferences and reunions	873	90
Day, College	558	57
Deacons, duties of	471	55
Deacons, quorums of	—	266

Deacons to convey emblems at sacrament, neither teachers nor	401	53
Deacons to preach, teachers and	449	54
Dead, baptism for the	308	46
Debts, members who contract	120	38
Defined, the church as	6	11
Delegate district conference	29	20
Delegates, Certification of	26	19
Delegates, Conferences, Missions or Regions	34	21
Delegates elected not appointed, General Conference	936	110
Delegates, qualifications for	25	19
Delegates, time for election of	1106	212
Delegates, to General Conference	23	18
Delegate voting	27	20
Democracy, theocratic	6, 849	11, 73
Department heads, nomination of	782	66
Departments and associations make financial report	901	93
Departments to prepare history, quorums	470	55
Designation of the field jurisdictions	32	21
Development of business from surplus, fund for	1040	162
Difficulties, officers (branch and district) to settle	59	32
Direct apostles, Presidency to counsel and	386	50
District Conference agenda	49	28
District conference, delegate	29	20
District conferences	46	27
District conferences, preside at	47	27
District conferences, stake and	19	16
District historians, church historian to appoint	498	56
District organization	44	26
District president	10, 45	12, 26
District where residing, members responsible to branch	594	59
Districts	44-49	26
Districts conducted by rules in law, branches	59	32
Divorce after adultery and remarriage, marriage	272	44
Divorce and remarriage, marriage	1034	156
Doctrine and Covenants, format, order of sections and historical appendage	1080, 1115	187, 216
Doctrine and Covenants standard of authority, Bible, Book of Mormon	215, 222	41, 42
Doctrine of Christ, church is exponent of	718	65

Doctrine of resurrection, preaching of	391	52
Doctrines, affirm basic	861	80
Doctrines necessary for salvation, elders to teach	222	42
Doctrines not a test of fellowship, abstract	222	42
Doctrines of the church	—	265
Dormitory construction, Graceland College Endowment Fund for	979	131
Drinking intoxicants and visiting saloons a test of fellowship	297	45
Drinks and tobacco, abstinence from intoxicating	92	37
Duplex envelope system recommended	1008	145
Duties, high priests'	386	50
Duties of church secretary	115	38
Duties of deacons	471	55
Duties of presiding officer (branch business meeting)	54	29
Duties, officers free to discharge	1014	146
Duty of members	57	30
Duty of presiding officers	48	28
Dynasty, imperial	308	46
Economic and moral problems, social	1045	164
Editorial policy to avoid abuse, *Saints' Herald*	298	45
Editors to conform to law, writers	379	50
Education in branch program, cradle roll and religious	872	89
Education in the church, higher	1024, 1065	148, 177
Education objectives and emphases, religious	919	103
Education, race relations	976	126
Education, Reserve Fund, higher	1024	148
Education, teaching objectives	918	101
Eight years old for baptism	552	57
Elderly, care of the	1038, 1130	162, 230
Elders administer ordinance of healing	132	38
Elders and Aaronic Priesthood, Conference organization	1125	225
Elders, Bishops' High Councils, courts	14	14
Elders bore testimony, the early	3	9
Elders' expense reports, appointee	804	70
Elders Expenses in Regions and Stakes	1101	210
Elders' expenses, printing of appointee family allowances	1006	144
Elders (in transgression), acts valid till silenced	90	37
Elders, quorums of	—	266

Elders to teach doctrines necessary for salvation	222	42
Elective offices, nominate all	834	71
Emblems at sacrament, neither teachers nor deacons to convey	401	53
Employment and use of architects	986	134
Endowment fund for dormitory construction, Graceland College	979	131
Endowments, temple and	308	46
Enemies, cursing and avenging	308	46
Enrollment of unknown memberships	910	95
Envelope system recommend, duplex	1008	145
Epitome of Faith and Doctrine	222	42
Equality, committee to study	1032	155
Equality, racial	963, 976	120, 126
Establish church building fund from surplus	863	84
Establishment of Zion through law of stewardships	851	74
Evangelists, and bishops, release of	884	91
Evangelists, bishops, high priests, ordinations of	1051	169
Evidence, witnesses of adultery as	343	48
Excommunicated, withdrawing and reinstated; members and ministers expelled	922	106
Executive body, First Presidency chief	861	80
Ex officio members of World Conference	22	18
Expelled, excommunicated, withdrawing and reinstated; members and ministers	922	106
Expression by people, General Conference instrument of	849	73
Expulsion for second offense of adultery and readmittance	864	85
Extension to Independence, Graceland College	1024	148
Faith of church, appointees to strengthen	298	45
Family allowance and elder's expense (maximum), appointee	1006	144
Family life, marriage and marital difficulties; home	972	125
Family Ministry, Coordinator for	1054, 1059	171, 174
Fellowship, abstract doctrines not a test of	222	42
Fermented wine and water in Sacrament	702	62
Field activities, planning	873	90
Field jurisdictions of Missions and Regions	32	21
File written confessions of adultery	713	63

Finances are used rightly, Presiding Bishopric to see	915	96
Financial assistance to students in higher education	1079	184
Financial law, priesthood should comply with	871	89
Financial policy	925, 940	107, 110
Financial policy affirmed	1035	158
Financial report, departments and associations make	901	93
Financing ministers	606	60
Financing of appointees; selecting, training, placement and	949	114
First Presidency (See Presidency)		
First Presidency, a president and two counselors	—	265
First Presidency chief executive body	10, 861	12, 80
First Presidency in charge of publications	852	75
First Presidency to fill vacancies in Standing High Council	853	75
Fiscal year, September 30	1062	174
Flag, church	887	92
Freedom, human, and injustice	1161	261
Fund, Auditorium construction	948	112
Fund authorized, Liahona Fellowship Student Emergency loan	1028	152
Fund authorized, Missions Abroad Capital	1041	163, 169, 170
Fund expanded, Missionary Reserve	1041	163
Fund for development of business from surplus	1040	162
Fund for dormitory construction, Graceland College Endowment	979	131
Fund for gathering and handling General Church money	1009	145
Fund from surplus, establish church building	863	84
Fund, Graceland College	948	113
Fund, Herald House Loan from Ministerial Reserve	1042	163
Fund, High Education Reserve	1024	148
Fund (General) income projection policy	1146	244
Fund, interest to Operating Reserve	1023	148
Fund, Lamoni church	948	113
Fund, Liahona Fellowship	1081	191
Fund, Ministerial Reserve	948, 1055, 1071, 1095	111, 172, 179, 206
Fund, Missionary Reserve	948	111

Fund, Missions Abroad Education	1102, 1153	211, 253
Fund, Operating Reserve	948	112
Fund, Radio-Television Development Reserve	1090	203
Fund, Sanitarium and Hospital	948	113
Funds for General Church projects on local level	1009	145
Funds for missionary program	1041	163
Funds, oblation	940	110
Funds, segregation of	940	110
Fund use for Resthaven, Oblation	1043	163
Gathering and handling General Church money, fund for	1009	145
Gathering to Zion, procedure and objectives of	917	97
General Assembly	17	16
General Assembly, who presides, General Conference	18	16
General Church activities, report on	985	134
General Church Building Commission authorized	1027	151
General Church missions and regions	30-34	21
General Church money, fund for gathering and handling	1009	145
General Church projects on local level, funds for	1009	145
General Conference (See World Conference)	16	16
General Conference, a body of spiritual authorities	61	37
General Conference, appointments submitted to	839	71
General Conference chief legislative body	861	80
General Conference Credentials Committee	617	60
General Conference delegates elected not appointed	936	110
General Conference, delegates to	23	18
General Conference, ex officio members of	22	18
General Conference, in General Assembly, who presides	18	16
General Conference instrument of expression by people	849	73
General Conference Organization Committee authorized	1025	150
General Conference, quorums report to	666	61
General Conference, time and place for	808	70

"General" use encouraged, "World" instead of	1021	148
Gospel, ministry to preach	387	52
Gospel to all mankind regardless of race or condition	171	39
Gospel to all world	1014	146
Gospel to racial and ethnic groups	1075	181
Government through priesthood by common consent	849	73
Government of the church includes	9	12
Government of the church . . . through priesthood	7	11
Graceland College and School of the Restoration to plan together	1024	148
Graceland College bond issue, authorize	1004	143
(Graceland) College Day offerings, use	1004	143
Graceland College endowment fund for dormitory construction	979	131
Graceland College extension to Independence	1024, 1079	148, 184
Graceland College Fund	948	113
Graceland College, incorporation of	—	278
Graceland College, ministry, spiritual nurture of students	1099	209
Graceland College program affirmed	1024	148
Graceland College, sell lands to meet obligation to	1003	142
Graceland College, support of operational budget	1065	177
Graceland College, transfer of Herald Hall and other property to	980	131
Graceland College Trustees	1069, 1140	178, 239
Headquarters office building	1113	214
Healing, elders administer ordinance of	132	38
Health and Nutrition, Committee on	1098	209
Health Ministries Commission authorized	1109	213
Health Ministries Commissioner, member of Sanitarium Corporation	1119	219
Health Ministries Day	1093	204
Herald editorial policy to avoid abuse, *Saints'*	298	45
Herald Hall and other property to Graceland College, transfer of	980	131
Herald House loan from Ministerial Reserve Fund	1042	163
Herald House trustees, selection of	911	96

Heritage people, commission to take Book of Mormon to	965, 970, 1131	121, 231
High Council, Presidency to preside over	386	50
High Councils; courts, elders, bishops	14	14
High Council, First Presidency to fill vacancies in Standing	853	75
High council, stake	40	24
Higher Education, Christian education, priesthood and leadership education, financial assistance to students	1079	184
Higher education in the church	1024	148
Higher Education Program	1024	148
Higher Education Reserve Fund	1024, 1127, 1135	148, 228, 235
Higher Education Scholarship Fund, assets transferred to Higher Education Reserve Fund	1127	228
Higher Education Study by Commission on Education	1065	177
High Priesthood, Prophet, Seer, Revelator, Joseph Smith sustained as President of	153	39
High Priests, calling and ordination of	638, 1051	60, 169
High Priests' duties	386	50
High Priests' Quorum	—	265
High Priests to preside over branches	111	38
Historian to appoint district historians, church	498	56
History, quorums and departments to prepare	470	55
Home, family life, marriage, and marital difficulties	972	125
Hospital fund, Sanitarium and	948	113
Houses of Worship Loans	1071, 1095	179, 206
Houses of Worship Loans, for stakes	1083	193
Houses of Worship Revolving Fund—Missions, loans	1096	207
Human freedom and injustice	1161	261
Incorporation of church in Australia and New Zealand	—	276
Incorporation of church in Canada	—	273
Incorporation of church in Illinois	—	265
Incorporation of church in Iowa	—	270
Incorporation of Graceland College	—	278
Incorporation of Independence Sanitarium and Hospital	—	289
Incorporation, purpose of	866	87
Increase; stewardship responsibilities, inventory, tithe, surplus, offerings	847, 851	72, 74

Indebtedness of church institutions and agencies	1035	158
Independence, Graceland College extension to	1024	148
Indians, ministry to	965, 1131	121, 231
Indians, needs of and work among	955, 1131	119, 231
Indians, objective of ministry among	970, 1131	121, 231
Individual sacrament service	747	65
Indorse Inspired Version of Bible	214	41
Inheritances, appointee allowances and	1001	139
Institutions and agencies, indebtedness of church	1035	158
Insurance, church	800	70
Insurance program study, self	1031	154
Inspiration not affirmed, plenary	308	46
Inspired Version of Bible, indorse	214	41
Integration in church activities	1142	241
Integration, racial	995	137
Interdenominational participation	1157	256
Interest to Operating Reserve Fund	1023	148
Interpreters and teachers of laws and revelations, Presidency	386	50
Interpret law, Standing High Council to	864	85
Intoxicating drinks and tobacco, abstinence from	92	37
Inventory tithe, surplus, offerings, increase; stewardship responsibilities	847, 851	72, 89
Investments; buildings and purchasing of churches, lands and investments	903	94
Investments, speculative	595	59
Imperial dynasty	308	46
Improvements, church and reunion grounds purchases and	954	118
Iowa, incorporation of church in	—	270
Jesus Christ, the Church of	1	9
Judicial body, Quorum (Council) of Twelve as	280	44
Judicial procedure	14	14
King, Tribute to Martin Luther, Jr.	1064	176
Labor of superannuated ministers	755	65
Lamanite Ministries	955, 965, 970	119, 121
Language, committee on clarity of Book of Mormon	993	136
Lamoni and Ozarks; Stewardship projects at Atherton	917	97
Lamoni church building	948	113
Lands and investments; building and purchasing of churches	903	94

Lands to meet obligation to Graceland College, sell	1003	142
Latin America ministry	970	121
Law, branches and districts conducted by rules in	59	32
Law, priesthood should comply with financial	871	89
Law of stewardships, establishment of Zion through	851	74
Laws and revelations, Presidency interpreters and teachers of	386	50
Law, Standing High Council to interpret	864	85
Law, writers, editors to conform to	379	50
Leading missionary quorum, Twelve is	386	50
Leading quorum — presides over church — Presidency	386	50
Legal alternatives to military service	1087, 1129	196, 229
Legislation, initiation of proposed conference	1155, 1160	255, 261
Legislation of mission (General Church) and regional conferences	34	21
Legislative assemblies, Conferences are	15	16
Legislative body, General Conference chief	16, 861	16, 80
Legislative functions	12	13
Liahona Fellowship Fund, per capita basis	1081	191
Liahona Fellowship Student Emergency Loan Fund authorized	1028	152
Libraries, placement of church literature in	1026	150
Literature for profit by ministers, publication of	550	56
Literature in libraries, placement of church	1026	150
Literature to be published by church	—	266
Loan Fund authorized, Liahona Fellowship Student Emergency	1028	152
Loan from Ministerial Reserve Fund, Herald House	1042	163
Loans, Houses of Worship	1071, 1095	179, 206
Local commandments not binding on Reorganization	282	44
Local organizations, stabilizing	949	114
Local treasurers to issue receipts for offerings	1008	145
Locate near branches, members	895	92
Locations for conferences and reunions, dates and	873	90
Marriage and marital difficulties; home, family life	972	125

Marriage, divorce after adultery and remarriage	272	44
Marriage, divorce and remarriage	1034	156
Meeting, quorum at branch business	56	30
Meetings, branch business	52, 58	29
Meetings, branch business, when held	55	30
Members and ministers expelled, excommunicated, withdrawing and reinstated	922	106
Members committed to missionary work	897	93
Members, duty of	57	30
Member of corporation shall not receive profit	—	253
Membership; church, organization, purpose and	1-5	9
Membership in secret society	175, 593	40, 59
Members locate near branches	895	92
Members, removal and enrollment of unknown	910	95
Members responsible to branch or district where residing	594	59
Members, retired, employment or utilization of	1053, 1130	171, 230
Members who contract debts	120	38
Members, withdrawal and reinstatement of	981	132
Member to be reconfirmed and reordained, rebaptized	133	39
Memorial to the prophets	999	138
Message, appointees and ministers with affirmative	854	76
Men created one blood and one race	963	120
Metropolitan branches	55	30
Mexico church properties	1137	238
Mexico, ministry in	970	121
Military service, legal alternatives to	1087, 1129	196, 229
Minister administratively in charge	33	21
Ministerial Reserve Fund	948, 1055, 1071, 1095	111, 172, 179, 206
Ministerial silences and appeals	1158	258
Ministers expelled, excommunicated, withdrawing and reinstated; members and	922	106
Ministers, financing	606	60
Minister in charge to direct appointees in stakes	551	57
Ministers, labor of superannuated	755	65
Ministers, publication of literature for profit by	550	56
Ministers with affirmative message, appointees and	854	76

337

Ministries to primitive cultures	1114	216
Ministries, youth	1084, 1129	193, 229
Ministry, Latin America (Mexico)	970	121
Ministry not to use tobacco	217	42
Ministry of Reconciliation	1132	231
Ministry, redemptive	1151	250
Ministry to College People, Committee on	1024	148
Ministry to preach gospel	387	52
Missionary Development Budget	1134	234
Missionary in charge to move appointees	367	49
Missionary Ministry in Twos	1123	223
Missionary opportunities, appointees to create	897	93
Missionary quorum, Twelve is leading	386	50
Missionary Reserve Fund	948	111
Missionary Reserve Fund expanded	1041	163
Missionary work, members committed to	897	93
Missionary work part of every function	897	93
Mission (General Church) and regional conferences, legislation	34	21
Missions Abroad Capital Fund authorized	1041	163
Missions Abroad Education Fund	1102, 1153	211, 253
Missions (General Church) and Regions	30-34	21
Missions (General Church) and Regions may be organized	31	21
Missions (General Church) and regions president	33	21
Moral problems; social, economic, and	1045	164
Move appointees, missionary in charge to	367	49
Multiple branches	50, 55	29
Name of the church	1144	242
Nature of stake organization	35	23
New Zealand, incorporation of church in Australia and	—	276
Nominate all elective offices	834	71
Nominate, presiding officers to	834	71
Nominate, right to	13	14
Nomination of department heads	782	66
No previous organization	21	17
Objections in conference	854	76
Objective of ministry among Indians	970	121
Objectives and emphasis, religious education	919	103
Objectives (education), teaching	918	101
Objectives of gathering to Zion, procedure and	917	97
Oblation funds	940	110
Oblation fund, use for Resthaven	1043	163

Oblation at Sacrament services	773	66
Offerings, increase; stewardship responsibilities, inventory, tithe, surplus	847, 851	72, 74
Offerings, local treasurers to issue receipts for	1008	145
Offerings, use (Graceland) College Day	1004	143
Offerings, printing lists and annual statements of tithing and	878	91
Office building, headquarters	1113	214
Office wing addition to Auditorium	1063, 1089, 1113	176, 201, 214
Officer (branch business meeting) duties of presiding	54	29
Officer to decide validity of charges	743	65
Officers, appointment of stake	551	57
Officers, branch	51	29
Officers (branch and district) respect presiding	59	32
Officers (branch and district) to settle difficulties	59	32
Officers free to discharge duties	1014	146
Officers to nominate, presiding	834	71
Officers in church, purpose for	386	50
Officers, sustaining General	1103	212
Offices, nominate all elective	834	71
Operate on approved budget, church subdivisions to	1008	145
Operating Reserve Fund	948, 1133	112, 232
Operating Reserve Fund, interest to	1023	148
Opinions with tolerance, present	308	46
Opportunities for Women	1116	217
Opposing the church, appointees	862	82
Ordained, presidents and counselors of quorums to be	109	38
Ordaining of priesthood, procedures in calling and	988	134
Order of Bishops, Bishopric and	788	69
Order of Bishops, Presiding Bishopric, Stake Bishopric	710	63
Orders, amend rules and	60	34
Ordinance of baptism, procedure in	212	41
Ordinance of blessing to children under eight	701	61
Ordinance of healing, Melchisedec priesthood administer	132	38
Ordinance, sealing up to eternal life not an	202	40
Ordination and release of Bishops	982	135, 136
Ordination of high priests, calling and	638, 1051	60, 176
Ordination of Seventy	966	121

Ordination of women to priesthood	564, 1141	58, 240
Ordinations, High priests, evangelists and bishops	1051	169
Ordinations void when rebaptized (baptized)	329	48
Organization and membership of delegate district conference	29	20
Organization Committee authorized, General Conference	1025	150
Organization, district	44	26
Organization, nature of stake	35	23
Organization, no previous	21	17
Organization of branches (includes multiple branches)	50	29
Organization, purpose, and membership, church	1-5	9
Organization, stabilizing local	949	114
Organized, Missions (General Church) may be	31	21
Organized on basis of administration not race, branches	995	137
Ozarks; Stewardship projects at Atherton, Lamoni, and	917	97
Park College relationship	1154	254
Parliamentary Procedure	1156	255
Peace, War, and the Use of Force	1052, 1087	170, 196
Petitions without reading, refer	640	61
Placement of church literature in libraries	1026	150
Plan together, Graceland College and School of the Restoration to	1024	148
Planning Field activities	873	90
Plenary inspiration not affirmed	308	46
Policy of 1932 affirmed, financial	1035	158
Policy, financial	925, 940	107, 110
Preach gospel, ministry to	387	52
Preaching of doctrine of resurrection	391	52
Preach, teachers and deacons to	449	54
Prejudice, and bigotry, eradicate	1064	176
Present opinions with tolerance	308	46
Presidency (See also First Presidency)		
Presidency in charge of publications, First	852	75
Presidency interpreters and teachers of laws and revelations	386	50
Presidency is leading quorum—presides over church	386	50
Presidency to fill vacancies in Standing High Council, First	853	75

Presidency, stake	39	24
Presidency to counsel and direct apostles	386	50
Presidency to preside over high council	386	50
Preside at branch business meeting	53	29
when held	55	30
Preside at district conferences	47	27
President appointed by revelation, confirmed by vote	386	50
President, district	10, 45	12, 26
President of High Priesthood, Prophet, Seer, Revelator, Joseph Smith sustained as	153	39
President, Mission (General Church) and Regions	33	21
Presidents and counselors of quorums to be ordained	109	38
Presidents, Branch	10	12
Presidents of Seventy, reorganization of	860	78
Presidents of Seventy, selection of	802	70
Presidents, Stake	10	12
President to receive revelations	386	50
Preside over branches, high priests to	111	38
Preside over high council, Presidency to	386	50
Presides, in General Conference, in General assembly, who	18	16
Presides over church—Presidency is leading quorum	386	50
Presiding Bishop and counselors are trustees	—	266
Presiding Bishop and counselors as trustees	866	87 266, 270, 273, 274
Presiding Bishopric create business associations as trustees	907	94
Presiding Bishopric, stake bishopric, Order of Bishops	10, 710	12, 63
Presiding Bishop to hold seal and sign conveyances	—	267
Presiding Bishopric to see finances are used rightly	915	96
Presiding officers (branch and district) respect	59	32
Presiding officer (branch business meeting), duties of	54	29
Presiding officer, duty of	48	28
Presiding officers to nominate	834	71
Presiding responsibilities, field administrative officers	1097	208
Priesthood and leadership education	1079	184
Priesthood authority, the reality and extent of	8	11

Priesthood by common consent, government through	849	73
Priesthood, Conference Organization of elders and Aaronic	1125	225
Priesthood, government of church ... through	7	11
Priesthood, procedures in calling and ordaining of	988	134
Priesthood, ordination of women to	564	58
Priesthood should comply with financial law	871	89
Priests, quorums of	—	266
Primitive cultures, ministries to	1114	216
Printing lists and annual statements of tithing and offerings	878	91
Printing of appointee family allowances and elders' expenses	1006	144
Principal place of business of church	—	268, 270
Procedure and objectives of gathering to Zion	917	97
Procedure in ordinance of baptism	212	41
Profit by ministers, publication of literature for	550	56
Profit, member of corporation shall not receive	—	271
Program affirmed, Graceland College	1024	148
Program for assisting young people	1047, 1084	166, 193
Programs for graduate students	1079	184
Programs of Reconciliation, proportion of church budget for	1128	228
Programs of specialized ministry for unmarried adults	1050, 1059	169, 174
Projects at Atherton, Lamoni, and Ozarks; stewardship	917	97
Projects, on local level, funds for General Church	1009	146
Property to be conveyed to corporation	—	268
Prophecies, publication of	709	62
Prophet, Seer, Revelator, Joseph Smith sustained as President of High Priesthood	153	39
Prophets, memorial to the	999	138
Publication of literature for profit by ministers	550	56
Publication of prophecies	709	62
Publication to manage, Committee (Board) of	—	267
Publications, advertisements in church	725	65
Publications, church responsible only for authorized	368	49
Publications, First Presidency in charge of	852	75
Published by church, literature to be	—	266

Purchases and improvements, church and reunion grounds	954	118
Purchasing of churches, lands and investments; building and	903	94
Purpose, and membership, church, organization	1-5	9
Purpose of church administration	849	73
Purpose of incorporation	866	87
Purposes for offices in church	386	50
Qualifications for delegates	25	19
Quorums and departments to prepare history	470	55
Quorum at branch business meeting	56	30
Quorum (Council) of Twelve as judicial body	280	44
Quorum, High Priests'	—	265
Quorums of deacons	—	266
Quorums of elders	—	266
Quorums of priests	—	266
Quorums of seventy	—	265
Quorum of seventy, second	990	135
Quorums of teachers	—	266
Quorum of Twelve	10	12, 265
Quorum—presides over church—Presidency leading	386	50
Quorums, release of seventy from	1163	263
Quorums report to General Conference	666	61
Quorums to be ordained, presidents and counselors of	109	38
Quorum, Twelve is leading missionary	386	50
Quorum, Twelve is second	386	50
Race, appoint persons of any	995	137
Race, branches organized on basis of administration, not	995	137
Race, men created one blood and one	963	120
Race or condition, gospel to all mankind regardless of	171, 1075	39, 181
Race relations education	976	126
Racial and ethnic groups, gospel to	1075	181
Racial equality	963, 976	120, 126
Racial integration	995	137
Radio broadcasting and station	960	120
Radio broadcasting station	971	124
Radio (ham) call signs	1149	248
Radio station	957	119
Radio-Television Development Reserve Fund	1090	203

Readers' Version of the Book of Mormon authorize	1002, 1058	141, 174
Readmittance, expulsion for second offense of adultery	864	85
Rebaptized (baptized), ordinations void when	329	48
Rebaptized member to be reconfirmed and reordained	133	39
Receipts for offerings, local treasurers to issue	1008	145
Reconciliation, ministry of	1132	231
Reconfirmed and reordained, rebaptized member to be	133	39
Refer petitions without reading	640	61
Regional Administrators	10	12
Regional Bishops	10	12
Regional Conferences	34	21
Reincorporation, Sanitarium and Hospital	1070	289
Reinstated; members and ministers expelled, excommunicated, withdrawing and	922	106
Reinstatement of members, withdrawal and	981	132
Release of bishops, ordination and	982	132
Release of evangelists and bishops	884	91
Release of seventy from quorums	1163	263
Religious education in branch program, cradle roll and	872	89
Religious Education materials, new curriculum	1094	205
Religious education objectives and emphases	919	103
Remarriage; marriage, divorce after adultery	272	44
Remarriage; marriage, divorce and	1034	156
Reordained, rebaptized member to be reconfirmed and	133	39
Reorganization, local commandments not binding on	282	44
Reorganization of Central Missouri and Center Stakes	1030	153
Reorganization of Presidents of Seventy	860	78
Reports, appointee elders' expense	804	70
Report, departments and associations make financial	901	93
Report on General Church activities	985	137
Report to General Conference, quorums	666	61
Representation, basis of	24	18
Representation, Rules of	22-29	18
Requirement for candidate for baptism	705	62
Research and service for Zion, bureau of	997	138

Research, Archaeological	1147	247
Reserve Fund, Missionary	948	111
Reserve Fund, Operating	948	112
Reserve Fund, Ministerial	948	111
Residing, members responsible to branch or district where	594	59
Resolutions, revision of book of *Rules and*	—	34
Resource material for church school curricula from Three Standard Books	1122	234, 235
Respect presiding officers (branch and district)	59	32
Responsible only for authorized publications, church	368	49
Responsible to branch or district where residing, members	594	59
Resthaven, oblation fund use for	1043	163
Restoration principles in church school materials	1122	234, 235
Restoration, the	2	9
Resurrection, preaching of doctrine	391	52
Retiring and superannuating appointees	560	58
Reunions, dates and locations for conferences and	873	90
Reunion ground purchases and improvements, church	954	118
Revelation, confirmed by vote; president appointed by	386	50
Revelations, presidency interpreters and teachers of laws and	386	50
Revelations, president to receive	386	50
Revelations (See "commandments")		
Revelator, Joseph Smith sustained as President of High Priesthood, Prophet, Seer	153	39
Revision of book of *Rules and Resolutions*	—	34
Rights of body are safeguarded in, church administration	11	13
Rules and orders, amend	60	34
Rules and restrictions of delegate voting	27	20
Rules and Resolutions, revision of book of	—	34
Rules in law, branches and districts conducted by	59	32
Rules of Order, Robert's	1156	255
Rules of representation	22-29	18
Sacrament, blessing of bread and wine at	172	39
Sacrament dignified, administration of	894	92
Sacrament, fermented wine and water in	702	61

Sacrament service, individual	747	65
Sacrament services, oblation at	773	66
Sacrament, teachers nor deacons to convey emblems	401	53
Sacrament, unbaptized not to partake	91	37
Safeguarded in, church administration, Rights of body are	11	13
Saints' Herald editorial policy to avoid abuse	298	45
Saints Herald to be used to inform on development of church school materials	1122	221
Saloons a test of fellowship, drinking intoxicants and visiting	297	45
Salvation, elders to teach doctrines necessary for	222	42
Sanitarium and Hospital addition	1055	172
Sanitarium and Hospital Corporate membership	1120	289
Sanitarium and Hospital Corporation, Health Ministries Commissioner member of	1119	219
Sanitarium and Hospital Fund	948	113
Sanitarium and Hospital, incorporation of	—	289
Sanitarium and Hospital Reincorporation	1070	289
School of the Restoration to plan together, Graceland College	1024	148
School of the Restoration, transfer to Temple School of Zion	1126	225
Scouting, World, distinctive emblem, officer to coordinate	1124	224
Seal and sign conveyances, Presiding Bishop to hold	—	267
Sealing up to eternal life not an ordinance	202	40
Second offense of adultery and readmittance, expulsion for	864	85
Second quorum of Seventy	990	135
Second quorum, Twelve is	386	50
Secretary, church	115, 411	38, 53
Secret society, membership in	175, 593	40, 58
Seer, Revelator, Joseph Smith sustained as President of High Priesthood, Prophet	153	39
Segregation of funds	940	110
Selection of Herald House trustees	911	96
Selection of Presidents of Seventy	802	70
Selecting, training, placement and financing of appointees	949	114
Self-insurance program study	1031	154
Sell lands to meet obligation to Graceland College	1003	142

Service to local community	1072	180
Settle difficulties, officers (branch and district) to	59	32
Seventy	10	12
Seventy from quorums, release of	1163	263
Seventy, ordination of	966	121
Seventy, quorums of	—	241
Seventy, reorganization of Presidents of	860	78
Seventy, selection of Presidents of	802	70
Seventy, second quorum of	990	135
Seventy, superannuated	1107	213
Silenced, elders' (in transgression) acts valid till silenced	90	37
Silences and appeals, ministerial	1158	258
Single adults, specialized ministry to	1050, 1059	175, 180
Single life-style task force	1143	241
Smith, Joseph, sustained as President of High Priesthood, Prophet, Seer, Revelator	153	39
Social, economic, and moral problems	1045	164
Society, membership in secret	175, 593	40, 58
Spanish, translation of Book of Mormon to	970	123
Special conferences, called by	20	17
Speculative investments	595	59
Speculative theories, avoid advancing	222	42
Spiritual authorities, General Conference a body of	61	37
Stabilizing local organizations	949	114
Stake and district conferences	19	16
Stake bishops	41	24
Stake Bishopric, Order of Bishops, Presiding Bishopric	10, 710	12, 63
Stake conferences	43	25
Stake high council	40	24
Stake officers, appointment of	551	57
Stake office, vacancy in	42	25
Stake organization, nature of	35	23
Stake presidency	39	24
Stake president	10	12
Stakes	35-43	23
Stakes and branches		266
Stakes, Houses of Worship loans	1083	193
Stakes, minister in charge to direct appointees in	551	57
Stakes, reorganization of Central Missouri and Center	1030	153
Standard of authority; Bible, Book of Mormon, Doctrine and Covenants	215, 222	41, 42

Standards of conduct by church members	1085	194
Standing Committee on World Peace	1087	196
Standing High Council, First Presidency to fill vacancies in	853	76
Standing High Council to interpret the law	864	85
Station, radio	957	119
Station, radio and broadcasting	960	120
Station, radio broadcasting	971	124
Stewardship, certificates of	722	64
Stewardship compliance	871	89
Stewardship projects at Atherton, Lamoni, and Ozarks	917	97
Stewardship responsibilities, inventory, tithe, surplus, offerings, increase	847, 851	72, 74
Stewardships, establishment of Zion through law of	851	74
Stewardship, tithing a voluntary	308	46
Storehouse treasury, consecration and use of surplus in	977	128
Strong drink, appointees not to use tobacco nor	463	54
Student Emergency Loan Fund authorized, Liahona Fellowship	1028	152
Superannuated ministers, labor of	755	65
Superannuated Seventy	1107	213
Superannuating appointees, retiring and	560	58
Surplus, established church fund from	863	84
Surplus, fund for development of business from	1040	162
Surplus, offerings, increase; stewardship responsibilities, inventory, tithe	847, 851	72, 74
Surplus in storehouse treasury, consecration and use of	977	128
Supreme directional control	849, 861	73, 80
Task Force on Aging	1130	230
Teach doctrines necessary for salvation, elders to	222	42
Teachers and deacons to preach	449	54
Teachers nor deacons to convey emblems at Sacrament	401	53
Teachers of laws and revelations, Presidency interpreters and	386	50
Teachers, quorums of	—	266
Teaching objectives (education)	918	101

Television authorized, committee on use of	1048	168
Television, encourage utilization of	1056	173
Temple and endowments	308	46
Temple, educational programs in relation to	1079, 1126	193, 225
Temple Fund, Christmas offering for	1088	201
Temple School, general purposes and basic structure	1126	225
Temple School of Zion, transfer from School of the Restoration	1126	225
Temporal jurisdiction, bishops having	—	274, 276
Testimony, the early elders bore	3	9
Testimony, those who received this	4	10
Test of fellowship, abstract doctrines not a	222	42
Test of fellowship, Visiting saloons and drinking intoxicants a	297	45
Theocratic democracy	6-14, 849	11, 73
Theories, avoid advancing speculative	222	42
Time and place for General Conference	808	70
Time for election of delegates	1106	212
Tithe, surplus, offerings, increase; stewardship responsibilities, inventory	847, 851	72, 74
Tithing and offerings, printing lists and annual statements of	878	91
Tithing a voluntary stewardship	308	46
Tobacco, abstinence from intoxicating drinks and	92	37
Tobacco, advertising and use of	1046	165
Tobacco, Ministry not to use	217	42
Tobacco nor strong drink, appointees not to use	463	54
Tolerance, present opinions with	308	46
Training, placement, and financing of appointees, selecting	949	114
Transfer of Herald Hall and other property to Graceland College	980	131
Translation of Book of Mormon into Spanish	970	123
Treasurers to issue receipts for offerings, local	1008	145
Tribute to Martin Luther King, Jr.	1064	176
Trustees, Graceland College	1069, 1140	178, 239
Trustees, selection of Herald House	911	96
Trustees, Presiding Bishop and counselors as	866	87, 266, 270, 273, 274
Trustees, Presiding Bishopric create business associations as	907	95

Twelve is leading missionary quorum	386	50
Twelve is second quorum	386	50
Twelve, quorum of	10	12, 265
Unbaptized not to partake of sacrament	91	37
Unions, credit	1039	162
Unity, Church of Christ committee to work for	1036	160
Unknown members, removal and enrollment of	910	95
Unmarried adults, programs for	1050, 1059	169, 174
Unordained men, Utilization of	1150	250
Urban renewal land purchase program	1037	161
Utilization of talents and time, retired members	1053, 1130	171, 230
Vacancies in Standing High Council, First Presidency to fill	853	76
Vacancy in stake office	42	25
Validity of charges, officer to decide	743	65
Vocational education	1152	251
Vote; president appointed by revelation, confirmed by	386	50
Voting Delegate	27	17
Water in sacrament, fermented wine and	702	61
Wine and water in sacrament, fermented	702	61
Wine, at sacrament, blessing of bread and	172	39
Wisdom, word of	933	110
Withdrawing and reinstated; members and ministers expelled, excommunicated	922	106
Withdraw and reinstatement of members	981	132
Witnesses of adultery as evidence	343	48
Women, opportunities for	1116	217
Women to priesthood, ordination of	564, 1141	58, 240
Women's Ministry Commission authorized	1118	219
Word of wisdom	933	110
Words to be used in baptism	48	37
World Conference (See "General Conference")		
World Conference role in policy statements	1057	173
"World" instead of "General" use encouraged	1021	148
World hunger	1148	247
World Peace Committee	1052, 1087, 1129	170, 196, 229
World Scouting, officer to coordinate	1124	224
World-wide worthy assistance	1019	147
World Witness, Church Mission and	1121	220
Worthy assistance, world-wide	1019	147
Writers, editors to conform to law	379	50

Year, Fiscal, September 30	1062	174
Young people, program for assisting	1047, 1084	166, 193
Youth Ministries (Day)	1084, 1129, 1162	193, 229, 262
Zion, agriculture colonization	940	111, 112
Zion, bureau of research and service for	997	138
Zion, procedure and objectives of gathering to	917	97
Zion through law of stewardships, establishment of	851	74
Zionic research and service	997	138